OF BOOKS AND BEASTS

A CRYPTOZOOLOGIST'S LIBRARY

MATT BILLE

Scientific Editor
DR. ANNE LARSEN

HANGAR 1 PUBLISHING

To Corey and Lauryn Bille
Keepers of the future

And to all the heroes who work to understand and preserve the wonders of
Planet Earth
May God bless you all

CONTENTS

Introduction	vii
SECTION 1	1
Cryptozoology Books	
A Basic Library of Cryptozoology	1
Primates	19
Land Animals	50
Lake and Sea Creatures	68
Others	90
SECTION 2	124
Related Sciences	
Paleontology and Evolution	125
Environment and Exploration	147
Zoology of Land, Sea, and Air	166
SECTION 3	221
Crypto-Fiction	
My Top Three	225
Other Crypto-Novels	228
SECTION 4	255
A Marvelous Miscellany	
AFTERWORDS	272
Cryptids and Me	272
A Few Contributions of My Own	273
Acknowledgments	279
Index	283

INTRODUCTION

Cryptozoology, the search for "hidden" animals, features prominently on all our modern social media platforms, not to mention television, movies, and publications. The amount of information available—good, exaggerated, or invented—is staggering. Fortunately, most of the useful information is available in a handy, durable format: books.

Books matter because this highly controversial field is barely 60 years old. Much information recorded before that, including the information in letters, diaries, telegrams, etc., is gone. While some have been preserved in institutions like Loren Coleman's International Cryptozoology Museum, relatively few can visit such archives. Scientific papers are valuable, but few peer-reviewed scientific journals take cryptozoological articles, and fewer still specialize in them. (At this writing, I'm aware of two, the *Journal of Cryptozoology* and the *Relict Hominid Inquiry*.) So, we're back to books.

This compilation does not cover all the cryptozoology books written. Such an endeavor, if possible at all, would take years. It collects the ones that have passed through my hands in the last four decades and have, in my view, been very influential and/or offered significant useful information. What I offer here is a collection of

Introduction

reviews from my books, my blog, my old newsletter *Exotic Zoology* (1994-99), and other sources, along with many recent reads.

Compiling this library is worthwhile because cryptozoology, when approached correctly, meets Karl Popper's classic definition of a science. Cryptozoology deals with all three of Thomas H. Huxley's divisions of zoology: morphology (including classification), distribution (the study of animals in relation to habitat or conditions), and, although to a lesser extent, physiology. Cryptozoological hypotheses can be proven false, even though the resources needed to disprove a proposition like "There is an unknown Himalayan ape species" may not be available. This quality of cryptozoology is why it should not be included under the heading of "the paranormal," which contains much that cannot be proven false.

Definitions

Here are two definitions of the field that demonstrate its uneasy status in the scientific community:

Cryptozoology (Wikipedia)

Cryptozoology is a pseudoscience and subculture that aims to prove the existence of entities from the folklore record, such as Bigfoot...

Cryptozoology (Bernard Heuvelmans)

The scientific study of hidden animals, i.e., of still unknown animal forms about which only testimonial and circumstantial evidence is available, or material evidence considered insufficient by some.

This is the definition I'd personally like to see used and consistently applied:

Introduction

Cryptozoology

A scientific endeavor that takes traditional zoological methods of animal location, collection, and identification (using fieldwork, local reports of animals, chance discovery of trophies, etc.) and widens the aperture to consider animals based on evidence not firm enough or consistent enough to draw interest from most zoologists.

The Wikipedia version is harsh but understandable. There are pseudoscientists all over cryptozoology, and there's certainly a subculture. While cryptozoology can and should be a science, it is too rarely practiced using robust scientific methods. It often looks more like a worldwide argument (sometimes, in the case of Sasquatch-hunters, a barroom brawl) where facts can come unmoored from the original context and be drowned in wild claims and speculations.

The internet both enables the exchange of information and exacerbates conflict. When I teach research classes, I always run into three uncomfortably common myths. The first is that information on the internet is mostly accurate, the second is that all important information is available online, and the third is that all sources are, with some variation, equally reliable. Any of these beliefs will ruin serious attempts to understand a scientific topic. So, I return, once again, to the books, where it's easier to make a useful selection and evaluate the sources the author used as well as their approach to this data.

While the great naturalist Louis Agassiz wrote, "Study nature, not books," the regions where new animal species might exist are inaccessible to most people in the industrialized world. Serious cryptozoological researchers who want to understand the field must start with reading. Almost all the books presented here are available in my favorite format–good old-fashioned paper, which doesn't care whether you have connectivity or what software you have. Many are also available in electronic form, but many aren't because converting old or obscure books isn't always profitable.

Part of the value of books is based on the simple fact that they

Introduction

take time to write. Yes, the interested high school student can cut and paste and upload a "book" in days or hours, but for serious writers, just the act of writing books offers some time for reflection. Furthermore, books from the pre-digital age had to pass the eyes of an editor, fact-checker, and often peer reviewers, whose attentions often weeded out shoddy data prior to publication. That hasn't saved us from a tsunami of ridiculous cryptozoology books from the 1960s on, including some from major publishers, so if I'm arguing with myself here, I'm not sure I'm winning. (Sometimes I think that, in cryptozoology, the plural of "anecdote" is "book.")

I've kept the present-tense form of review, even with books from a long time ago, because it provides a consistency that improves the readability, and, I hope, the utility of this library.

In assembling this library, the first challenge was to keep the books to a reasonable number. I've read zoology and cryptozoology ever since I could access elementary school libraries. One easy rule was limiting it to books published in English. It's a failing of mine that I can't read any other languages, but so it is. Also, I review only books I've personally read, although I mention some others.

I decided on three other rules to keep the reviews to a manageable number. One was to focus on books under 100 years old. R.T. Gould's *The Case for the Sea-Serpent* (1930) turned out to be the oldest nonfiction book I kept. The second is that most state-by-state books were out, although I kept a few of the better ones. Finally, I also left out annuals published by periodicals: they certainly have value, but I must again plead "too many books."

The reader will notice these books are almost entirely written by North American or European authors. There is a scarcity of books available in English from people who live in areas like South America and Africa. These are, ironically, the regions most likely to house unknown species. I've done my best to collect such books.

It was not logistically or financially possible to get the newest editions of some reprinted books, so the date on each review is the date of the edition I reviewed.

Introduction

Books are borrowed minds, and because they capture the soul of a people, they explore and celebrate all it means to be human. – Diane Ackerman, poet and naturalist

Section 1 covers the cryptozoology books per se. This is the biggest room in our putative library. It's chronologically organized but divided into A Basic Library, Primates, Land Animals (non-primate), Sea and Lake Creatures, and Other, a category for books that deal with other cryptids or cover the whole field.

I passed over or culled many of the Sasquatch and Loch Ness books because they'd overwhelm this entire book, let alone this section. If Sasquatch is ever proven real, I'm willing to bet the number of related books exceeds the number of living Sasquatches by a considerable margin.

There are far more books in this section that argue for the existence of cryptids than there are books that dispute them. This isn't me taking sides. "Pro-cryptid" books outnumber the other kind at least a hundred to one, which means most of the information (if not always the most reliable information) is in the former. Not all the authors here call themselves cryptozoologists or even have any use for the field, but all provide relevant information.

This is a good place to mention that books offering mundane explanations deserve the same scrutiny as pro-cryptid books. Joe Nickell, in his book *Tracking the Man-Beasts*, shows a clear "suit-glove" interface on a line drawing of the creature in the famous 1969 Patterson-Gimlin film. I can't see that on enlargements or enhancements, and Nickell doesn't show the reader any imagery from the film or even discuss the topic in the text. It may be there, but he does not prove it.

For cryptozoology to gain wide acceptance within zoology, it must end its entanglement with the paranormal. Apparitions and extrasensory contact are matters for the parapsychologists: if it's not zoology, it's not cryptozoology. Some prominent cryptozoologists, though, are Forteans: they share the late author Charles Fort's interest in many types of oddities, both physical and paranormal, and

xi

Introduction

that's reflected in their work. I also understand cryptozoologist Loren Coleman's point that if someone reports an apparently physical animal, it's part of cryptozoology until determined otherwise. I kept a minority of the mixed-topic books based on their cryptozoological value or influence.

Section 2, books on the relevant science in this field, holds a collection of books in zoology and related sciences of interest to the cryptozoological researcher. The lines between these categories can get fuzzy. For example, thylacines are a proven and almost certainly extinct species, but you'll find some books on them in Section 1 because cryptozoologists still seek the animal out. I've largely set aside textbooks and scientific conference proceedings to focus on authoritative books which are also understandable and available to a broad audience.

Section 3 is our Fiction room. Crypto-fiction is a broad slice of literature that includes thrillers, mainstream fiction, science fiction, and horror. (Sections 3 and 4 are alphabetized by author.) When thousands of novels are uploaded to Amazon per day, no one can read a fraction of the cryptozoological ones, much less review them, so this is a tiny slice of the genre. I believe fiction is more important to cryptozoology than to established fields like geology. Where hard information is scarce, speculation must serve, and fiction allows cryptozoological writers to suggest how Sasquatches might live or how lake creatures could end up where they did.

I ruled out "creatures munching humans" novels, even if *Pterodon Mall* is one of the best titles ever. Also out were novels involving human-created creatures (I made an exception for the enormously influential *Jurassic Park*), aliens, magic, or time travel. A few of those pop up in Section 4, a room for books that didn't fit into the other classifications but are too interesting or too much fun to leave out. Some books on unknown primates are shelved here to keep that category from overwhelming Section 1.

If a book title mentioned in another review is in boldface, that book has a separate review. A short review does not mean the book is of lesser quality: since circumstances did not permit my re-acquiring books with older reviews and reading them again, it reflects what I wrote when I had that book in hand.

I stress that this is "A" Cryptozoologist's Library and not "The" Cryptozoologist's Library. This collection was driven by my own curiosity. In addition to reading on cryptozoology and zoology practically since I could read, I've written two very well-received books on the topic along with several articles and presentations. I've talked and corresponded with researchers inside and outside cryptozoology, and some of their names are listed in the Acknowledgements. I've been a science and technology writer since the 1990s, publishing on topics from Martian soil to prehistoric fish.

With that said, this is not an authoritative list of the best books. Every well-read cryptozoologist (and many a cryptozoology author) will have disagreements with my list of books and the content of my reviews. This is an effort by one researcher to provide current and future generations with a useful guide to the books I've read. While book reviews, by definition, are opinions, I tried to read everything as a skeptic in the proper sense of the word: someone who wants to see new scientific discoveries but needs convincing evidence.

Onwards!

Ignorance more frequently begets confidence than does knowledge: it is those who know little, and not those who know much, who so positively assert that this or that problem will never be solved by science. – Charles Darwin, naturalist, author of *On the Origin of Species*

SECTION 1
CRYPTOZOOLOGY BOOKS

A Basic Library of Cryptozoology

The most solid piece of scientific truth I know of is that we are profoundly ignorant about nature. – Lewis Thomas, physician and naturalist, author of *The Lives of a Cell*

I have said that I'm not prescribing a canon. Still, those new to cryptozoology can profit from the advice of someone who has waded through much of the relevant literature. This section contains reviews of books that I believe form a basic reading list of the classics in the field.

Any list of must-read cryptozoology starts with Dr. Bernard Heuvelmans' *On the Track of Unknown Animals*, which came out in English in 1958. Heuvelmans' collection of cryptozoological reports from every inhabited continent is invaluable, even if few of the animals he surveyed turn out to be real. I recommend the revised 1995 edition from Kegan Paul International.

A second excellent book from the founding years of cryptozoology is Willy Ley's *Exotic Zoology*. Published in 1959, this

I

book collected zoological and cryptozoological material from Ley's several books on scientific oddities. While some of the information is outdated, the book remains a fascinating collection of discoveries and mysteries. There are several books from the 1950s with similar themes, but this is my favorite example.

Dr. Karl Shuker's *Encyclopedia of New and Rediscovered Animals* (2012) describes the variety of animal finds made in the 20th and 21st centuries. The modern bookend for Heuvelmans' *On the Track* is Shuker's *Still in Search of Prehistoric Survivors: The Creatures That Time Forgot?* (2016). The final survey book is the skeptical *Abominable Science! Origins of the Yeti, Nessie, and Other Famous Cryptids* by Daniel Loxton and Donald Prothero (2013).

There are several important books concerning large marine cryptids. A good collection starts with Gould's 1930, *The Case for the Sea Serpent*. Writing when he still could correspond with some witnesses to the "classic" cases, Gould presented a formidable brief in favor of one or more "monsters." Four decades later, Bernard Heuvelmans assembled all the known information on the subject in his massive *In the Wake of the Sea Serpents* (1968). Heuvelmans is still a vital resource, although few cryptozoologists accepted his belief in seven or more unknowns. Richard Ellis made a major contribution with *Monsters of the Sea* (1994), an open-minded treatment of the subject.

Henry Bauer's *The Enigma of Loch Ness* (1991) is one of the most useful Nessie books, and Gareth Williams' *A Monstrous Commotion* (1997) explores the people and events in depth. The books reach opposite conclusions, so reading them as a pair presents a balanced view of the topic.

Sasquatch: Legend Meets Science by Dr. Jeff Meldrum (Forge, 2006) is a presentation of the evidence by a qualified scientist convinced the animal is real.

These titles, reviewed below, are my suggested foundation texts. Please note that I often use the broader term "primate" rather than the commonly-seen term "hominin" because it's often unclear where on the family tree a cryptid primate would be classified if caught.

On the Track of Unknown Animals

Heuvelmans, Bernard (1955: reviewed edition was 1995: Kegan Paul International, 677pp.)

This is an update to the founding work of cryptozoology. The updating, unfortunately, consists only of a 13-page preface to the original text, plus some new illustrations. Still, the amount of material here is impressive: the bibliography fills 26 pages. Heuvelmans, a zoologist, is famous for opening with Baron George's Cuvier's (1769-1832) "rash dictum" from his 1812 monograph *Recherches sur les ossemens fossiles,* "There is little hope of discovering new species of large quadrupeds." There were plenty of spectacular examples that proved Cuvier was wrong. A more recent equivalent is Dr. George Gaylord Simpson's 1984 dictum that only a "few small and unimportant mammals" awaited discovery. There, too, Heuvelmans disagreed, and new species from Southeast Asia in the 1990s supported his dissent.

It is rare to say that a book created a discipline, but such was Heuvelmans' aim. There were older books on unknown animals, some of them very good, but *On the Track* was by far the most influential and comprehensive "survey" book. The book includes alleged animals from all the inhabited continents, ranging from celebrities like the Yeti to little-known ones like Australia's dinosaur-like *gauarge*. In general, in cases as varied as the bunyip, the giant anaconda, and the ground sloth, Heuvelmans comes down on the side of there being at least one unknown species involved. He includes some hoaxes, too, like a taxidermically-reworked langur monkey passed off as an *orang-pendek* in 1932. He uses that specimen to make the point that "The fact that a forger of genius painted Vermeers which took in experts... does not mean the great Dutch painter never existed." Heuvelmans does good work in his examination of matters like the "Nandi bear" of Africa. He patiently untangles a welter of contradictory reports, explains most of them, and offers candidates for the ones he feels remain unexplained.

How does he do, given what he knew in 1955, at predicting new findings? It must be said that the score is close to zero. The extremely rare *marozi*, or spotted lion, appears to be an interesting oddity, as does the strikingly marked king cheetah. Some of the undescribed species may still be out there: the *orang-pendek* and the Queensland marsupial tiger are candidates, and one or two of the "extinct" mammals of Madagascar just might be hanging on. The pygmy elephant exists, but modern zoologists reject the idea that it is a distinct species or subspecies. Heuvelmans did correctly predict more species of lemurs, but that wasn't a reach.

History has nevertheless vindicated Heuvelmans' belief that new animals await, many of which will be found by listening to local reports around the world. Heuvelmans makes the important point that indigenous descriptions of animals aren't necessarily invalidated by unrealistic or supernatural details. We may say a lion roared like thunder. If you translate that into, say, Warlpiri for an Australian Aborigine, the distinction between facts and flourishes might be lost, and so the other way around.

Despite the lack of success in finding Heuvelmans' creatures, the book remains the literary foundation of cryptozoology. Heuvelmans introduced the world to animals (confirmed and unconfirmed) many had never heard of in the age when travel was often arduous, communications limited, and the colonial-era Western view that "natives" just told fairy tales still prevailed. We may yet meet a few animals that make us say, "Oh, that's what he was talking about!" I hope so.

Exotic Zoology

Ley, Willy (1959: Viking Books, 468pp.)

In this early survey of cryptozoology, science and space writer Willy Ley (1906-1969) offers sections taken from his earlier works *The Lungfish, the Dodo, & the Unicorn: An Excursion into Romantic Zoology* (Viking Press, 1948); *Dragons in Amber: Further Adventures of a Romantic Naturalist* (Sidgwick & Jackson, 1951); and *Salamanders and Other Wonders* (Viking Press, 1955). His interests range from Pacific Islander stories of giant sharks to the discovery of the Congo peacock by a scientist whose imagination was fired by two enigmatic feathers. Ley's discussion of a "dragon" frieze on the Ishtar Gate that once guarded an entrance to Babylon is just one of many items in this book that are still discussed by cryptozoologists in 2021. He explores folkloric creatures as well. How did the legend of a tree that bore lambs ever get started? What does the unicorn myth represent? He gives sea serpents a careful look and thinks at least one species will likely be identified. The book is well written, well organized, and fun.

Encyclopedia of New and Rediscovered Animals

Shuker, Karl (2012: Coachwhip Publications, 368pp.)

Building on two of Dr. Shuker's earlier works, *The Lost Ark: New and Rediscovered Animals of the 20th Century* (HarperCollins, 1993) and *The New Zoo: New and Rediscovered Animals of the Twentieth Century* (House of Stratus, 2002), the *Encyclopedia* deserves its title. This is a mammoth collection of scientific achievements from 1900 to the present. It's information-packed, thoroughly illustrated, and most enjoyable. Shuker does not try to include all discoveries since the beetles alone would merit a library. He goes for creatures that are relatively large or scientifically important, and those are more than sufficient to fill this large-format book.

Shuker is a highly knowledgeable writer, as you'd expect from a Ph.D. who has been poking into the odd corners of zoology for four decades. He discusses both species and important subspecies, including those where there is some dispute about taxonomy (e.g., it's not clear whether Rothschild's giraffe is a subspecies, species, or just a local variation). The zoologically inclined reader will enjoy every page of this romp through monk seals, giant stick insects, megamouth sharks, monitor lizards, and other discoveries simply too numerous to mention. One thing Shuker does not do is provide context by discussing species discovery curves or just how many new species are being found. He does, though, amply demonstrate his main theme: that discovery didn't end with the "golden age" of the 1800s—indeed, it's continued at a steady and often surprising pace right up to the present day.

This book has plenty of mysteries along with definite discoveries. Some are well-known. Others, like a slow loris with a thick bushy tail, a species not yet taxonomically described although it's been held in captivity and photographed, surprised even a well-read aficionado like myself. Likewise, some of the stories of discovery, like the coelacanth's, have been told many times, but few people know the tragic tale behind the discovery of Flecker's sea wasp jellyfish or how Rudie Kuiter discovered an octopus pretending to be a flounder. Shuker also includes stories of animals that didn't live up to their hype as new species, like Mexico's onza, which is not a new species of big cat, just an odd puma.

He closes with a few words on possible future discoveries, a note on taxonomy, and a 33-page bibliography. The book includes hundreds of images, ranging from photos to Bill Rebsamen's wonderful color illustrations. This is one of the classic books, not just of cryptozoology but of zoology and conservation biology. Readers will revisit it many times. It's a great achievement.

Still in Search of Prehistoric Survivors: The Creatures That Time Forgot?

Shuker, Karl (2016: Coachwhip Publications, 612pp.)

Shuker, one of the few academically-credentialed zoologists to pitch his intellectual tent in cryptid territory, has assembled the most ambitious single volume on cryptozoology since Bernard Heuvelmans' original *On the Track of Unknown Animals*. It's also one of the most sumptuously illustrated cryptozoology books ever, thanks to Bill Rebsamen and several other artists.

Shuker, in this massive rewrite and expansion of his previous books, does not cover all reported cryptids. He is interested primarily in those who may be unrecognized survivors from past eras. This eliminates, for example, the intriguing giant fish of Lake Iliamna, and both Sasquatch and Yeti also get only brief treatments.

Shuker makes the most persuasive case for Australia's marsupial cat, the *yarri*, a possible survivor from the genus *Thylacoleo*. It does seem likely this animal existed into the 20th century and just maybe still does. Shuker does not accept every survivor theory: he doubts the late survival of the Irish elk, the mammoth, and the American lion *Panthera atrox*, among others. However, he seems accepting, to my mind, of a few too many. He makes the strongest case possible for the African "dinosaur," most commonly called *mokele-mbembe*, but widespread similarities in stories and art can exist even with completely mythical animals. Also, paleontologist Louis Jacobs's argument that the region involved is not a "lost world" where time has stood still for millennia needs more discussion.

All that said, this is a magnificent compendium of information, and Shuker is to be commended for his exhaustive research and clear writing. Though I'm a cryptozoological reader and writer with decades of experience, Shuker here offers a great deal that's new to me. Notable examples are some reports of the North American *waheela* (a scary predator like a wolf on steroids, which may have been a late survivor of the "bear-dogs" or Amphicyonidae) and several African and Chinese animals.

Some of the subjects are famous, while some you've likely never heard of. Shuker builds interesting cases for lesser-known cryptids ranging from several large Indonesian birds to (relying a great deal on Professor Christine Janis' work) a pig-sized hyrax from China.

I doubt we will find more than a few of these animals alive, but I will be surprised if we don't find any. Shuker has poured many years of effort into this book, and the result is one of the foundational works of cryptozoology.

Abominable Science! Origins of the Yeti, Nessie, and Other Famous Cryptids

Loxton, Daniel, and Donald R. Prothero (2013: Columbia University Press, 411pp.)

Loxton and Prothero have written a very useful book. There's nothing else in this niche—that of the scientific, skeptical examination of the entire field and the most spectacular cryptids.

Dr. Prothero, a prominent geologist and paleontologist, and Loxton, a science writer, start with the question of whether cryptozoology is a science or pseudoscience. They come down on the latter side, arguing that cryptozoology as practiced includes some of the sketchiest "science" being written today.

The authors alternate being the primary authors of chapters, and it's not hard to discern them. Loxton is a bit wistful, thinking cryptozoologists are overwhelmingly wrong but hoping that's not entirely true. He thinks cryptozoology is harmless at worst and may offer benefits, like increased knowledge of the environments being searched. Prothero believes cryptozoology has no purpose and no redeeming features. He argues it contributes to a general belief in pseudoscience, including the paranormal and scientific illiteracy.

This is certainly one of the most controversial books among cryptozoologists. To cite only one response, Jeff Meldrum complains that "... these self-proclaimed experts set out to write an authoritative evaluation and produce such dribble and get it published through academic presses!" The authors relied on secondary sources and had little contact with working cryptozoologists, although that's because their focus was largely historical.

There are long chapters on Bigfoot, the Yeti, Nessie, the sea serpent, and Africa's sauropod-like *mokele-mbembe*.

The authors agree with author Greg Long in ***The Making of Bigfoot*** (Prometheus, 2004) in his debunking of the Patterson-Gimlin film, although they should have mentioned that Long presents two contradictory accounts (a modified theatrical costume vs. a heavy horsehide suit) without reconciling them. They debunk the claim we don't find bones of other animals, like bears, and reject the idea that Bigfoot must bury its dead as special pleading.

Loxton and Prothero dismiss the Yeti, saying it's hard to find real evidence for an unknown animal in the jumble of differing reports and folktales. They believe the famous tracks photographed by Eric Shipton in 1951 were a hoax. Nitpick: They cite climber Reinhold Messner's belief that the Yeti is a brown bear without mentioning he means a bizarre bipedal whistling species, not *Ursus arctos*.

The Nessie chapter won't surprise anyone. Suffice to say, the authors consider it a mixture of hoaxes, claims made to boost tourism and misidentifications. They are certainly all the evidence, including Tim Dinsdale's 1960 film, can be dismissed.

On the sea serpent, the authors trace the subject's origin as a compendium of now-known creatures and heroic myths. They argue that, if we can't technically disprove the sea serpent, we can still dismiss it. While they reject two touchstone cases, the 1848 HMS *Daedalus* sighting and the modern Cadborosuarus, they ignore two others, the 1817-1819 New England sightings and the 1907 *Valhalla* case. [Loxton told me in an email they meant to include New England, but it got lost in the time crunch. Loxton said they left out the most-cited sea serpent case, the 1907 sighting by two naturalists on the yacht *Valhalla*, because it was an unusual description that didn't fit in with the main sea serpent story. I can't understand that at all.]

The authors effectively shred the case for *mokele-mbembe*. The few existing images could be anything, the contamination of local witnesses has been going on for years, and the ecology and paleontology don't work. They blame interest in this cryptid on young-Earth creationists, although seekers like Roy Mackal and Redmon O'Hanlon mention no such motives.

There are 56 pages of endnotes and citations included. Despite its flaws, this is a very important book. Even cryptozoologists who think the authors are flat-out wrong need to read it. A 2015 paperback edition has numerous minor tweaks.

Matt's Musings: The word "skeptic" is defined in the Oxford Advanced Learner's Dictionary as "a person who usually doubts that claims or statements are true, especially those that other people believe in." That's too broad to be of much use in cryptozoology. I'd summarize the current usage as "Someone who examines facts and theories carefully, balancing an open mind with a demand for empirical evidence." Whether that's applied in practice is a hotly debated topic among cryptozoologists. Many believe those labeling themselves skeptics are closed-minded: some even change the word to "scofftic." Skeptics respond cryptozoologists are too credulous. This chasm will, I hope, be narrowed, although it's unlikely to be closed.

I am inclined to think that the realm of mythology is where the Yeti rightly belongs. – Sir Edmund Hillary, mountaineer

The Case for the Sea Serpent

Gould, Rupert (1930: Phillip Allan Publishers, 211pp.) (Reprinted by Coachwhip Publications in 2008)

Writing at a time when he could correspond with many witnesses to the "classic" cases, Gould conducted a great deal of research for this book. He offers here a brief for the animal's existence that might still eclipse any later single book, even Heuvelmans'. He includes full chapters on the most important sightings, like those from the ships *Daedalus* and *Valhalla*. He is not uncritically accepting of reports: he includes the famous tale of a creature seen in its entirety by the HMS *Fly* in the late 1830s but cautions that the tale depends on one person's secondhand account of what one of the *Fly's* officers said, with nothing to corroborate it.

Gould concludes there are three species at large: a long-necked seal, a reptile descended from (or convergently evolved to resemble) a plesiosaur, and a "gigantic turtle-like creature," which depends heavily on one closeup description of the Australian *moha moha*. The *moha moha* was described by an Australian teacher when she saw the animal on the beach. Unfortunately, it's an impossible chimera with a high-domed shell and a fishlike tail. The seal and plesiosaur ideas, while not original to Gould, found their footings (so to speak) here and have been discussed in some form in every book on the topic written since.

In the Wake of the Sea-Serpents

Heuvelmans, Bernard (1968: Hill & Wang, 645pp.)

In this massive volume, Heuvelmans laid the foundation of marine cryptozoology, as he did for land animals in *On the Track*. It wasn't the first good book on the subject, but was the most comprehensive and remains so as I write this in 2021. Sifting through 358 "good" cases, Heuvelmans provides a worthy starting point for all researchers of the topic. He suggests the *Valhalla* sighting involved a huge eel or eel-shaped fish swimming with its head and forebody out of the water. Heuvelmans concluded there were at least seven new species involved (five mammals, a reptile, and an eel): he includes two others here, a giant turtle and an anomaly called the yellow-belly, but omitted them in his later works. Understandably, Heuvelmans' fellow zoologists found the idea of a whole zoo of huge unknown animals hard to swallow. It didn't help that he went out on a limb with the science, suggesting the ancient whale Basilosaurus had armor and side-fins (highly speculative in 1965 and known to be incorrect now) and saying that "eels are powerful constrictors," which they are not.

Alas, as with *On the Track*, no new species have been found that fit any of Heuvelmans' types. His brief tour of mystery cetaceans notes a few sightings that may match now-identified species, and this was my first introduction to Wilson's whale, an Antarctic animal that remains a genuine mystery. He focuses on the unknown species, though, and any that exist are still undiscovered. Nevertheless, this book is a trove of information, gathering most of the known sightings going back centuries. Heuvelmans tries to match these to order and family, even though his proposed genus and species names are invalid without holotypes (physical type specimens used in the formal description of species). Subsequent cryptozoologists have proposed both more and fewer categories in their own views. One common approach has been to collapse his mammals down to one possible species, as I did in **Shadows of Existence** (Hancock House Publishers, 2006) and Rob Cornes and Gary Cunningham did in **The Seal Serpent: the Search for a Long-necked Pinniped** (Independently published, 2019). But *In the Wake of the Sea-Serpents* is where modern marine cryptozoology started. It's essential reading for those studying the unknown animals of the deep.

Monsters of the Sea

Ellis, Richard (1994: Alfred A. Knopf, 429pp.)

Ellis covers a broad range of sea monsters real, fictitious, and alleged. The book is thoroughly referenced, expertly written, and fascinating. Ellis believes most sea monster sightings are mistakes, often involving giant squid. He puts the *Daedalus* creature and, less convincingly, the *Valhalla* monster down to squids behaving strangely. He accepts, though, that the repeated sightings off Gloucester in 1817 represent something unusual. Ellis also surveys the modern reports of "Cadborosuarus" from the coastal Pacific. He offers a summary line I've been stealing ever since because it applies so well to much of cryptozoology: "If I were a betting man, I would bet against it. (I would, however, like nothing better than to lose the bet)." Ellis reviews the Saint Augustine, Florida "giant octopus" carcass from 1896 with great thoroughness, including in this book a previously unpublished photograph, and concludes a genuine giant octopus had washed ashore. Ellis has written an enjoyable and important book, whether all his conclusions are correct or not. The extensive bibliography shows the kind of research only the best writers put into their work.

The Enigma of Loch Ness

Bauer, Henry (1986: University of Illinois Press, 242pp.)

Bauer, an emeritus professor of chemistry and science studies at Virginia Polytechnic Institute, offers an intriguing look at the creature of Loch Ness. He starts with opposing chapters, one with the premise Nessie does not exist and in the following chapter counters his own thinking to argue it does exist. This dichotomy, and his musings on the nature of science and of truth, recurs throughout the book. He spends a few chapters later on similar thoughts, in between a historical listing of major monster news and the interesting people and events of the quest. Two late chapters cover "Bad Reasons for Not Believing" and "Bad Reasons for Believing."

Bauer presents himself in the Introduction as an ex-skeptic who now believes that an unidentified species exists in Loch Ness, but he strives for a balanced look at the evidence throughout. He doesn't go into that evidence as thoroughly as most Nessie writers do because he's more interested in setting the question into its complex context of science, belief, etc. Bauer doesn't claim scientists are closed-minded, but he does believe science, especially during generational shifts of old to new thinking, can leave behind some useful thoughts and procedures. If the events of 1933 had happened a half-century earlier, he thinks, scientists would have swarmed over it and discovered the creature.

At the loch, he spends considerable time trying to understand hoaxer Frank Searle, wondering how much damage he did to the pursuit of Nessie as a serious enterprise. He also interviews Tim Dinsdale, whom he considers to be a reliable witness. He takes some shots at Maurice Burton's skeptical book *The Elusive Monster* (Rupert Hart-Davis, 1961), complaining Burton should have mentioned he knew Dinsdale and offered his opinion of the latter's veracity. Bauer believes Lester Smith, who has claimed to be the monster's founder/publicist, boosted interest in something that already existed. Appendices, notes, bibliography, and a chronology of sightings take up a good half of the book, and *The Enigma of Loch Ness* will be perpetually useful for this alone. In 2007, Bauer published a book disputing the AIDS-HIV connection, which cast a permanent pall over his career and work. However, this misguided work does not invalidate his Loch Ness research.

A Monstrous Commotion

Williams, Gareth (2017: Orion Publishing Group, 320pp.)

This book goes deep into the history of the region around Loch Ness, its people, and the lore and legend that culminated in the famous modern sightings and films. Even people familiar with the history of Nessie will enjoy new material, especially in the biographies. My favorite example is R. Kenneth Wilson, who was not merely a doctor when approached to participate in a photo hoax. He was a decorated World War I veteran, both as a doctor and as a combatant. He had other achievements, including writing a history of the machine pistol. His accomplishments and reputation made him a person of unassailable character and so perfect for presenting the pictures to the UK public. (In World War II, he returned to combat, parachuting into occupied France.)

Williams' historical account of Nessie is thorough. If the Nessie of the 1930s was a hoax to draw tourists, she was a brilliantly successful one, as people flocked to the lake even in hard economic times. Almost forgotten during the war, the monster stormed back onto the stage in the 1950s, particularly after Constance Whyte's book *More than a Legend* (Hamish Hamilton, 1957) and then the 1960 Dinsdale film.

Along the way, Williams describes personalities, expeditions, hoaxes, and the ups and downs of Nessie-hunters' relationships with scientists. These interactions were not always contentious as the two groups overlapped at several points. Williams' fascinating narrative of the developments of the 60s and 70s, the interplay of people like Dinsdale and Sir Peter Scott, and how the clash of human beliefs and sometimes shoved the monster into the background is the heart of the book. He includes the proposal to name the monster for Queen Elizabeth, the efforts to get more scientists to accept its existence to sign on, the tireless promotion of the monster's cause by Dinsdale, the role of eccentrics like Alistair Crowley and Ted Holliday, and much more.

Williams isn't perfect. His mention of the whale shark includes three major errors in two sentences. He has an irksome habit of presenting stories and witnesses as genuine and then mentioning the doubts about them chapters later. In the end, Williams accepts a publicist's claim that he invented the monster back in the 1930s. While no one living knows the whole truth, read this book for yourself and ponder it.

Abominable Snowmen: Legend Come to Life - The Story of Sub-Humans on Five Continents from The Early Ice Age Until Today

Sanderson, Ivan (1961: Chilton, 525pp.)

You can guess from the title that this is an ambitious book, and the publication date is part of the book's value. Like Stonor's ***The Sherpa and the Snowman*** (Hollis & Carter, 1955), this was written before the media and cryptid enthusiasts made these creatures (or myths) world-famous in a way that makes it hard to separate fact from fiction.

Sanderson draws on decades of fieldwork and travel to put things into environmental and cultural context. In this book, he pulls together disparate traditions, myths, reports, and evidence from all over the globe. He is interested in any eyewitness reports, even odd ones like a "wild man" wearing clothes and Canadian Albert Ostman's story of being kidnapped by Sasquatches, which Sanderson finds possible despite some discrepancies. (He also writes that one Native American asked about Sasquatch responded sarcastically, "Don't tell me the white men have finally gotten around to *that*.")

Sanderson accepted there were four creatures, with numerous local variations all over the world. They were 1) Sub-Humans (the Asian *almas* being most famous); 2) Proto-Pygmies, with Asian, African, and American versions; 3) Neo-Giants (Sasquatches and the like); and 4) *Meh-Teh*, the classic abominable snowman, which Sanderson would bet "gold bars against stale doughnuts" was real. He reports information from expeditions that have pursued the Yeti. A famous desiccated hand from the Pangboche monastery, he thinks, is human but ancient. (We now know it's human.)

When he guesses at lineages, he is handicapped by 1961's knowledge of ancient humans, but he is knowledgeable about a great many things from footprints to human abnormalities and evaluates evidence with the science available. Some of Sanderson's terminology about "natives" is offensive today, but he deplores xenophobia and considers information from indigenous people to be more accurate than that gathered by foreigners.

Sanderson had no patience with those he felt ignored cryptozoology. He divided science into "True Scientists" and "Experts," the former being open-minded and the latter refusing to look at anything odd enough to damage their standing, reputation, or career.

There are no footnotes, but many sources are given in the text and there is a bibliography.

The breadth of this book can't be adequately described in a short review. From the first hardcover release in 1961 (I was lucky to find a copy in a thrift shop), the book went through many printings and at least two more editions in the 20th century and three more already in the 21st. There is a 2017 edition from Cosimo, part of a series of republished crypto books with the added title *Loren Coleman Presents*, and the latest, out in 2018, is from Adventures Unlimited Press.

Sasquatch: Legend Meets Science

Meldrum, Jeffrey (2006: Forge Books, 297pp.)

I look at the evidence with a naturalist's eye. I am neither a believer nor can I reject all the evidence and conclude that a novel ape-like being could not exist. – George Schaller, mammalogist, in the Foreword to *Sasquatch: Legend Meets Science*

If you want to submit one book as a brief for Sasquatch's existence, this is it. Meldrum is well-qualified, being a zoologist and anthropologist with special expertise in how primates walk. He is dedicated to the pursuit of the truth that he's sure is out there and tries to be scientific in his approach. He devotes chapters to different types of evidence—footprints, sounds, etc.—and breaks down some of the famous film and video claims. Meldrum is convinced the famous 1969 Patterson-Gimlin Sasquatch film is real, although not every point convinces me, and he doesn't mention Heuvelmans' criticism that the subject's coat reflects light in all directions, like artificial rather than natural hair. Meldrum also finds a few video clips and some of the footprint evidence compelling.

On the subject of footprints, he argues that many of the tracks show flexibility and variation unlikely to be possible with fake feet and that the depth some prints are pressed into the soil indicates the walker was much heavier than a human. Like John Napier, an expert with similar credentials, he accepts the famous Bossburg, Washington, "cripplefoot" tracks, though Meldrum diagnoses the abnormality in the right foot as stemming from a congenital abnormality, where Napier thought it was from a childhood injury. He also thinks the so-called "Skookum cast" in mud, found in 2000 in Washington state, was left by a reclining Bigfoot.

Concerning acoustic evidence, Meldrum makes an interesting point about "wood knocking." This is commonly thought to be a Sasquatch habit and is often used by those trying to attract the creature. While such knocking is believable primate behavior, Meldrum writes that no one has reported seeing a Sasquatch actually doing it.

Meldrum argues that a human or a descendant of the giant Asian ape *Gigantopithecus blacki* could have made it across to North America, as there have been several times in prehistory when land or ice allowed animals to migrate between the continents. Meldrum thinks the species might have accomplished this while leaving very few fossils for us to find. One of his examples is the red panda, strictly an Asian creature today, whose U.S. version is known only from a few fossil teeth. As those teeth pre-date any of the Sasquatch candidates by millions of years, though, I am not certain how useful the parallel is.

Meldrum's evidence has been disputed, and he does acknowledge some shortcomings (e.g., hair isn't conclusive unless there's a Sasquatch hair to compare it with) and mentions some of the hoaxes. He makes the point that, while many of the Bigfoot researchers and promoters don't have a strong scientific background, neither do many of the skeptics. For instance, some researchers and skeptics failed to consider specific zoological details like the feeding behavior of apes before pronouncing on a related Bigfoot point. He doesn't take the "science is closed-minded" route but does mention some individuals who he believes take the attitude, "It isn't because it can't be." Meldrum does not deal with one of my own common complaints, that of people are finding one track, or a few tracks, where there should be a trail. However, he answered a query from me by saying it's surprising how few surfaces produce good footprints: a lone print or a few tracks crossing a walking trail in a forest may be genuine, but such solitary prints in areas of dirt, sand, or snow are red flags. If this book does not make his case airtight, it's still, in 2021, the best pro-Sasquatch book yet written.

. . .

There is nothing like looking, if you want to find something. You certainly usually find something, if you look, but it is not always quite the something you were after. – J.R.R. Tolkien, *The Hobbit*

Primates

Humans are narcissists, and we like a cryptid that resembles us. Sea monsters, globsters, out-of-place animals, the potentially not-extinct, and mythic beasts do not hold a candle to an ape-man. – Thomm Quackenbush, author, *Holidays with Bigfoot*

In Pursuit of the Abominable Snowman

Tchernine, Odette (1971: Taplinger Publishing, 184pp.)

This is one of several books for general readers written in the golden days of snowman-hunting. *In Pursuit* made a mark on me as a young teenager. Don't let the page count fool you: Tchernine packs the book with information. It opens with the Minnesota Iceman corpse story (the author thinks this exhibit was a model), then jumps continents to delve deeply into reports from Russia and adjoining territories to the south and east. She reaches into the Pamirs, the Himalayas, China, and Mongolia and touches on Borneo, Africa, etc. She incorporates findings by leading researchers Professor Marie-Jeanne Koffmann and Dr. Boris Porshnev, leaning most heavily on accounts gathered by the latter. Though the evidence is overwhelmingly anecdotal, this is at least a good collection of it, with a useful dictionary of names at the end. She throws barbs at both religion and "Science" along the way but muses at the end whether we are somehow not meant to find our more primitive relations.

Bigfoot

Napier, John (1972: Berkley Publishing, 240pp.)

Napier, a primatologist and authority on primate locomotion, was the perfect scientist to take a good look at Bigfoot. Napier mentions some other cryptid primates but focuses on the Yeti, Bigfoot, and the *almas* of south-central Asia. What he reports here is a bit surprising. He considers the evidence for the Yeti to be so scant he would dismiss it, except "The Shipton footprint is the one item in the whole improbable saga that simply sticks in my throat" (p. 207). Napier suggests the photographed print was a composite, made by a naked human foot stepping in a shoeprint, with the sun melting the two together. He decides the Yeti is all myth and no monster.

Concerning the *almas*, it seems to Napier that the inhabitants of its rugged homeland make the animal sound too plentiful as if it should be easy to find. Napier recounts the story of one Caucasus resident who was asked if the *almas* were mythical. The man, proud of his people's rich mythology, was actually offended that anyone would think that heritage included something as common and boring as the *almas*. Common or not, no one has found it, and Napier doubts anyone will.

Considering the Sasquatch and related accounts in North America, Napier rejects the two most substantive pieces of evidence offered. To him, the Minnesota Iceman has an unworkable mix of features from different primates. The 1967 Patterson-Gimlin film from a California sighting, while the creature in it was very different, provokes the same response from Napier. If the film is a hoax, he writes, it's an impressive one. If not, it shows an animal with human legs and gait but a massive, apelike upper body, plus an exaggerated stride he doesn't see as natural. While he "can't see the zipper," he thinks the footage is bogus.

In contrast, he does not think the famous footprints found in Bossburg, Washington, in 1969 were fabricated. He believes the anomalous right foot shows an anatomically accurate clubfoot deformity and it was extremely unlikely a hoaxer would have the required knowledge and skill. [The involvement of Bigfoot-hunter Ivan Marx, who certainly hoaxed other evidence, has raised some doubts.] Napier rejects the idea the hundreds of reports and thousands of tracks could all be bogus. While he does not commit to the idea that an overlooked giant primate exists in North America, he certainly leans in that direction.

North America's Great Ape: The Sasquatch

Bindernagel, John (1998: Beachcomber Books, 270pp.)

Rather than argue Sasquatch's existence, Bindernagel essentially accepts that as a given and instead focuses on analyzing behavior, anatomy, and other zoological characteristics of the animal. The result is intriguing but necessarily speculative. Even the most ardent Sasquatch proponents agree there are many hoaxes and mistakes, and there's no way Bindernagel can be certain all the evidence on which his theories rest is genuine. Many of his points are based on the disputed Patterson-Gimlin film. He followed this up with a broader book, *The Discovery of the Sasquatch* (Beachcomber Books, 2010), in which he reached back into pre-colonial times to build an account of Bigfoot through history, culminating in his explanation of why the most probable hypothesis is that an unknown primate exists in North America.

What are we doing in a snowstorm tracking something that might be 800 pounds? And what do we do if we catch it? – Student accompanying Grover Krantz after a sighting, quoted by anthropologist Gary Breschini

The Field Guide to Bigfoot, Yeti, and Other Mystery Primates Worldwide

Coleman, Loren, and Patrick Huyghe (1999: Avon Publications, 207pp.)

A year before this book was published, Loren Coleman told an interviewer that "Cryptozoology is really the study of those things that lead up to the discovery and verification of a creature." To further that end, Coleman and Huyghe devised a classification system that sorts over fifty reported unknown primates into nine groups: Neo-Giant (the group including Sasquatch), True Giant, Marked Hominid, Neanderthaloid, Erectus Hominid, Proto-Pygmy, Unknown Pongid, Giant Monkey, and Merbeing. The authors do not claim that each group or each example represents a valid animal, a point some of the book's harsher critics have overlooked. This book is useful for studying cryptid-primate reports because it lets the researcher put them in context with reports similar in description and/or location. The authors believe (and I agree) the top prospect for discovering a real animal is the *orang-pendek* of Sumatra. I think reports in two of their nine categories, those concerning True Giants 15 to 18 feet (4.6-5.5 meters) tall and Merbeings, are very unlikely to reward further research. Whatever the truth may be, any cryptozoologist trying to understand the subject of unclassified large primates will want this book. A good bibliography and a list of contacts around the world add to its value. A slightly revised version, the *Annotated Edition*, came out from Anomalist Books in 2006.

True Giants: Is Gigantopithecus Still Alive?

Hall, Mark, and Loren Coleman (2010: Anomalist Books, 188pp.)

In *True Giants*, Coleman and Hall tackle a question that lurks at the edge of primate cryptozoology: Are Sasquatch and it's ilk (assuming they exist) the tallest primates on Earth, or could there be an additional species, presumably a modern descendant of *Gigantopithecus blacki*, that forms the basis for worldwide legends of much taller giants? I respect Coleman, and the late Mr. Hall was a prodigious researcher, but this book doesn't convince me.

The authors admit that we don't know what kind of skeleton works in such an animal. They suggest a honeycomb bone structure for lightness, but there's no precedent for that in mammals. Developing it would have required a long line of evolution which we've never detected. Anthropologists and paleontologists consider *Gigantopithecus to be* a heavily-built orangutan relative with a quadrupedal stance. Speculation about the posture of "Giganto" draws on its relationship to orangutans plus the sheer size indicated by its sparse fossils, so the degree to which it might stand or walk short distances is not certain. Regardless, it would take a lot of evolving to get to a bipedal ape of this size, even assuming the existence of evolutionary pressures that might produce it.

The authors have done a great deal of research, unearthing animal reports from the Solomon Islands to South America. The eyewitness reports and footprints, while not enough to make me take the True Giant seriously, will be of interest to those wanting to understand the full spectrum of unknown-primate reports.

Matt's Musings: There's a limit to the size of even hypothetical bipedal primates. To me, a practical knee joint for a 10-foot creature is especially hard to visualize. Tall humans are plagued with knee problems (just ask me). The largest and strongest healthy human on record, Barnum's strongman Angus McAskill, was seven feet nine inches (2.36 m) and 405 pounds (183 kilograms). If there are unknown bipeds, I think it's reasonable to presume they never exceed eight feet or so.

Tracking the Man-Beasts

Nickell, Joe (2011: Prometheus Books, 239pp.)

Well-known skeptical investigator Nickell pokes into an interesting, if loosely-related, collection of topics: Sasquatch, Yeti, vampires, werewolves, etc. (Nickell's bio says he's been called "the real-life Scully." Sorry, Joe, but there are other aspects to Dana Scully's appeal.)

Nickell, not surprisingly, doesn't think much of any of the apelike or manlike cryptids of the world. While the relevant chapters in this book are too short to cover the subject in-depth, I wasn't terribly impressed, even where I agree with him. You can't spend a couple of days in the woods and expect it to contribute in any meaningful way to proving or disproving the existence of a particular species. It took Jane Goodall months to get good sightings of her chimpanzees even though she knew where they were. Nickell fails to close the gap between the two accounts of the Patterson-Gimlin film suit (commercial costume vs. homemade horsehide), and his drawing of the figure points to things like "suit-glove interface" that I can't see on any blowup of the actual film. I have a similar problem with his endorsing the "melted out" explanation for the Shipton Yeti tracks. Nickell has done a lot of good with his investigations of pseudoscience. This time, he only partially succeeds in dismantling his target.

The Nature of The Beast: The First Genetic Evidence on The Survival of Apemen, Yeti, Bigfoot and Other Mysterious Creatures into Modern Times

Sykes, Bryan (2015: Coronet Books, 336pp.)

Oxford genetics professor Bryan Sykes brought the tools of his specialty to bear on the contentious issues surrounding physical evidence of cryptids. He invited those investigating unknown primates to send him their best samples of hair, saliva, blood, etc., and, using techniques which he pioneered, he would extract DNA and identify the species. Most of what he received were hair samples. He discarded those he could identify as known species as well as samples of doubtful provenance, then tested the rest of the specimens. Results: every single one was from a known species. He found bear, horse, wolf, and human hair, and even a raccoon sample from Russia but found nothing to indicate a nonhuman primate.

Sykes criticizes cryptozoologists for overvaluing hair samples that are not identifiable and for ignoring contamination of specimens, citing as an example an *orang-pendek* report that got some people (including me) genuinely excited. He finds the genetic work "proving" Sasquatch published by Dr. Melba Ketchum in 2013 to be a complete mess. This book also tells us a lot about genetics and a little about the odd corners of said science. Surprisingly, Sykes thinks human-chimpanzee crosses are not 100% impossible. He debunks the Russian tale of an "ape-woman" named Zana as a legend built on a horribly mistreated African slave. Sykes is adamant that no one sent him a sample of any kind of nonhuman primate, even though he clearly wants there to be something incredible behind all this hominid-hunting. Sykes does discuss some samples that appeared to be a polar bear in the Himalayas, though re-analysis by Dr. Ron Pine and other scientists determined these samples were from brown bears.

Sykes does his best to give cryptozoologists the benefit of the doubt. He's intrigued by the fieldwork conducted by my friend Lori Sakshaug of Washington, who pursues a Sasquatch she calls "the Big Guy," although he concludes most of the reported Sasquatch activities could be otherwise explained. This is an excellent book that explains the science very well and should be every cryptozoologist's companion. The paperback version came out with the new title *Bigfoot, Yeti, and The Last Neanderthal: A Geneticist's Search for Modern Apemen* (Disinformation Books, 2016).

Sasquatch: The Apes Among Us

Green, John (2017: Hancock House Publishers, 492pp.) (Original edition 1978 from Cheam Publishing)

No one put more time and energy into Sasquatch-hunting than the late John W. Green (1927-2016). Green was a newspaperman in

Agassiz, BC, when he started investigating reports of Sasquatch tracks in 1957. In this massive book (it's published in rather dense print to keep the length reasonable), he presents everything he learned in decades of research. Green had no doubt the animal is real. He relates his adventures traveling far and wide, looking into cases both famous (e.g., the Patterson-Gimlin encounter) and obscure, and talking to every witness, researcher, and scientist that he could find. Green was interested in every aspect of the phenomenon, which even led him to Pennsylvania to ask Stan Gordon about Bigfoot+UFO cases, which, he says, "I will happily leave to the UFO people."

Sometimes the pages blur as Green recounts every discussion and report, but clearly, he intends to create the most detailed record possible in a single book. He breaks down reports of things like eyeshine, color, eating habits, and so forth. He asserts there must be thousands of animals with a wide distribution. Given the lack of luck so far in getting definitive evidence, he muses that it may be necessary to kill a specimen to establish the species and get protection for it, although he knows there would still be legions of people seeking a glimpse of the creature. Capturing and/or killing a specimen would be ethically permissible because he believes Bigfoot, despite being clearly bipedal, is "all beast" and not any form of human. (If it were, he suggests wryly, it would be subject to all the characteristics of the human world, from being eligible for food stamps to having to send Bigfoot children to school.) As comprehensive as it is, the book could use more illustrations, although the one of a footprint from 1947 is certainly interesting.

Far-Out, Shaggy, Funky Monsters: A What-It-Is History of Bigfoot in the 1970s

Green, Daniel (2018: Coachwhip Publications, 1,188pp.)

This is a unique book, and not only because you could stop a charging Bigfoot by braining him with this monster-sized tome. The 1970s were the real heyday for Bigfoot, Sasquatch, and other primate cryptids when the topic drew massive public interest in the wake of the Patterson-Gimlin film and even some scientific respectability. Green has uncovered seemingly every significant report, footprint claim, book, movie, and miscellaneous cultural artifact and presents them a year-by-year chronicle of North America's favorite monster.

The Sasquatch Festival of 1938 is our (little-known) kickoff point for a short pre-1970s history of public interest. In 1967, when the Patterson-Gimlin film appeared, the real fun began. We heard of sightings all over the country. One new to me was a report by three Marines in 1973, and while young Marines like their jokes, they filed an official report, which seems a bit iffy for a prank. Green covers the first films and documentaries, especially the shoestring hit film *The Legend of Boggy Creek*, and of course the Minnesota Iceman and the changing stories attached to it. He discusses the scientists who took an interest in the phenomena, as well as the first serious scientific book, Napier's 1973 *Bigfoot*, and the major tomes that followed it up through skeptical anthropologist Kenneth Wylie's *Bigfoot: A Personal Inquiry into a Phenomenon* (Viking Press, 1980). Green introduces us to many of the colorful characters, from hoaxers Jon and Tom Biscardi to completely serious—if not always scientific—searchers for knowledge, and finally, those like Stan Gordon who connected Bigfoot to UFOs and other oddities.

Green cites publications others have overlooked, like the *Baltimore Afro-American* newspaper, as he chases all over North America, from Alaska down to the Honey Island Swamp Monster and the Florida Skunk Ape. He takes us through the first conferences and meetings, the "kill-no kill" debate, and of course, more sightings, from Ogden, Utah, to Powderly, Texas. Green's best section header, without doubt, is "The Tunnel Monster of Cabbagetown."

The sheer weight of the material Green presents here is enough to make one hope that there is some creature behind all of it, but Green doesn't offer any final thoughts on whether there is or not. He includes over 100 pages of annexes, blogography, notes, and so forth. Green's evenhanded, sometimes bemused approach and mass of data may not make many converts one way or the other, but he has created an unsurpassed cultural history of the monster's most famous decade. This is a must-have reference on the phenomenon that was, and still is, Bigfoot himself, both monster and myth.

Okay, so let's talk about the E-word. You all know which word I mean. That pesky E-word that skeptics like my cousin Theodore just love to throw around to try to make the family cryptid enthusiast look like a total loser. That's right. I'm talking about evidence. – Jacqueline E. Smith, author, Trashy Suspense Novel

Giants, Cannibals and Monsters: Bigfoot in Native Culture

Strain, Kathy Moskowitz (2020: Hancock House Publishers, 288pp.)

Anthropologist Kathy Strain has collected stories from Native American tribes all over North America. They refer to a variety of dangerous creatures, from hairy dwarfs to "Hairy Man," from "giant Indians" to "giants" who can straddle rivers and tower over trees. Strain presents these by tribe, with Native names and tribal-area maps. Many of the stories could refer to a Bigfoot-like creature, while others concern shape-shifters which can appear animal or human when it suits them. Strain suggests this body of information has roots in both knowledge of strange hominins and a tradition of using giants and cannibals as bogeymen to keep children safe and teach other lessons. Several themes run through the stories passed down through generations: 1) trickery—many people and things are tricky, as sometimes the non-humans are duped and sometimes the humans, 2) listen to your parents, 3) family is paramount, and 4) not everyone is who they appear to be.

There are interesting motifs that parallel European folklore, like a giant being vulnerable only at his heel. The book has an index of names used by each tribe. Sources for the tales appear in the text. Some stories are from Native-written works, as with the book *Kwakiutl Legends* (Chief James Wallas with Pamela Whitaker

(Hancock House Publishers, 1982), although most are secondary, and some sources are unknown.

Strain acknowledges that basing conclusions about real animals on the folklore of a culture not your own is a tricky business. As there is no similar compilation by a Native American author, though, anyone interested in "Native American traditions" of Bigfoot outside a single tribe or region should start here.

Matt's Musings: The word "Sasquatch" began as one English speaker's approximation of a Coast Salish word. According to www.native-languages. org/sasquatch.htm, the spelling of names found in Coast Salish languages (Coast Salish, Halkomelem, Squamish, Sto:lo, and Cowichan) include Sasq'ets, Sesq'ec, Sesqec, Sacsquec, Saskehavas, and Sesquac, and the most common pronunciation is sess-k-uts.

The Sherpa and the Snowman

Stonor, Charles (1955, Hollis & Carter, 209pp.)

This book dates from a time when Western culture considered the rest of the world exotic and fascinating, but also primitive and unenlightened, and Western scientists and travelers believed there was much to be discovered. Anthropologist Charles Robert Stonor led an expedition in 1953-54 looking for the Yeti. He spent months in Nepal talking to witnesses, often living with local people, and gathering modern reports, old tales, and myths, as well as tromping through the snows looking at tracks and excrement and hoping to see the creature. He failed on the latter count but came away convinced that the Yeti existed. What makes this meandering book valuable is that Stonor documented the cultural context of the Yeti before radio, TV, and countless other expeditions and explorers mucked it up.

. . .

Matt's Musings: The Sherpa and the Snowman is one of the old hardcover books I cherish, although I have no recollection of where I got it. I have a fondness for hardcovers: I can't afford to fill a library with them, and I read paperbacks and ebooks too, but hardcovers to me have intrinsic value, and I get them when I can.

The Search for Bigfoot

Byrne, Peter (1975: Acropolis Books, 263pp.)

In this book, hunter and conservationist Byrne presents his unsuccessful efforts to find North America's reported ape. The most distinctive aspect of the book is not in the narrative, which is good, but the many illustrations, maps, and documents Byrne collected. Byrne, a man with enormous field experience, was a major popularizer of the subject. He has written other crypto books and led expeditions in Nepal as well as North America. My favorite Byrne book, although it does not deal with cryptids, is *Tula Hatti: The Last Great Elephant* (Faber & Faber, 1991).

On the Track of the Sasquatch

Green, John (1980: Hancock House Publishers, 64pp.)

In this slender collection, Green offers the highlights of his first two decades of Sasquatch-hunting. Whatever the explanation for Sasquatch turns out to be, this is an interesting recap by one of the creature's most effective popularizers and most ardent pursuers.

Yes, everyone know Bigfoot smell like shit. Please make effort not to point out every time you see Bigfoot. Thank you. – Graham Roumieu, author, *Me Write Book: It Bigfoot Memoir*

Manlike Monsters on Trial: Early Records and Modern Evidence

Halpin, Marjorie (editor) (1980: University of British Columbia Press, 336pp.)

This is a unique collection of papers from the 1978 university-hosted conference "Sasquatch and Similar Phenomena." The papers here focus mainly on Sasquatch, with occasional excursions. The names may surprise you: almost all the authors except John Green were university professors or instructors, and none of them became prominent in the Sasquatch-hunting community as we know it in 2021. There are papers on Sasquatch as a cultural phenomenon, Native American accounts and beliefs, and six papers on the state of Sasquatch investigations. An interesting one by anthropologist Vaughn Bryant, Jr. and ecologist Burleigh Trevor-Deutsch reports the authors have three specimens of purported Sasquatch feces and one of hair they couldn't ascribe to known animals. There's a rich bibliography included.

I'm a romantic; I would like Bigfoot to exist. I've met people who swear they've seen Bigfoot, and I think the interesting thing is, every single continent, there's an equivalent of Bigfoot or Sasquatch. There's the Yeti, the Yowie in Australia, the Chinese Wildman, and on and on and on. – Jane Goodall, primatologist and anthropologist

Wild Man: China's Yeti

Zhenxin, Yuan, and Huang Wanpo (1981: Fortean Times, 23pp.)

This booklet is a collection of articles on China's reported unknown primate, with a helpful glossary of Chinese "monster" names and types. It includes analysis of hair and other evidence.

. . .

I don't think there is a Loch Ness Monster ...But I am absolutely baffled by the abominable snowman, which was also called the Yeti or Sasquatch, because very, very convincing footprints have been found. – Sir David Attenborough, naturalist, 2020

Still Living? Yeti, Sasquatch, and the Neanderthal Enigma

Shackley, Myra (1983: Thames & Hudson Publishing, 192pp.)

This book offers a detailed review of the evidence for mystery primates worldwide, focusing on Eurasia. (Sasquatch gets one chapter.) Shackley, an archeologist, devoted years of research, correspondence, and travel into remote regions to solving the mystery. She concludes that there are two mystery primates. One is a surviving Neanderthal, called *almas* and by many other names. The other, the Yeti, is quite different, a tall upright ape probably evolved from *Gigantopithecus*, and she feels that Sasquatch is a close relation of this species. She considers the existence of the *almas* a certainty. Her evidence, though, is limited to reports and footprints, plus the belief that the Zana story referred to an *almas*. Zana has since been shown by DNA analysis to have been an African slave. Still, anyone studying the *almas* should definitely read this book.

Big Footprints: A Comprehensive Bibliography Concerning Bigfoot, the Abominable Snowman, and Related Beings

Perez, Danny (1988: DPP, 189pp.)

Perez provides an extensive bibliography, with no annotations but with useful divisions by type of item and time period. He begins with "Books: 1556 to 1983," listed by author, e.g., Paul Belloni du Chaillu, *Stories of the Gorilla Country*, Harper and Brothers, 1868. (This is still available as an ebook, by the way.) Perez continues through thousands of entries of magazines, journals, newspapers, records and tapes, radio programs, TV shows (he lists an episode of the animated

Superman, but misses *Jonny Quest*), encyclopedias, audiovisual items like a Marlin Perkins slide presentation on the Yeti, etc., all the way to a handful of comic books. This is a treasure vault for researchers of this topic and era, and technology that didn't exist in 1988 makes it easier to find some of the items. Who knew that a singer named Rex North once cut a record entitled "Oh, Please, Mr. Bigfoot, Put Me Down?" It's available online, and it's a hoot.

...the ye-teh, or Yeti, has met with a storm of disapproval from upset scientists around the world. But as with the Sasquatch of the vast rain forests of the Pacific Northwest, the case against the existence of the Yeti— entirely speculative, and necessarily based on assumptions of foolishness or mendacity in many observers of good reputation—is even less 'scientific' than the evidence that it exists. – Peter Matthiessen, author of The Snow Leopard

Lore and Legend of the Yeti

Rall, Kesar (1988: Pilgrims Book House [Thamjel, Kathmandu, Nepal], 89pp.)

In this slender but valuable book, Rall presents a collection of reports, lore, and legend concerning the variety of primates that reside either in the valleys of the high Himalayas or in the folklore of its people. There is a 1999 reprint.

Matt's Musings: Lore and Legend of the Yeti *is an example of the kind of serendipitous find a researcher can make by walking through libraries and bookstores. I spotted this one in the Los Angeles city library around 1992 and photocopied much of it in the ancient days before cell phone cameras or Amazon.*

Tom Slick and the Search for the Yeti

Coleman, Loren (1989: Faber & Faber, 171pp.)

Cryptozoologist Coleman traces the Yeti and Sasquatch expeditions financed by oil tycoon and outdoorsman Tom Slick, which began in 1956.

Slick was a colorful and fascinating character, and this book offers creature reports, adventure, and intrigue. For instance, negotiating with local governments to allow a Yeti search was often difficult, if not chaotic, and it turns out the Central Intelligence Agency (CIA) was involved quite a bit. Slick's curiosity extended to other cryptids, including my favorite mystery, the giant fish of Alaska's Lake Iliamna. He died in 1962 in a light-plane crash. There are appendices on all aspects of Slick's work and the CIA connection, plus a very good bibliography. Updated and reprinted as *Tom Slick: True Life Encounters in Cryptozoology* (Craven Street Books, 2002)

In the Tracks of the Yeti

Hutchison, Robert (1989: MacDonald and Company [Publishers], 285pp.)

Hutchison is an avid Yeti-seeker who understands the people and cultures forming the backdrop to the Yeti reports. He is positive the creature exists. On his expedition, Hutchison found several sets of what he thought were Yeti tracks and examined a mummified "Yeti foot," which he thought was very strange but which he fails to describe in detail. Most valuable if read in company with Daniel Taylor-Ide's similarly thorough, more skeptical work, ***Something Hidden Behind the Ranges*** (Mercury House, 2000). Taken together, these two books present most of what is known about the Yeti mystery and introduce the reader to the cultural milieu in which it exists, providing vital information for evaluating reports of unknown primates.

. . .

But there's no such thing as the unknown, only things temporarily hidden, temporarily not understood. – "Captain James Kirk," *Star Trek* (original series)

Big Footprints: A Scientific Inquiry into the Reality of Sasquatch

Krantz, Grover (1992: Johnson Books, 300pp.)

Anthropologist Krantz sifts through Sasquatch reports and tries to deduce the animal's lifestyle and characteristics based on what he considered the most reliable information. It's a good effort, although necessarily speculative. Krantz, who made major contributions to the study of human evolution, is famous among cryptozoologists for his paper "A Species Named from Footprints" (*Northwest Anthropological Research Notes*, 19: 1986). He stands by that paper's conclusion that he's pursuing an evolved *Gigantopithecus*. At that time, he named it *G. blacki*, but as that name belongs to an existing species, he later shifted to *G. canadensis*. We have neither feet nor footprints of Giganto, but Krantz believes there is no way to account for Sasquatch tracks as other than primate, and Giganto, which Krantz argues is bipedal, is the only known species that might have been big enough. Krantz weakens his argument by accepting partial evidence in two cases where some faking was involved, but this is still an important work on the subject.

Something Hidden Behind the Ranges

Taylor-Ide, Daniel (1995: Mercury House, 298pp.)

Taylor-Ide, born in the shadow of the Himalayas, recounts his personal search for the Yeti. He never did find it and eventually reached the conclusion that no such primate existed. Along the way, however, he made important discoveries about bears, conservation, and the unique place the Yeti holds in the human mind and spirit.

. . .

It is highly possible that that kind of creature may exist. – Soyam Prakash Shrestha, Nepal Agricultural Research Council

If the idea of a gorilla-like creature striding on two legs through the mountains of Nepal is unbelievable, some people argue it's not impossible... [but] There's no food; there's no shelter; it'd freeze to death. – Gerry Moffat, filmmaker and Himalayan guide

Where Bigfoot Walks

Pyle, Robert (1995: Houghton Mifflin Publishing, 338pp.)

A unique exploration of the myth and reality surrounding Sasquatch. Pyle, an ecologist and lepidopterist, does not attempt to prove or disprove the animal's existence. He goes exploring with an open mind and, while providing insights on conservation, spotted owls, and dedicated Sasquatch hunters ("They don't want to find Bigfoot. They want to *be* Bigfoot"), he makes the best argument I've read that such primates could find food and remain hidden in the Northwestern US.

Bigfoot Sasquatch Evidence

Krantz, Grover (1999: Hancock House Publishers, 348pp.)

This is a revised and updated version of *Big Footprints*. Krantz vigorously defends the veracity of the Patterson-Gimlin film and some of the trackways he's examined. Krantz is more cautious than some cryptozoologists when discussing worldwide reports of such creatures: he sees no reason to accept the Yeti or to assume there is more than one species of unknown primate. Krantz added changes at the back of the book instead of rewriting the text, which makes the book a little hard to follow. It's still worth reading, though, as it summarizes the best arguments on the pro-Sasquatch side.

. . .

Sasquatch is ridiculous. But the alternative of a hoaxer is impossible. Therefore—the ridiculous must be true. – Grover Krantz, anthropologist

The basic reason why some of the faculty didn't support him (Grover Krantz) for full professor was not so much because of Bigfoot, but because he stayed with it when his evidence never got any better. – Donald Tyler, anthropologist and former student of Krantz

Living Fossils: The Survival of Homo gardarensis, Neandertal Man, and Homo erectus

Hall, Mark (1999: Mark A. Hall Publications:131pp.)

Dedicated cryptozoological researcher Mark Hall thinks several unknown primates exist, including *Homo gardarensis*. Anthropologists consider this an invalid type based on the misidentified skull of a Norseman with acromegaly, but Hall argues it's not only genuine but living and the source of reports he classifies as "Taller-hominid." He investigated the Minnesota Iceman in person. Noting differences between the original specimen and the model now on display in a museum, he argues it was genuine and a type of *Homo erectus*. Hall classes Bigfoot as a "Neo-Giant," a descendant of the species called *Paranthropus boisei* or *Australopithecus robustus*.

Hall puts a foot wrong on Kennewick Man, a skeleton of seemingly confusing origin found in 1996 that Hall thinks is closely tied to the Ainu of Japan and an unidentified people allegedly represented by finds in Nevada caves. In fairness, Hall did not have the benefit of more recent DNA studies, which placed the skeleton with the Colville tribe of eastern Washington, to whom it has been repatriated. Hall argues his species are all supported by fossil evidence, even if it hasn't been found yet in the places they live now, and suggests, "Perhaps it is not Justice that should be depicted as wearing a blindfold, but the figure that embodies modern Science." Most of Hall's speculations, if sometimes far-fetched and unevenly supported, do make interesting reading. *Living Fossils* offers 229 endnotes.

My Quest for the Yeti

Messner, Reinhold (translated by Peter Constantine) (2000: St. Martin's Press, 169pp.)

This is really two books: one, an adventure tale by a great mountaineer; the other, a confusing attempt to show that the Yeti is a large and very strange type of brown bear. Messner is a legend among climbers as the first human to summit Mt. Everest without oxygen, but his zoology is slipshod at best. Whatever one thinks of the Yeti, Messner's version of the bear hypothesis is a poor fit. He describes bear-Yetis routinely walking and running on two feet, not to mention whistling to each other. He includes photographs of an ordinary-looking brown bear he claims is the mysterious *chemo* or Yeti.

Bigfoot! The True Story of Apes in America

Coleman, Loren (2003: Pocket Books, 288pp.)

Coleman's book is a cogent argument for the reality of an unclassified primate, as well as a good portrait of the often-fractious world of Sasquatch hunters. Coleman thinks there are three types of North American primates. The book begins with the most recent cases, like the "Skookum cast." It's a nice change from the books that go by straight chronology. Coleman does get to the famous incidents, of course. He treats the 1924 "battle" at Ape Canyon, the 1958 Jerry Crew footprints, etc., cautiously, thinking it likely there was Bigfoot involvement but acknowledging good reasons for "the mountain fog" of doubt surrounding these cases. Coleman, who has an interest in other reported phenomena, acknowledges a bit ruefully that his own earlier writings were partly responsible for the Bigfoot-UFO connection: here, he mentions a couple of cases but otherwise focuses on his big hairy quarry. He writes about some of his own efforts contacting witnesses, and he includes some things generally passed over or missed. One example is the transcript of a radio interview with Roger Patterson and Bob Gimlin done right after their film was first shown. Another is his story of chancing on a California fruit label many decades-old showing a hairy near-human giant for reasons he can't uncover.

Coleman suggests that one of the dryopithecine groups was in North America a long time ago and has evolved into the present forms, but we have no certain answers. (Assuming for a moment that an undiscovered North American primate exists, the chimp-size dryopithecines are logical ancestors, although that doesn't rule out much since that group may be ancestral to all the higher primates. The smaller ones flourished for millions of years, expanding to at least a dozen species that ranged widely over Africa and Eurasia until about 2.6 million years ago (MYA). It's not impossible to imagine a larger descendant *if* a group ever made it to North America.)

As to why no one has found a body, here Coleman ducks a bit, he cites a claim by the late Grover Krantz that no one's found a dead bear (inaccurate), and that's about it, although he emphasizes how good the footprint evidence is. He does not address the lack of fossils. Coleman rejects the idea that we should shoot one to get a specimen. Good appendices and a bibliography fill out this useful addition to the Bigfoot library.

Bigfoot Exposed: An Anthropologist Examines America's Enduring Legend

Daegling, David (2004: AltiaMira Press, 288pp.)

Daegling starts off by agreeing that thousands of tracks and reports can't just be dismissed, but unknown giant primates are unsupported by hard evidence, and that's a baffling situation. As he goes through the evidence and descriptions, though, he can't find a real animal. He's bothered not only by the quality of reports but who makes them. "I have always been impressed with the ability of wildlife photographers to be able to splice together thirty- and sixty-minute segments on such rare creatures as the wolverine. These people apparently don't ever see Bigfoot." He doesn't like the P & G film creature's proportions or what he sees as an exaggerated human walk. Daegling thinks the paranormal/UFO aspect weakens any effort to take Bigfoot seriously (which it does), although he never claims this rules out a physical creature. He mentions many of the known or suspected hoaxes. He does, though, give too much credit to Ray Wallace's claim to have virtually invented Bigfoot in 1958. In the end, he suggests Bigfoot is a modern myth, sustained in part by our desire for a living ecological symbol, like us but untainted by what we call civilization.

The Making of Bigfoot

Long, Greg, and Karl Korff (2004: Prometheus Books, 475pp.)

Long and Korff put an enormous amount of research into this "unmasking" of the Patterson film, although they can't quite nail down all the details. They do a good job of pointing out problems with the accounts of Patterson and Gimlin and show convincingly that the events were not well investigated by cryptozoologists, who were too quick to embrace the film. There is no convincing explanation, though, of the contradictory stories of the man who claims to have made the suit and the man who says he was in it. Cryptozoologists have pointed out errors in dates and locations that seem odd for a book of such depth. In the end, Sasquatch escapes, battered but not yet dead.

Of Books and Beasts

Meet the Sasquatch

Murphy, Christopher, with John Green and Thomas Steenburg (2004: Hancock House Publishers, 239pp.)

This is a unique book featuring good enlargements from the Patterson film and a lot of technical analysis of footprints, biomechanics, etc. It is a brief for the defense: critics of Sasquatch are summarily dismissed. I think too much is made of details and measurements based on enlargements of a figure captured by a low-priced 1960s 16-mm camera, but this book provides a lot to look at and some things to think about for anyone interested in the topic.

The Bigfoot Casebook: Updated Sightings and Encounters from 1818 to 2004

Bord, Janet and Colin, with Loren Coleman (2005: Pine Winds Press, 343pp.)

This book, updated from the Bords' original *The Bigfoot Casebook* (Stackpole Books, 1982), offers hundreds of reported Bigfoot (or possible Bigfoot) events, some mentioned very briefly and some explored in detail. The authors include their evaluation of the creatures' origins, locations, and so on, but the primary utility here lies in the mass of sighting data. The paranormal and UFO parts are distracting, but the trove of reports is unmatched. Those, plus the accompanying notes and bibliography, make the *Casebook* very useful for the Bigfoot researcher.

Searching for Sasquatch: Crackpots, Eggheads, and Cryptozoology

Regal, Brian (2011: Palgrave Macmillan, 260pp.)

Regal, a science historian, takes a unique look at cryptozoology's most famous (and now dominant) topic. He doesn't focus on the reality of Sasquatch but on the people and the scientific milieu in which it exists. Grover Krantz (1931-2002) is at the center of his narrative, but he presents all the major personalities involved in Sasquatch and its Asian counterparts. He explores how they interacted with more conventional scientists, each other, and (in the Yeti case) the CIA. Regal includes criticism of cryptozoologists for offering weak evidence and sometimes acting as though the skeptics have the burden of proof. However, he also cites instances where critics have dismissed or insulted cryptozoologists without examining their topic in any depth. The resulting "crackpots vs. eggheads" feud has lived on despite the interest in cryptozoology shown by a handful of well-qualified individuals, including Krantz, anthropologists like Carleton Coon, and primatologists like John Napier and W.C. Osman-Hill. This well-documented book makes a very important contribution to the scientific understanding of cryptozoology and cryptozoologists' understanding of science.

The Beast of Boggy Creek: The True Story of the Fouke Monster

Blackburn, Lyle (2012: Anomalist Books, 237pp.)

Lyle Blackburn does an admirable job here of chronicling one of the most famous Bigfoot cases. He tells how a primate sighting turned into a national phenomenon thanks to a low-budget film that succeeded beyond all expectations. He chronicles sightings in the area near Fouke, Arkansas, before the famous events, the impact of the film, the rush to make money with sequels, souvenirs, tourist attractions, and hoaxes, the many sighting reports made since the film, and the major personalities involved. Blackburn recounts how star witness Smokey Crabtree showed off the headless skeleton of a *tiger* as a Bigfoot, how bands wrote music about it, and many other incidents. About the most famous sighting, by the Ford family, he says, "No one will ever be able to prove whether the Fords actually came face-to-face with an unknown creature that night in 1971, but it doesn't matter." While Blackburn suspects a real creature is involved (assuming, he notes, that the famous three-toed footprints, in this case, were hoaxed), one thing is for certain: the legend will go on. This is the best account of Boggy Creek and the best of Blackburn's cryptozoology books.

Matt's Musings: The Boggy Creek case is an early example of a multimedia cryptozoology sensation. The whole affair would be just another sighting event recorded in a few books were it not for a low-budget film that became a monster hit (how else could I say that?) with an irresistibly hummable title tune written by Earl E. Smith. "And this is where the creature goes / safe within a world he knows" isn't exactly Bob Dylan, but it can stay in your head for days. And so, we have about 15 books, by my count, based on the events in Fouke, Arkansas.

The Sasquatch Seeker's Field Manual

Gordon, David (2015: Mountaineers Books, 172pp.)

Acclaimed science writer David George Gordon doubts Sasquatch's reality but sincerely hopes he's wrong. Here he offers a unique and very informative guide on how citizen scientists can aid in the search. After a recap of the basic story, he muses on cryptozoology. He rejects the idea that it is a pseudoscience pursued only by kooks. He discusses fieldwork, the needed tools and preparations, and the art of deciding where to look. Gordon includes everything from hiking safety to proper interviewing, along with often-humorous asides about topics from the tabloid headline "I Had Bigfoot's Baby" to the suit for the film *Harry and the Hendersons*. He closes with a list of suggested expeditions sites and routes. Sometimes serious, sometimes tongue-in-cheek, this is a book for everyone who wants to find the elusive beast.

MATT BILLE

Neanderthal: The Strange Saga of the Minnesota Iceman

Heuvelmans, Bernard, translated by Paul LeBlond, Afterword by Loren Coleman (2016: Anomalist Books, 284pp.)

Whatever Bernard Heuvelmans and Ivan Sanderson saw at a Minnesota carnival exhibit in 1968, one can't fault the effort Heuvelmans put into studying it. The book describes the enormous lengths he went to analyze the images they took and compare every anatomical trait and measurement to living and extinct primates. Writing in 1973, he was handicapped by the knowledge of his time. He thought Neanderthal was the only viable candidate, even though some items, notably the upturned nose, did not match 1973 reconstructions Heuvelmans thought were wrong. As a non-expert, I won't critique his anatomical discussion except to say the book indicates he cherry-picked the data. That's not as wrong as it sounds given that he was sure he had the decisive evidence, namely, the creature, and it was logical that everything had to match that. He also works out where he thinks the Iceman was from and how it got to Minnesota. No step in the long chain of events he describes is impossible, but none is verifiable, and the story isn't convincing to me. After going missing for decades, the model appeared on eBay in 2013 and is now in a Texas museum. Although Heuvelmans is wrong about the original specimen being a real animal, this is a fascinating tale of discovery, trickery, media, government, and much else in the first decade of cryptozoology.

Yeti: An Abominable History

Hoyland, Graham (2018: William Collins, 310pp.)

Hoyland, the writer/director/climber who was instrumental in finding George Mallory's body on Mount Everest, offers his thorough thrashing of our friend the Yeti.

Initially intrigued, he becomes very skeptical, challenging most of the accounts and all of the proffered evidence. Hoyland believes the

1952 Shipton-Ward tracks were a joke that got out of hand. While the only three men (Eric Shipton, Michael Ward, and Sen Tensing) who know for certain are dead, Hoyland makes an intriguing case. He goes on to review the files on Nessie and other cryptids, none of which he finds worth pursuing. There are some shortcomings here, most notably that discussing Sasquatch without mentioning the work of Meldrum or Krantz is inexplicable. Hoyland thinks little of the cryptozoologists he mentions. To him, Ivan Sanderson was zoology's version of the trickster-god Loki, and even John Napier was sloppy.

In the larger context, Hoyland talks about our need for monsters and cryptids in media. He rambles a bit on fake news and a post-truth world, straying widely from zoology. He laments the decline of scientific knowledge among journalists as well as the Western public, a fact far more solid than anything on shows like *Mountain Monsters*.

Matt's Musings: I did some experiments in North Dakota and concluded that the Shipton tracks could not be artifacts of melting since they showed clear toes. The first thing that happened to my tracks in sunlight was that the toes melted into a blob. Hoyland says that, under Himalayan conditions, the sides melt out first. I'm not sure of the physics, but he's the one who's been there.

The Essential Guide to Bigfoot

Gerhard, Ken (2019: Crypto Excursions, 246pp.)

If you want a book that introduces you to the Sasquatch world and is pro-creature without being dogmatic, this is a good one. Gerhard is a long-time searcher who is "90 percent sure" Sasquatch exists, withholding 10 percent because he hasn't seen one for himself. Here he gives a highly readable survey of the history, personalities, evidence, and other aspects of the phenomenon. The skeptics, although mentioned in specific cases, get too little ink here, but otherwise, the tone is pretty matter-of-fact. He includes the sightings and events he thinks are impressive, and not all of them are the famous cases. Bigfoot books tend to fall into a litany of similar-sounding reports, but Gerhard is a good writer, and his unadorned recaps make you understand why he's intrigued.

There's a good discussion of what Sasquatch (if real) is like given the trends in sighting reports, plus a review of suggested ancestors. Gerhard also examines the sociological questions of where Bigfoot fits in culture and the human psyche.

Gerhard spends most of the time on the U.S. and Canada, but mentions travel to other nations to look into their local versions of Sasquatch. He reviews the worldwide presence in the folklore of smaller hominins, and, while he thinks the idea of such a widespread species or group of them with minimal evidence "utterly unbelievable," it's not quite impossible. He rejects, correctly, the idea that a "hide the Bigfoot" conspiracy could go on this long. One subpar chapter is "Why No Remains?" Gerhard gets kudos for putting this topic upfront, but he spends most of it reviewing claims of bodies that weren't recovered and passes over the hard question too lightly.

The author mentions the weird aspects of UFO buffs and Sasquatch-cultist-types ("the Woo people") and thinks the former are irrelevant and the latter a significant distraction. There's a brief appendix by a scientist on DNA, a good addition. I don't expect footnotes in a book of this sort, but chapter notes would have been valuable.

The suppression of science by scientists contradicts the essence of the method, and the illogic of the government 'suppressing' evidence of cryptids when they have plenty of other work to do is nonsense. The problem is that people without formal scientific training get frustrated because without evidence and structured data they can't get their findings widely accepted, or they can't find what they want to use as evidence. This frustration makes them easy prey for the lurking anaconda of conspiracy. – Anne Larsen, Life Sciences Historian

In the Valleys of the Noble Beyond: In Search of the Sasquatch

Zada, John (2019: Atlantic Monthly Press, 320pp.)

The Great Bear Rainforest of British Columbia is the setting for this beautifully written travelogue as one man scours the area, talking to locals, especially First Nations people, hiking through remote country, and learning as much about himself and human belief as about Sasquatch. Zada hears all kinds of stories of creatures, footprints, and what I call "smells and yells" evidence. The author wonders how it's possible something that doesn't exist could be so omnipresent and how, on the other (hairy) hand, people can steadfastly believe in something when hard evidence is so elusive. Zada explores zones with multiple Sasquatch reports, although he never tries camping out for a few days in a promising area. (I can't blame him, though, given he's already been charged by a grizzly bear.)

He decides that Sasquatch is both real and unreal: "human logic simply doesn't apply here." Sasquatch is an animal, symbol, and myth all at once, something that exists when the spirit of nature and the observer are aligned just right. That's hardly satisfying in a scientific sense, but the book demonstrates how complex the phenomenon is. While nearly all the details are different, this reminded me thematically of Peter Matthiessen's *The Snow Leopard*. It's well worth reading, no matter what you think of Sasquatch.

The Soviet Sasquatch

Porshnev, Boris (translated by Lars Thomas, edited by Chris Clark) (2021: CFZ Press, 281pp.)

Porshnev, a social scientist and historian, was a member of the official Soviet Academy of Sciences' "snowman" committee, which he proposed in 1957. This committee included two other key figures in

Eurasian snowman lore, Dmitri Bayonov and Dr. Marie-Jeanne Koffmann, whose book is reviewed elsewhere. This book is an incomplete manuscript from 1963, lost for over half a century until dedicated cryptozoologists found a rare copy, translated it, and edited it. While there are a few gaps and deletions, this is a very dense collection of reports and analyses not just from the Union of Soviet Socialist Republics (U.S.S.R.) but most of Asia. Beginning with reports in the 19th century, Porshnev traces encounters with the snowman, known regionally by many names including *almas* (which appears in several languages spoken from Mongolia to Iraq) *hum-yavoi* (Tajik), *ksy-gik* (Kazak), and of course Yeti. Although the book deals with vast distances and rugged terrain, I still thought of John Napier's suspicion that the creature appeared in so many places and cultures that the lack of a specimen was very hard to explain.

Porshnev provides a very detailed description of his main piece of physical evidence, a desiccated hand from a monastery in Pangboche, Nepal. (The hand has since been stolen, but a *previously* stolen bone has been identified as a modern human.) As Clark notes, Porshnev was working with an antiquated "ape-man" concept of Neanderthals, and this is what the author believes the snowman basically is: a degenerate, bestial offshoot of the line that led to modern humans. Despite many differences in the description, he thinks we are dealing with variations within a single species. That species is not strictly Neanderthal but *Homo troglodytes*, a name proposed by Linnaeus for "wild men." Clark has fleshed out the surviving text with illustrations and maps and added an index. There's some fascinating material in here. Other books from the Russian/Soviet perspective include Dmitri Bayanov's *In the Footsteps of the Russian Snowman: A Record of Investigation* (Crypto-Logos Publishers, 1996) and the same author's *The Making of Hominology: A Science Whose Time Has Come* (Hancock House Publishers, 2019).

Bigfoot in Maine

Souliere, Michelle (Introduction by Loren Coleman) (2021: History Press, 190pp.)

Maine native Michelle Souliere has talked to everyone from witnesses to government biologists to assemble this enjoyable excursion into the woods of my birth state.

In his Introduction, Loren Coleman of the Portland-based International Cryptozoology Museum provides some background on Maine's oddities. Souliere starts with a list of reasons why the state contains viable habitat for a big primate. She covers the habits and appearances of black bears, the most likely source of mistaken reports, then offers her insights about how and where Bigfoot is most often encountered and the commonalities in witnesses' descriptions.

Next, she presents the accounts. Maine has "wildman" traditions going back to the 1780s. She admits that she hasn't yet developed relationships with Native American tribes residing in Maine to learn what they think. That creates a gap in the relevant history, but she opted not to offer her own interpretations of their accounts and traditions, which is rather refreshing. *Souliere* covers nineteen accounts in depth. Some of the events, like the Durham Gorilla from the early 1970s, are relatively famous. Interestingly, **Souliere** learned that there were two exotic wildlife menageries in the area, but no evidence either had lost an ape. Other reports appear here for the first time. One is the story from a woman named Suzy about numerous childhood encounters with a creature that became accustomed to her. Bigfoot stories often include some odd elements (besides the Bigfoot), and one man claims he saw a giant, dead, hairy foot sticking out between two pulled-over cars of an official-looking convoy.

Souliere adds some notes about Bigfoot-hunters and hoaxers in the state. In offering her tentative conclusion, she doesn't overreach the evidence or her own expertise. She says, simply, "Mainers are encountering something in the woods that does not match known large mammals."

If you're a Bigfoot researcher, a Mainer, a folklorist, or anyone else with an interest, you'll appreciate this well-written book.

Sasquatch Central: High Strangeness at a Minnesota Homestead

Quast, Mike (2021: Untold Publishing, 168pp.)

I don't follow the Sasquatch "habituation" literature because such cases should be the perfect opportunity for clear photos, film, and DNA but never do produce that evidence. I read this one by Mike Quast, though, to get a recent example and to look at the line between zoology and everything else that's attached to the putative primate.

This case starts conventionally enough, with sightings around a remote homestead. Quast, a veteran Bigfoot hunter who is sure he's pursuing a real animal, runs full tilt into weirdness. Animals don't leave finger marks in peanut butter while remaining invisible to three trail cams. (The publisher told me the peanut butter was saved and will be tested for DNA when funding permits.) While there's one picture of an animal's back and a partial shot of what might be fingers, the non-triggering of motion sensors and witness reports of strange lights and apparitions bewilder Quast and, while it's hardly his fault, ensure no scientist is going to look at this case unless that DNA shows something special.

Land Animals

"Pliny suggested that the ostrich, then newly discovered, was the result of a cross between a giraffe and a gnat. In practice, there must be many such crosses which have not been attempted because of a certain understandable lack of motivation." – Carl Sagan, *The Dragons of Eden*

Animal Treasure: A Naturalist in Search of Strange Creatures

Sanderson, Ivan (1937: Viking Press, 325pp.)

This first book by Ivan Sanderson, who went on to become an important and controversial figure in cryptozoology, is delightful reading for animal lovers of all sorts. Sanderson was part of the generation of Western zoologists that finally abandoned the "collect everything you can shoot" mentality and turned to studying animals *in situ*. This book followed his first major expedition to British Cameroon (now split between Nigeria and Cameroon). Everything here fascinates Sanderson: he pays as much attention to ants as to antelopes. In vivid language, he recounts adventures from being trapped and lost in a cave of bats to trying to befriend a troop of baboons. The animals pop off the page into the reader's imagination. His writing shows the typical 1930s condescension of Westerners toward the indigenous tribes, although he never says they aren't his equals as people.

Two incidents in his expedition are especially memorable. On one occasion, men who wanted to show Sanderson they were better fishermen than a rival tribe dragged ashore a stingray over 11 feet [3.4 meters (m)] long. Sanderson had no idea such giants lived in African rivers. The second is Sanderson's account of a giant black bat that swooped toward him at head level. He describes it here as the size of an eagle. He wrote much later that he and fellow witness Gerald Russell later compared their diaries and agreed it was 12 feet (3.6 m) across. He closes by saying he was saddened by the destruction of the forest, a rare sentiment in 1937.

Matt's Musings: ***Animal Treasure*** *launched Ivan T. Sanderson on a career as a popular naturalist in print, radio, and television, and it's easy to see why. Sanderson would later get too colorful, claiming, among other things, to have met an African dinosaur. Yet* ***Animal Treasure*** *predates those excesses and remains readable and fun.*

Monsters of the Gévaudan: The Making of a Beast

Smith, Jay (2011: Harvard University Press, 391pp.)

A popular pursuit among cryptozoologists is wondering what sort of beast was responsible for as many as a hundred deaths in rural south-central France from 1764 to 1767. Jay Smith, a historian, has done extensive research and succeeds admirably in explaining the cultural forces which made this mystery a huge national story. I am not quite sure he has killed the Beast, though. Smith opens by saying that he will not ascribe the Beast "myth" to the backwardness of the peasants living under its spell, but in the end, he basically does. He shows that the killings of humans by wolves certainly happened, then proceeds to the conclusion that the press and local panic shaped ordinary events into an extraordinary affair. He doesn't ask why the locals grew up familiar with wolves and yet few people, farmers or officials, thought this was what they were dealing with. It's possible the killings involved a really exceptional wolf or wolf-dog hybrid or an escaped or released exotic animal. In the end, I think Smith is too dismissive of those ideas. A hyena loose in France seems unlikely, but so does an entire region panicking over a threat they'd always known about. We may never nail this particular hide to a barn.

Gold Rush in the Jungle: The Race to Discover and Defend the Rarest Animals of Vietnam's "Lost World"

Drollette, Dan (2013: Crown, 336pp.)

The "gold rush" of large mammals in and around the Vu Quang region of Vietnam and Laos in the early 1990s was like nothing zoologists had seen since before World War I. Finding new species of large mammals had become a rare event, and the Vu Quang ox or *saola* was not just a new species but a new genus with no close living relatives. At 100 kg, it's easily the largest new mammal from all of Eurasia since the now-disputed kouprey in 1937. The animals identified included new deer species (belonging to a group of relatively small species, the muntjacs), a mysterious bovid with high-rise horns like motorcycle handlebars, new or rediscovered monkeys, a rediscovered wild pig, and the identification of the world's biggest freshwater turtle in a shallow, polluted lake in the midst of Hanoi. Nothing seemed too outlandish.

Dan Drollette Jr. undertook several trips into Vietnam, meeting with the Western and Vietnamese scientists and lay researchers trying to identify and protect the remnants of the closest thing the Earth still has to offer to a genuine "lost world." In this book, he visits sites from the Hanoi Hilton prison to the Endangered Primate Research Center, trying to understand the modern nation of Vietnam, its culture, and how those factors affect the mixed attitudes toward wildlife. Some animals draw crowds who want to see them alive: others are ruthlessly poached. Some Vietnamese condemn poaching, while others aid poachers for money (a tiger can be worth $250,000), and some elites have an attitude that everything in Vietnam is theirs to eat.

Drollette loves Vietnam's endemic species of langur monkeys but also devotes chapters to several unique cases. These include the bizarre discovery of a giant turtle in Hoan Kiem Lake; the kouprey, which some scientists now doubt is a species but rather a hybrid of other cattle; and the rediscovered Vietnamese population of the Javan rhinoceros, quickly hunted back into extinction. He includes the *nguoi rung*, an upright ape that has not been proven to exist but remains intriguing. It may be a species of orangutan or something equally exciting. Drollette notes that it's hard to dismiss anything in an area that has seen an average of two new species discovered each week for ten years. The author also offers perspectives from internationally acclaimed scientists and conservationists about habitat protection vs. species protection, zoos vs. original habitats and reserves, and captive breeding.

Drollette reports that the war, which ended in 1975, need no longer concern Americans who want to seek the local wildlife, and he closes on a cautiously hopeful note. Vietnamese children are now being taught the value and richness of their nation's wildlife, and a new generation of rangers and scientists is expanding conservation efforts. A thorough reference section with a glossary, bibliography, and index round out this indispensable book.

The Last Unicorn: A Search for One of Earth's Rarest Creatures

deBuys, William (2015: Little, Brown and Company, 364pp.)

Anyone pondering a trek into the wild after a rare or reported animal can learn what to expect in deBuys' account of his travels in search of the *saola*. The *saola* or Vu Quang ox (*Pseudoryx nghetinhensis*) was discovered by Western science only in 1992. In 2011, journalist deBuys was invited to join a small team led by conservation biologist William Robichaud. Robichaud's objective was to survey the watershed of a river called Nam Nyang, a place no Westerner has ever seen. They wanted to examine probable *saola* habitat, understand the health of the ecosystem, collect as much information as they could to appeal for conservation, and remove the snares and traps of poachers when possible. The journey by boat and foot into central Laos includes an unending series of dangers, including unreliable companions, treacherous terrain, and unexploded bombs, yet deBuys finds human friendship and natural beauty even in the worst of circumstances.

Elsewhere in this book, deBuys chronicles the discovery of the *saola* and the other new mammals from Vietnam and Laos. He explains how little science knows about wild-living *saolas*. Occasional kills or lucky captures, plus some camera-trap photos, are all science has to go on. (Interesting note for cryptozoologists: the saola is extremely rare, smaller than many popular cryptids like Sasquatch, and a dweller in one of the most remote places on Earth. It's arduous work to get a handful of camera traps in there, much less keep them functioning. Nonetheless, they get at least occasional results.)

The author also describes the precarious context, natural, economic, and political, in which the animal and its remaining habitat exist. The saola's already-tiny population appears to be shrinking. Poachers don't target saolas, but snares are indiscriminate, and resource extraction is nudging deeper into the remote, relatively undisturbed regions of the country. One Laotian guide mentioned the *phi kong koy*, a red-haired, humanlike primate known as *nguoi rung* in Vietnam. Everyone, it seems, believes in this animal, although none of the guides or the people they know have seen one.

The expedition ends without any of the members seeing a *saola*, but accomplishes its other objectives, and one of the fortunate legacies is this gripping and informative book.

Anthropology and Cryptozoology: Exploring Encounters with Mysterious Creatures

Hurn, Samantha (editor) (2016: Routledge, 263pp.)

This is a rare academic tome on cryptozoology and a very useful book indeed. There's a lot in here, most of it based on years of fieldwork, about how different cultures see cryptids and how cryptozoology interacts with anthropology and other fields of study. The authors take cryptozoology seriously, with some praising Bernard Heuvelmans for his work defining the field. There's some fairly dense anthropological jargon (e.g., "...the processes of becoming that are co-created through ingestive relationships..."), but most of the writing is accessible. Subjects include the hairy "bush dwarves" of Africa and the Zanzibar leopard. In the leopard's case, authors Martin Walsh and Helle Goldman held out a slim hope for the "extinct" population in this book and were vindicated when it was videotaped two years later. They also recorded there were no less than 21 names in Swahili for leopards or leopardlike animals in the area.

There's a very thorough study of an unknown cat reported from the "hobbit" island of Flores. This includes notes on the enigmatic "little people," the *ebu gogo*, and the relevant fact that local people showed scientists the Komodo dragon lived in areas where it had never been officially recorded. Two authors examine alien big cats

(ABCs) in the British Isles and come away convinced some sightings are genuine. Also included are several broader discussions of cryptozoology and the zone between the physical and the mythical. Does cryptozoology include physical animals only (my view), or does it include those which are factual to certain cultures even though they'll never be caught? Finally, this book is superbly referenced.

Copper State Monsters: Cryptids and Legends of Arizona

Weatherly, David (2019: Eerie Lights Publishing, 208pp.)
  This is the best example of the many state-by-state books I've read. It's comprehensive and offers some intriguing stuff. Many of the accounts are recent and include the names of those involved. Weatherly spent a lot of time running down these topics in person, including exposing some hoaxes. The bibliography is short and not linked to particular reports, but additional sources are given in the text.
  Weatherly includes some items concerning known wildlife that make for interesting reading. There are chapters on Arizona's particularly nasty population of Africanized bees, the slow return of the jaguar to its old range, and an especially enjoyable treatment of the camels left behind by the Army and private entrepreneurs. These lingered and reproduced, with reports of their presence running into the 1940s.
  There are a lot of reports of Sasquatches and the like here. It's common to think of Arizona as all desert and mountains, but there are substantial forests, river valleys, and other places more in keeping with the habitat of this cryptid primate. One of the interesting reports is of a trackway two miles long: far too many footprint reports involve one or a few tracks, which can be highly suspicious depending on the terrain. There are several reports of primates peeking in windows at night. Those, at least, are unlikely to be pranksters in suits since there's no better way to get yourself shot in the face. There are a few reports that could be interpreted as unaccompanied juveniles,

something unusual in Bigfoot lore. One report that demands follow-up or documentation is a claim that a toenail produced DNA of a human-nonhuman hybrid. Tested by what lab, when, and where is the paperwork?

Arizona has some tales of thunderbirds and pterodactyls. It would take more than a few witness reports to make surviving pterodactyls worth serious consideration, but it's a fun topic. The author spends some time, of course, on the Tombstone "thunderbird photograph." Like many people, he's convinced he saw this photograph before modern fakes were in circulation. Many years of work by cryptozoologists have failed to find a trace of it, and Weatherly leaves the topic there. He also includes some accounts of the Chupacabra, a critter based on mange-stricken canids and media hype.

Weatherly includes accounts and beliefs of Arizona's Native Americans. He respectfully refers to specific tribes in the region instead of dumping this material into a generic "Indian legends" category. The reports are mostly from Navajo, Hopi, and Apache witnesses. Some are firsthand, while other information comes from scholars of these cultures. Many Native American cultures have mixed views about the accuracy of white scholars, even trusted ones, but Weatherly certainly makes a better effort than many writers have.

To summarize, this is the best of Weatherly's books I've read so far. Even if you doubt every critter involved, it makes for enjoyable reading and the occasional spooky moment. Sam Shearon's great cover art is a welcome addition.

Thylacine: The Tragedy of the Tasmanian Tiger

Guiler, Eric (1985: Oxford University Press, 218pp.)

Dr. Guiler, a zoologist who spent his professional life studying the thylacine and trying to determine if it still existed, tells the story of the animal and his quest for it in this book. In 1998 he released *Tasmanian Tiger: A Lesson to Be Learnt* (Abrolhos Publishing, 256pp.) In both books, Guiler demonstrates convincingly that the species survived its official demise in 1936. In *Tragedy*, though, he still hopes to rediscover the animal: in *Lesson*, he offers the reluctant conclusion that the thylacine is no longer alive. Guiler may have known more about the species than anyone else ever has, and these books are a treasure trove for the Anzac cryptozoologist.

A Living Dinosaur?

Mackal, Roy (1987: E.J. Brill, 340pp.)

Mackal chronicles his arduous expeditions in search of reported unknown animals in the swampy Likouala region of the Congo. While the evidence reviewed in this book is limited to eyewitness reports and a single trail of strange footprints, Mackal believes there are as many as three large unclassified animals in this area. His most controversial belief is that one of these could be a small sauropod dinosaur. He also discusses several animals from local folklore he feels are exaggerations of known species.

Natural Mysteries: Monster Lizards, English Dragons, and Other Puzzling Animals

Hall, Mark (1991: Mark A. Hall Publications, 93pp.)

Mark A. Hall self-published several short volumes on animal mysteries, this being the most intriguing. Hall makes some very puzzling leaps, from basing animal distribution on a crackpot geological theory to endorsing a flying reptile in England based on one witness. However, there are enduring lessons here for the crypto-researcher. Hall emphasizes the use of old maps to see, not just where woods and swamps are, but where they were centuries ago. Hall makes researching an extreme sport. He describes driving to tiny towns and looking through old newspaper morgues and microfiche to find overlooked reports – a skill that remains relevant today because material like this hasn't been digitized. Many reports of oddities like huge lizards and Hall's special focus, the thunderbird, are among those summarized here. The third lesson from Hall's work is his provision of citations and endnotes. One example concerns a freakish alligator snapping turtle from Kansas that weighed 403 pounds (it must have looked like a Civil War ironclad). Hall cites the 1947 scientific society paper making the claim and presents three books, one by the legendary Archie Carr, that discuss it, albeit cautiously. Many writers in this age of global information databases and networks don't document or cross-reference nearly as well. I've yet to read Hall's most famous book, *Thunderbirds: America's Living Legends of Giant Birds* (1994: updated and reissued as part of the Loren Coleman Presents series from Cosimo Classics in 2008.)

The Beast of Exmoor

Francis, Di (1993: Jonathan Cape, 160pp.)

Francis' first book, 1983's ***Cat Country***, advanced the highly controversial theory that Britain had an indigenous unclassified big cat. In *The Beast of Exmoor*, she broadens her scope to include the Kellas cat and a bizarre skull from Dufftown, Scotland, that scientists consider a deformed freak. Francis' tenacious support of the indigenous big cat—a difficult theory to swallow, even for other cryptozoologists—will turn off some readers, but there are a lot of interesting reports here.

Out of the Shadows: Mystery Animals of Australia

Healy, Tony, and Paul Cropper (1994: Ironbark Press, 200pp.)

Cryptozoologists love Australia, where all kinds of truly strange animals exist or existed, and there are remote forests and mountains still not well surveyed. Healy and Cropper provide a balanced and thoroughly-researched study of the region's six most interesting cryptozoological puzzles. These include the thylacine's survival in

Tasmania, the same animal's possible survival in Australia, alien big cats, the Queensland "tiger," the ape-like "Yowie," and the legendary bunyip. The authors assign them credibility in about that order, although they actually build the strongest case for the introduced American puma.

On the thylacine, the authors feel it is slipping further from possible rediscovery on Tasmania as new sighting reports diminish: the last detailed one here is from 1986. The mainland thylacine, presumed long extinct, has a better case for survival. The authors list several sightings into the early 1990s, some very clear, others a bit ambiguous, from several areas of the country. They doubt the photographs by Kevin Cameron (1984), but they're still intrigued by a film clip from 1969 and other evidence.

Australia seems infested with unidentified big cats—leopards, pumas, and some that don't match up well to any known species. The Queensland tiger or *yarri* gets, and deserves, its own chapter. The authors are cautious about reports of killed or wounded "tigers" where the evidence seems to have disappeared but are intrigued by the similarity of the descriptions.

Then it's on to the Yowie. While reports and traditions go back centuries, only a handful of non-Aboriginal Australians (who largely ignored or dismissed Aboriginal accounts) paid attention to it until the late 1970s. Then modern sightings exploded, old accounts were unearthed, and the whole thing turned into a smaller-scale Bigfoot hunt. The authors analyze 85 reports for patterns in height and color. Solutions offered by Yowie researchers range from *Homo erectus* to hoaxes to an unknown marsupial, which would be quite a find. They close the zoological part of the book with a chapter on the bunyip, but the body of reports is too vague and varied to make much out of. There is a final chapter on "psychic animals" (apparitions), but I hope zoologists don't dismiss this book because of that. It is essential reading on Australian cryptozoology, and I think one or two of the animals discussed will eventually be confirmed. May photographs and some amusing cartoons illustrate this valuable work.

. . .

"I admit freely that I have tried to "explain away" the [Yowie] reports. It is important to try to do so; if they cannot be explained away, then what we are faced with is Evidence...the best real evidence is consistency." – Dr. Colin P. Groves, mammalogist

Ghost Grizzlies

Peterson, David (1995: Henry Holt, 296pp.)

This enthralling zoological detective story takes readers on the trail of a possible relict population of grizzly bears in Colorado's San Juan Mountains. While the proof is not final, the reader will learn much about bears, conservation, and animal tracking in this book.

Matt's Musings: I once presented on surviving Colorado grizzlies to the Colorado-Wyoming Academy of Sciences. I cited a close-up witness I considered well-qualified and unimpeachable but who didn't want his name used after a wildlife officer rejected his sighting. This illustrates a common problem in cryptozoology: not everyone who reports Bigfoot, for example, wants the sighting attributed to them. There's no satisfactory resolution for this. The reader has to make a judgment about whether to trust the author (whom they usually don't know) to decide whether witnesses who they certainly don't know are credible. I still believe my friend saw a grizzly.

The Lost Grizzlies

Bass, Rick (1995: Houghton Mifflin, 240pp.)

There's a great deal of cryptozoological interest in any book about finding large animals thought extinct. This is one of two books on the possible survival of the grizzly bear (*Ursus arctos horribilis*) in the state of Colorado, where the species was supposedly exterminated in the 1950s. Bass, a first-rate wilderness writer, believes he personally got a brief glimpse of one of these wary bruins.

Onza!

Carmony, Neil (1995: High-Lonesome Books, 204pp.)

In this enjoyable book, Carmony chronicles a century of interest in Mexico's legendary big cat. Carmony concludes, with obvious regret, that the onza specimens collected so far show the cat is just an atypical puma.

Mammoth Hunt

Blashford-Snell, John, and Rula Lenska (1996: HarperCollins Publishers, 263pp.)

Explorer Blashford-Snell recounts his successful quest for the rumored "monster elephants" of Nepal's Bardia National Park. Blashford-Snell does not discover the ancestral elephant species he had hoped to find, but he documents an isolated population whose distinctiveness was previously unknown to Western scientists. The Bardia elephants include some huge specimens, and the twin domes on top of the head that appear in older Asian elephants are unusually prominent. Add to that a nasal bridge that protrudes at the base of the trunk, and they are striking animals indeed. This book combines an exciting travelogue with a good study of the elephants.

Proceedings of the Eastern Cougar Conference, 1994

Tischendorf, Jay, and Steven J. Ropski (editors) (1996: Aerie Publishing, 245pp.)

This book collects papers on all aspects of the Eastern cougar question up to 1996. The conference was not repeated, but this volume contains information on sighting reports, some well-attested individual animals that might or might not be true wild cougars, ecological niches, the idea of reintroduction, and Loren Coleman's paper on the "black panther escapes a circus train wreck" motif that has popped up several times but has never actually happened. A valuable resource.

No Mercy: A Journey to the Heart of the Congo

O'Hanlon, Redmond (1997: Alfred A. Knopf, 480pp.)

In this travelogue, O'Hanlon undertakes a serious (although often humorously recounted) exploration of the Lake Tele region of the Congo, the supposed home of a giant reptile. O'Hanlon never saw the creature, but he provides some fascinating background on the area. He also describes a reported animal called the *Yombe*, which may be an unclassified ape.

"To learn something from you, the forest silently observes you and quietly listens to you! If you want to learn something from the forest, do the same thing!" – Mehmet Murat ildan, Turkish writer

The Eastern Panther: Mystery Cat of the Appalachians

Parker, Gerry (1998: Nimbus Publishing, 210pp.)

A history of the Eastern panther controversy, with detailed records of the last proven killings and an even-handed examination of the continuing debate over the animal's survival. Parker, a retired wildlife biologist, finds the evidence to be inconclusive. Still, he says, "I remain encouraged that the panther may again be among us."

The Last Tasmanian Tiger

Paddle, Robert (2002: Cambridge University Press, 284pp.)

A comprehensive account of the thylacine, with special emphasis on the circumstances surrounding its head-on collision with human expansion. In addition to the factual record of the animal's deliberate extermination, Paddle offers his own theories on why the scientific world essentially ignored the thylacine until it was too late.

Mothman and Other Curious Encounters

Coleman, Loren (2002: ParaView Press, 205pp.)

This is a collection of stories and sightings from around the U.S. It's a mix of cryptozoology and paranormal weirdness, but the cryptozoology is interesting enough to plant it here. I've never gotten excited about West Virginia's Mothman because I can't picture it as a real animal, but Coleman argues the term "cryptid" should encompass reports of things that might be animals until we can label them as something more specific. He writes for comparison that local myths and exaggerations about gorillas initially led Europeans to discount the beast. The book also covers "thunderbird" reports. While it is virtually impossible that the largest bird in North America is undiscovered, there's something about the topic that fascinates me.

Matt's Musings: To me, descriptions of physically unlikely cryptids like Dogman or Mothman should be considered highly suspect from the beginning, as should anything large in North America (where a new shrew would be a sensation) without repeated independent sightings. However, it's not always a bright line: reports of a cryptid may be wrong, but they may point to a released/escaped oddity or something else interesting. Such events are, but a truck crash once lost a polar bear overnight.

Varmints: Mystery Carnivores of North America

Arment, Chad (2010: Coachwhip, 686pp.)

Mr. Arment, an indefatigable cryptozoology writer and publisher, has combed countless publications old and new to explore the weird, undiscovered, or out-of-place carnivores of the continent. As he provides nuggets on mystery lions, black panthers, wolflike creatures where there are no wolves, and ten-legged polar bears, he discusses the way such animals are both enthoknown (known by some human community) and folkloric (carrying the cultural baggage of their milieu).

A geographical compilation will have everyone looking for their home state. Mine, Colorado, is *very* unimpressive, although the Colorado Springs lion sighting of 2008 (a case in which I was misquoted in the local paper) slips in. Chad also discusses how known animals can be mistaken for mysterious ones and how to consider tracks. He finishes with a very good bibliography. This is a great reference book for any cryptid sightings of predators.

Lizard Man: The True Story of the Bishopville Monster

Blackburn, Lyle (2013: Anomalist Books, 208pp.)

Blackburn recounts his travels in search of the truth behind a popular but rather weakly supported modern cryptid. Indeed, the book is better than the topic deserves. It all started with a 1998 report by a teenager near the Scape Ore Swamp adjacent to Bishopville, South Carolina, and became a national sensation. Blackburn and his co-researcher Cindy Lee talk to everyone who claims a sighting and look over the swamp region for themselves. He's aware that the Lizard Man if described accurately, is very difficult to square with any plausible animal, but he believes many of the witnesses are sincere people who saw something odd.

Monsters of Patagonia

Whittall, Austin (2013: Zagier & Urruty Publications, 256pp.)

This is an overlooked treasure among cryptozoology books. Whittall, who lives in Buenos Aires, has done a monumental amount of research into this fabled region spanning much of Argentina and Chile. He describes the region and its peoples, then goes on to probe or at least document every cryptid and cryptid-like story in this million-square-kilometer land. Some, like giants, readers will be familiar with, while the *cagua-cagua*, a huge snake with a hairy tail, will be new. Whitall explores water-tigers, lake monsters, apes, giant snakes, and countless other mysteries. His writing is clear and objective: depending on the cryptid, he suggests unknown species, known species, exaggeration, hoax, and myth as explanations. Whittall thinks tales of giants and dwarfs may come from unusually tall or short tribes now extinct, although he also speculates whether *Homo erectus* could have made it to South America. Every entry is backed by footnotes and endnotes, and there's also a bibliography. Most sources are historical or scientific, and there are very few cryptozoologists who go to such lengths in documentation. The bibliography alone is 20 pages. Anyone interested in South American cryptids *must* have this book.

Beyond the Secret Elephants: On mystery, elephants and discovery

Patterson, Gareth (2020: Tracey McDonald Publishers, Kindle only)

Patterson is a conservationist who made the amazing discovery that a population of South African elephants thought extinct, or nearly so, was instead stable and healthy. He recounted this in *The Secret Elephants: The Rediscovery of the World's Most Southerly Elephants* (Penguin Global, 2010). In *Beyond*, he adds accounts of newly observed and unusual elephant behavior, including possible self-medication. If the news that wildlife authorities missed a herd of elephants was not enough for cryptozoologists, he also learns that both indigenous people and visitors have many accounts of a hairy manlike creature called *Otang*. Patterson collects reports and even has his own sightings, one of them especially intriguing. He writes, "less than three or four meters away from me, I saw a bipedal hominid being. *Otang*! It was approximately five and a half feet in height (though hunched as it leapt away) and had dark brown-black hair…" This seems a cryptid well worth investigating.

Beasts of Britain

McGrath, Andy (2021: Hangar 1 Publishing, 331pp.)

If you want to know what British cryptozoologists are interested in, here's the whole collection. The cast runs from famous names (e.g., Nessie, unidentified black cats) to a menagerie of understudies, including dogmen, wildmen, owlmen, eels, monkeys, and so on. McGrath also visits faerie folk and demonic dogs and considers real creatures that might inspire such legends. He adds a long list of wayward beasts, like whales in the Thames, and invasive species. I didn't know there was alligator snapping turtles in Britain! McGrath includes a section of "Beastly Theories" accompanying each group.

The author passes on some reports without comment but has put considerable research into the ones that intrigued him. In one interesting case, he is not convinced the famous Stronsay carcass of 1808 was a decaying basking shark. While the shark explanation is almost universally accepted (including by me), McGrath believes it's still a mystery based on the eyewitness descriptions. The preserved vertebrae certainly look like a shark's, but he notes they haven't been tested for DNA.

Some cryptids here are single-witness-single-encounter reports, while others like the mystery cats come from all over the country. It's all very readable and referenced and illustrated.

Lake and Sea Creatures

Loch Ness: For centuries, it's been home to one of the most enduring legends. Hundreds of eyewitnesses have reported a monster moving through these waters, yet countless scientific studies have failed to find it. – Philippe Cousteau, *The Loch Ness Monster Revealed*, Discovery Science, 2015

I don't believe in that bullshit. – Jacques Cousteau, ~ 45 years earlier, on the same topic

In the Domain of the Lake Monsters: The Search for Denizens of the Deep

Kirk, John (1998: Key Porter Books, 302pp.)

Kirk, President of the British Columbia Scientific Cryptozoology Club, recounts his own search for "Ogopogo," the alleged inhabitant of Lake Okanagan, and discusses other lake monster reports and tales from around the world. It's not enough to make me believe the animal is real, but he does make the case that Lake Okanagan is more likely than the more famous Loch Ness to house an unknown animal. Kirk has created a very readable introduction to the lake monster world. He includes photographs, but all are open to interpretation, and the story is still based mainly on anecdotal evidence. Kirk, though, has several Ogopogo sightings of his own and is very certain.

For marine life, the age of discovery is not over. – Jesse Ausubel, founding chair of the Encyclopedia of Life project

The Great New England Sea Serpent

O'Neill, June (1999: Down East Books, 256pp.)

This is a marvelous little book—thoroughly researched, enjoyable, and open-minded—about the great sea creature whose appearances off Cape Ann in the early 1800s captivated all of New

England. O'Neill shows how sightings of a similar creature far predated the famous flurry of activity in 1817 and have continued, albeit much less frequently, into modern times. June O'Neill accomplished the very difficult feat of writing a book on a cryptozoological subject and making that book balanced, readable, and highly entertaining. This book is enough to make even the most hardened skeptic gaze out to sea and ponder whether we may have overlooked a spectacular discovery. O'Neill doesn't try to argue the case for a large, unknown animal. She lets the witnesses speak for her and lets the reader draw conclusions.

The Field Guide to Lake Monsters, Sea Serpents, and Other Mystery Denizens of the Deep

Coleman, Loren, and Patrick Huyghe (2003: Penguin Books, 358pp.)

I said in the Basic Library that I didn't think there was a truly great water-cryptid book since Ellis's, but this one is extremely useful and perhaps just misses that cut. Similar to Coleman and Huyghe's book on mystery primates, this volume offers a classification system for all kinds of alleged denizens of seas, lakes, and rivers. Such beasts are so varied, though, that fourteen categories are needed, and even this approach requires grouping some unrelated reports together. As in their primate book, the authors are not saying these are all valid species, but that they're a useful way to sort the cases.

The research that went into this is prodigious. There are some types of sightings not normally looked at, which are always welcome: "Mystery Monitors," "Cryptid Chelonians," and so on. If you like such tales from the seas and coasts as I do (most lake creatures to me are more dubious and thus less interesting), you could be browsing this all day.

An early section deals with known creatures that could be mistaken for cryptids, from sturgeon to a mass of writhing sea snakes. I wish the authors had screened some cases more skeptically, although they don't just accept all the reports. Other times, I could nitpick the categorization: I don't think the Lake Iliamna creature fits under "Giant Sharks," although Coleman, like me, has talked to people who've seen it, and it's his choice how to interpret the information in his own book.

There are some interesting extras in this book: best places to look for a lake monster, best places to look for a sea serpent, what to do if you see something, and so on. The sighting maps are another valuable addition, and the list of lake, river, and sea monster locations worldwide fills a startling 35 pages. The bibliography is very good, too. Bottom line: not perfect, but if the subject interests you at all, you want this book.

If people would make an effort to learn about the wonders that did exist, he thought, their appetite for dragons would be well satisfied. – Peter Benchley, author, *Beast*

In the Wake of Bernard Heuvelmans

Woodley, Michael (2008: CFZ Press, 176pp.)

The title comes from Heuvelmans' book *In the Wake of the Sea-Serpents* and examines several alternative schemes used by that author and others to group sightings of large unknown marine animals in ways that may point to a particular type of creature, thus biasing their descriptions of these cases. Although such a study is necessarily incomplete with no actual creatures to examine, it has value as an intellectual exercise to help focus our thinking on the subject.

Woodley summarizes theories about "sea serpents" in general and goes through Heuvelmans' classifications, the types of creatures that might be behind them, and the way other researchers have classified the same types of reports. As Woodley acknowledges, Heuvelmans' bestowing of scientific names on creatures with no type specimens is invalid. Woodley offers thoughts on the plausibility of Heuvelmans' types and suggests modifications to his categories. The whole effort is well written, although I have some quibbles about what cases Woodley thinks are worth including. The report of the ship *Pauline*, which describes a huge serpent wrapped around the body of a sperm whale, is either a fabrication or a very confused sighting of a giant squid/whale battle, and the story from the German submarine *U-28* never made sense. Still, the point of Woodley's work is to take a good look at Heuvelmans' categories, and in that sense, the book is worth your time.

Weird Waters: The Lake and Sea Monsters of Scandinavia and the Baltic States

Thomas, Lars, with Jacob Rask (2011: CFZ Press, 148pp.)

This book is an engaging tour of Scandinavian waters with a lot of firsthand accounts and some bits of information I've not seen anywhere else. Thomas is a marine biologist, and it shows in his proper handling of zoological terms, species identification, etc. The only point I didn't understand was when he remarks on a pendant made from the hooks from a giant squid's suckers (left embedded in a boat), even though that species has no hooks. Thomas also wanders off the purely zoological into some specters and other "things," but the physical cryptozoology is intriguing enough to keep him in this section.

Being of Danish ancestry, I was intrigued by the 16th-century episode in which a "sea monk" (large squid) was caught and sent alive to King Christian III, a distant relation of mine. The king put it in the castle moat and attempted to talk to it. (Okay, so my ancestors were kings, not rocket scientists. The fact that Danish legend includes a "mercow" doesn't say much for the nation, either.) To his credit, Thomas tries hard to suggest known species in creature reports.

The most intriguing bit here is a series of sightings on the coast and in a lake near the ocean in Iceland of a creature resembling a very large, long-necked seal. I've thought that such a creature was at least possible: it's still a long shot, but these reports "keep the file open" in my head.

Thomas throws in some science about known species. He has, for example, seen a bottlenose dolphin and pilot whales with two dorsal fins. He adds a good bibliography, although I would have liked more direct source notes. Some of his eyewitness reports are from people who remained anonymous, always a bit frustrating, but would you tell everyone you'd seen a mercow? If you're interested in legends of seas and lakes, Scandinavian history, or the possibility of large unknown species, you are going to like this book.

The Untold Story of Champ

Bartholomew, Robert (2012: State University of New York [SUNY] Press, 253pp.)

I'm always cautious about sociological explanations of cryptozoological creatures: not that they are wrong, but that they may be used to close a case prematurely. Robert Bartholomew, though, does a good job of both establishing the cultural background and investigating the best-known eyewitness accounts. He shows that the history of something in the lake, going back to early "pioneer" days and then further into Native American lore, is real, even though the enduring tale of a monster sighting by Samuel de Champlain himself is a fabrication. He takes the story into modern times, presents the encounters fairly, and ends up offering prosaic explanations for most of them that seemed convincing to me.

A centerpiece of the Champ mystery is the photograph by Sandra Mansi. The author looks at the many theories and perspectives offered on this and interviewed Mansi. He concludes there are so many changes in her story over the years that it's hard to figure out exactly what happened. He thinks she photographed a real object (a floating log, perhaps?) and succumbed to the temptation to add drama and detail as the years went by.

Bartholomew has not put a definitive end to the mystery. There's at least one videotape that remains puzzling, as do some acoustic data and a subset of the witness reports. He does, though, make the case that this mystery is a lot less substantial than many cryptozoologists believe, and he has convinced this reader that (sadly) his view of Champ as a creature of folklore rather than zoology is very close to the truth.

The Loch Ness monster is famous all over the world ... It's a timeless brand because the monster has been around forever. It's a prehistoric dinosaur; it will be around for some time to come. – David Martin-Jones, University of St Andrews

Discovering Cadborosaurus

LeBlond, Paul, John Kirk, and Jason Walton (2014: Hancock House Publishers, 172pp.)

The late Dr. LeBlond and his colleagues wrote this book convinced that there is a large, unidentified marine animal off the coast of British Columbia and points north and south. They won't persuade everyone of that, but they do argue strongly that there's a puzzle here. This book builds on LeBlond and Edward Bousfield's **Cadborosaurus: Survivor from the Deep** (Heritage House, 2000).

The authors open by emphasizing that marine zoologists expect many more species from the sea, even though most will be tiny invertebrates. The evidence for Caddy is mostly anecdotal, and the authors list sightings from 1791 to 2013 they consider valid.

The authors start with Native American traditions of sea creatures and take the story through the 1930s when Caddy became famous and got its name, thanks in large part to newspaperman Archie Wills. They continue through the modern era of books and TV specials and more sightings, including John Kirk's own. They discuss a lot of the evidence in the context of the Naden Harbor carcass. While the item fished out of a sperm whale's stomach was dismissed as a fetal baleen whale (wrongly, as the authors demonstrate with a photo of a real one) and a basking shark (perhaps correctly), it is odd how well the skeleton held together.

They also look at the Kelly Nash video from 2007. The video certainly shows a number of living creatures, but their identity is not clear, and the part that should answer that question—which Kirk and LeBlond insist shows a head with bulging eyes on a long neck—has been recorded over or lost. There's no reason to doubt the authors' veracity, but the "missing evidence" part reduces a case to one that's intriguing but not game-changing.

To put my skeptic glasses on when reading these two books, the head in Alan Chikite's 1987 sketch looks like a swimming moose (indeed, several Caddy descriptions and illustrations feature a rather moose-like head). A more puzzling bit is the repeated detail of Caddy chomping, or trying to chomp, on birds either on the surface or flying.

The authors don't attempt to assign a zoological identity, saying the animal's existence needs to be proven first. They suggest there is more than one species involved, which is required if all the sightings here are accurate: the solid-body animal with a humped back and the very slender "coiled" animal aren't compatible. The authors buttress the anecdotes with maps, photographs, and drawings, plus references and a bibliography. If their case remains unproven, it's also hard to lock away as "solved."

Men really need sea-monsters in their personal oceans. An ocean without its unnamed monsters would be like a completely dreamless sleep. – John Steinbeck, *The Log From the Sea of Cortez*

The Seal Serpent (Revised): The Search for a Long Necked Pinniped

Cornes, Rob, and Gary Cunningham (2018: CFZ Publishing, 330pp.)

Cornes and Cunningham have written one of the best contributions to the "sea serpent" literature in decades. The authors focus on one of the most common and plausible theories of what sort of unknown animal (if there is one) might be responsible: an undescribed species of long-necked pinniped. There are hints of such an animal in paleontology, although Dr. Darren Naish, a cryptozoology-friendly paleontologist, is *very* cautious about connecting the modestly long-necked Late Miocene seal *Acrophoca longirostris* with any modern sightings. There is also a description of a dead pinniped with a long neck once exhibited in London. Physician and naturalist James Parsons (1705-1770) wrote of this as a species in 1751, but it was never formally described, and the specimen is lost.

The authors collect reports of sea serpents, odd seals/sea lions, escaped specimens (I didn't know they could climb fences), and out-of-place pinnipeds (what was a Northern fur seal doing in Vietnam?). They discuss which known pinnipeds could have accounted for some of the sighting reports. In far-southern latitudes, one of my favorite animals, the leopard seal (*Hydrurga leptonyx*), comes up a lot. Leopard seals, which visit Australia on occasion, look serpentine and strikingly reptilian. They can also be aggressive and do not shy from humans or boats: they have attacked humans and have killed at least one. If you double the known length of 3.5 m, you'd get a fine sea serpent, although presumably not applicable to the reports of giants 30-100 feet (9.1-30.5 m) long. The leopard seal that killed biologist Kristy Brown in 2003 was huge: the estimate of length cited in this book is an outsized 14 feet (4.3m).

The authors are properly cautious about eyewitness reports. For example, they spend considerable time with the Australian bunyip but believe sightings represent just a mélange of known species. Other sea-creature sightings, notably the whole-body description made from a British fishing boat in 1929 by J. Mackintosh Bell, impress them. They also look at "lake monsters" but conclude there aren't any, although wandering pinnipeds are one of the explanations for reports.

The authors say they have not solved the question by any means, but the seal hypothesis is backed by "a small body of evidence" and is plausible, and they speculate on the ancestry, lifestyle, and environment of a possible candidate. The book is well illustrated and thoroughly referenced, with a large bibliography, and the authors' tone is properly scientific throughout. Excellent work.

The potential for fundamental discoveries is high for anyone who goes into the field of deep-sea research with open eyes and an intuitive mind. – Cindy Lee Van Dover, marine biologist

Without funding, we will never have investigations or results. Without results, we will never have funding. – Sir Peter Scott, conservationist, referring to Loch Ness

Sun, Sand, and Sea Serpents

Goudsward, David (2020: Anomalist Books, 298pp.)

This book on the sea, lake, and river monsters of Florida and the surrounding lands and waters really impresses me. Goudsward has done a superb job of assembling tales and tracking them to their sources. I grew up in Florida, was a monster buff, and yet never heard of most of these. Some episodes are famous among cryptozoologists: the St. Augustine "octopus" carcass, the sightings in the St. Johns River, the giant penguin footprint hoax, and so on. But how many people know of the Muck Monster from the Lake Worth Lagoon? Wherever there's a report, the author tracks down everything he can and suggests non-monster explanations while still leaving open the most intriguing episodes. Some of the lake monsters, in particular, were made up to have an excuse to hold festivals and sell T-shirts, while others were one-time reports and the "creature" was never heard of again. An interesting point is that the author is often critical of Bernard Heuvelmans, the closest thing this topic has to a lawgiver, arguing Heuvelmans several times forced a vague or explainable report into one of his categories.

On the most divisive Florida monster report, Brian McCleary claimed his four friends were killed by a sea monster in 1962 while snorkeling; Goudsward reinforces my own thinking. The particulars kept getting more detailed over time (improbably so, given that McCleary was an admittedly panicking teen and it was a foggy night), and there's no evidence for anything but a tragic accident.

The author ventures afield to the Caribbean to look at giant octopus stories and to the Georgia haunts of the Altamaha-ha monster. He also looks at Thomas Helm's report of a long-necked creature with a head like an earless cat in the Gulf of Mexico. Here Goudsward notes the usual problems with distance and size estimates at sea but can't nail down the animal for certain.

A very good bibliography divided by subject completes a very good book. The lack of illustrations is the only deficiency.

When, upon the closed system of normal preoccupations, a story of a sea serpent appears, it is inhospitably treated. To us of the wider cordialities, it has recommendations for kinder reception. I think that we shall be noted in recognitions of good works for our bizarre charities. – Charles Fort, author of *The Book of the Damned* and other studies of oddities

Monsters of the Deep

Helm, Thomas (1962: Dodd, Mead and Company, 232pp.)

Helm wrote several books on the sea, including one on the famous U.S.S. *Indianapolis* sinking (he served on the ship before the war). In this one, he spends time with known animals that might be mistaken for "monsters" then reviews the most interesting cases. There are some errors in the science, but the book's value lies in a few incidents. Helm 1) chased what he and a friend were dead certain was a living, breathing sea monster down a beach until dawn showed them a floating tree trunk with an extended root, 2) talked to someone involved in the 1948 Florida monster-tracks hoax decades before hoaxer Tony Signorini's confession, and 3) with his wife, Helm saw from a sailboat in the Gulf of Mexico in 1943 a mammal with a round head the size of a tiger's (eyes in front, whiskers but no seal-like snout, and no visible ears) on a four-foot neck. The range was short and the conditions perfect, so the prosaic explanation of a pinniped may or may not be definitive.

Monster Hunt

Dinsdale, Tim (1972: Acropolis Books, 295pp.)

Dinsdale, the most famous Loch Ness monster hunter, traces the history of Nessie and similar creatures around the world. He discusses the scientific expeditions to investigate Loch Ness, which took place in the 1960s and 1970s. Dinsdale was a photographer on some of these expeditions. He has, as you would expect, no doubt Nessie is real. He lets his speculation roam beyond Scotland here, visiting cases around the world, including the crocodile-like *buru*, the sea serpent, one mermaid claim, disappearances in a South American river (he suggests a giant catfish, which is not completely out of the question), and so on. He reviews and accepts two disputed photographs of supposed giant anacondas. His non-Ness writings don't offer conclusive evidence of anything, but he tells the stories well. (An earlier edition is called *The Leviathans*.)

... some of the serpents in similar Irish tales may have been real water monsters, which are still seen from time to time... These eerie, ugly monsters, with their aura of primeval mystery, appropriately symbolize the uncouth savagery which the Christians attributed to all non-Christian beliefs; but that is not to say that the monsters were totally symbolic and did not have a reality of their own. – Janet and Colin Bord, Sacred Waters: Holy Wells and Water Lore in Britain and Ireland

The Loch Ness Story

Witchell, Nicholas (1975: Penguin Books, 156pp.)

This book influenced me tremendously when I first became curious about Loch Ness. The 1975 edition altered the original 1974 one by adding a Postscript reporting on the 1975 photographs from Robert Rines' group. Witchell's lively history includes interesting oddities like "monster-sniffing dogs" and a Japanese expedition that arrived with no idea how big the loch was and how muddled the water was. In the main, though, it's a brief (Witchell was in law school) for a pro-monster viewpoint, with the Postscript declaring all doubt was removed and there were definitely plesiosaurs in the Loch. While sources are sometimes given in the text, there are almost no footnotes and no bibliography. Still valuable for the photographs and the accounts of early sightings.

The Monster of Loch Ness

Mackal, Roy (1976: Swallow Press, 401pp.)

When this book came out, it was hailed by *Publishers Weekly* as "the best book on the subject." It's still a very useful one. Mackal, a biochemist and biologist, tells us he has always been curious about what we now call cryptids, but it's a quick visit to Loch Ness that really draws him in. He works with David James of the Loch Ness Phenomena Investigation Bureau (LNPIB, later just LNIB) to improve search methods and seek better evidence, even as he remains skeptical of the candidates put forward by Nessie hunters. He recounts his experiences in year-by-year searches through 1970. He then goes into themed chapters: still photographs, memorable eyewitness reports, etc. He rejects many still photos, including the Surgeon's photograph and the 1955 Peter McNab photograph, although he likes the Rines photographs and a few others. Next come chapters on the morphology and behavior of the animal, then another look at candidates. He finishes with appendices listing sightings, films, sonar contacts, ecological information on the lake, and other supporting topics.

His candidate for the creature is an amphibian, like a giant salamander with fins instead of feet, proffering a thick-bodied giant eel as a secondary candidate. There are no footnotes or endnotes to external sources, although he does include a good bibliography. This book is less well-known today, bobbing in the wake of a hundred newer Nessie books, but it's worth tracking down.

The Loch Ness Mystery Solved

Binns, Ronald (1984: Prometheus Books, 288pp.)

Binns believes there is no evidence of monsters in Loch Ness that can't be explained as known phenomena. Here he explains why he thinks most if not all sightings are actually of birds, roe deer, large fish, otters, and wave or wake phenomena. He argues that more hoaxing has gone on than monster investigators usually believe. Binns explores the personalities and events going back into the 1930s and generally argues that, after the initial burst of excitement, all too many people and expeditions saw what they expected or wanted to see. That human dimension is sometimes missing from Loch Ness books, but Binns' arguments are necessarily (admit it, you thought I was going to make a Nessie pun there) speculative when so many people involved have died. If Binns can't quite throw the monster case completely out of court, though, he introduces reasonable doubt. I've not read the follow-ups: *The Loch Ness Mystery Reloaded* (Zoilus Press, 2017) or the grandly titled *Decline and Fall of the Loch Ness Monster: Contested Histories and Revisionist Tales* (Zoilus Press, 2019.).

Monster Wrecks of Loch Ness and Lake Champlain

Zarzynski, Joseph (1986: M-Z Information, 112pp.)
 Unusual collection of short items about the two lakes in the title. The subjects include shipwrecks, archeology, history, and, of course, the search for "monsters."

Ogopogo

Gaal, Arlene (1986: Hancock House Publishers, 128pp.)
 Gaal, who believes she has seen Ogopogo several times, is the closest thing this cryptid has to an official historian. This is a brief but lively account of the Canadian lake monster, with an excellent photo section and a table of sightings from 1860 to 1984. She followed up with *In Search of Ogopogo* (Hancock House Publishers, 2001, reissued 2019). This book on the creature of Lake Okanagan includes a detailed chronology and many photographs. The author argues the evidence in totality is very convincing and the presence of unknown animals "can no longer be disputed." She tries hard to prove that point here, but she can't quite bring her catch to the dock.

Lake Monster Traditions: A Cross-Cultural Analysis

Meurger, Michel, and Claude Gagnon (1988: Fortean Tomes, 320pp.)

This unique scholarly work surveys monster reports and folklore from around the world and explores the common themes involved. While not entirely rejecting the possibility of "real" lake monsters, the authors trace the cultural roots of the subject in a way no one else has done. I have my reservations about applying a sociological analysis too broadly, as a given witness might never have heard of a supposed tradition concerning the creature they are reporting, but this well-referenced book is valuable nonetheless.

There Are Giants in the Sea: Monsters and Mysteries of the Depths Explored

Bright, Michael (1989: Robson Books, 224pp.)

Bright, a biologist, offers an enjoyable survey of large and unusual sea creatures (the known and the unknown). He writes well and includes many things I've seen nowhere else, like basking and whale sharks well beyond the official record sizes, and I like any book with a chapter titled "The Big Blob." The book is seriously weakened by the lack of references. Bright says a Soviet whale-spotting helicopter crew saw a squid with arms one meter (3.3 feet) *in diameter*: I'd need a clear photo to even consider that one. Still, a good book overall.

Living Fossil: The Story of the Coelacanth

Thomson, Keith (1991: W.W. Norton & Company, 252pp.)

Dr. Thompson covers nearly everything about *Latimeria chalumnae*, including its ancestry, scientific importance, and unique features and lifestyle. He also addresses the question of distribution in this authoritative book. The only topic cryptozoologists may note he does not address is the hint of a New World population. He had written this book before additional populations were found in African waters and a second species in Indonesia, but the book's value remains intact.

Matt's Musings: The coelacanth was a marvelous discovery, and the subsequent finding of a second species and several new populations is likewise wonderful, and yet I grow tired of the creature's constant presence in cryptozoology books. Authors need to stop citing it as proof there could be undiscovered plesiosaurs surviving from the same epoch.

The Loch Ness Monster: The Evidence

Campbell, Steuart (1997: Prometheus Books, 128pp.)

Campbell surveys all the evidence concerning Loch Ness and finds it wanting. His skepticism can verge on the dogmatic, and some items are dismissed too briefly when I'd like him to explain his reasoning further. (A film taken by Gwen Smith in 1977, for instance, is dismissed as evidence because a hoax was possible and is, therefore, assumed.) His habit of using "L" for "loch" and "N" for Nessie is distracting, and he seems to automatically assume researchers like Roy Mackal are right when they assign a conventional explanation and wrong when they don't.

Campbell looks at all the major Loch Ness events, including photos and films, sonar readings, and some of the eyewitness reports. He also spends one chapter dismissing other lake monsters around the world. His discussion of the mistakes witnesses can make and why they make them, though, is very good. His main point at the end is that Nessie is seen less often even as more people look for it, which he argues is solid evidence Nessie does not exist.

. . .

MATT BILLE

I cannot give any scientist of any age better advice than this: the intensity of the conviction that a hypothesis is true has no bearing on whether it is true or not. – Sir Peter B. Medawar, biologist

The Book of Sea Monsters

Eggleton, Bob, and Nigel Suckling (1998: Overlook Press, 112pp.)

This unique book does not offer any special insight or information in its text, but I'll keep it always. It's a showcase for Eggleton's paintings of sea and lake monsters, real, reported, and mythical. Suckling's text is merely fair, but Eggleton's visions of Nessie, plesiosaurs, Ogopogo, etc., are beautiful works of talent and imagination.

The giant squid is the perfect embodiment of a sea monster: it is huge, it has tentacles, it has big eyes, and it is absolutely frightening-looking. But, most important, it is real. Unlike the Loch Ness monster, we know it's out there. – David Grann, author, in *The New Yorker*

Nessie: The Surgeon's Photograph Exposed

Martin, David, and Alastair Boyd (1999: Thorne Printing, 100pp.)

This small self-published book makes a convincing argument, starting with Ian Wetherell's story of how it was done, that the most famous Loch Ness photo was a fake. They argue previous authors who took it seriously didn't pay attention to warning signs.

A Fish Caught in Time

Weinberg, Samantha (2000: HarperCollins Publishers, 220pp.)

Superbly written history of the coelacanth and the people who have pursued it. Less technical than Keith Thomson's coelacanth book, this volume is filled with details about the effect this unique fish has had on those caught in its prehistoric aura. Weinberg includes a thorough account of the discovery of the second population in Indonesia, along with evidence for other populations.

Sea Serpents and Lake Monsters of the British Isles

Harrison, Paul (2001: Robert Hale, 253pp.)

    Harrison, president of the Loch Ness Monster Society, has written a readable collection of the more interesting accounts of the titular creatures, arranged geographically. It's a worthwhile contribution with a lot of information (I see 11-page markers I planted in my copy). However, maps (or any kind of illustrations) and footnotes would have strengthened it considerably. There is a good bibliography.

The monster—if there was one—never revealed itself to me again. But what I had learned over the past year was that monsters abound, usually in plain sight. – Sara Gruen, author, *At the Water's Edge*

River Monsters: True Stories of the Ones that Didn't Get Away

Wade, Jeremy (2011: Da Capo Press, 304pp.)

    The host of the television show *River Monsters* here unspools his adventures with rod and reel. Wade is clearly a master at the craft of fishing, although it's refreshing that he also admits sometimes he's benefited from dumb luck. He has caught (and, when practical, released) the largest freshwater fishes on every inhabited continent. Along the way, he has harrowing adventures in the water and out. Wade explains conservation issues and fish biology (for example, adapting to fresh vs. saltwater) very well. He also has some tidbits for the cryptozoologist. Remember, Wade is the man who filmed an "impossible animal," a river dolphin with a weird sawtooth back, most likely an unlikely survivor of severe injuries inflicted by a fisherman's machete. He investigates Lake Iliamna (finding some data I did not) and comes to the same conclusion I did that it's probably an undocumented population of white sturgeon. This book is fun from beginning to end.

Sea Monsters on Medieval and Renaissance Maps

Van Duzer, Chet (2013: British Library Publishing, 144pp.)

A beautiful book, to say the very least. Van Duzer shows us how sea creatures, real, intended-to-be-real, and wholly imaginary, decorated maps from the earliest surviving Western examples, are as much as 1,200 years old. The practice may be much older.

Van Duzer's focus is on the sixth through tenth centuries. Cartographers decorated maps with creatures both real and fantastic to show dangers believed to be in specific areas, to emphasize the breadth and wonder of Creation, or just as ornaments, especially on maps commissioned by the wealthy as art. The creatures are sometimes absurd, sometimes intriguing, and sometimes even believable—a swordfish and a whale on the Gough map of Britain, c. 1400, are very accurate. An illustrated copy of Ptolemy's *Geography*, made about 1560, was the pinnacle of sea monster art, including in its maps 476 creatures. Often creatures shown on maps turn up in other places, such as illuminated manuscripts, bestiaries, and church decorations.

Monsters on maps declined in the more scientific era that followed the Renaissance, but the older maps left us some gorgeous illustrations as well as a window to the thinking of their times. Do any possibly indicate cryptozoological creatures, the modern sea serpents that never quite vanish into myth? They might: there is something in here to match up with almost any hypothesis, although I don't know what one artist used as a guide for a half-fish half-rooster, a literal chicken of the sea. This is a great reference to the monster beliefs of the period as well as a thing of sometimes-breathtaking beauty. The 299 endnotes add many interesting details.

Monsters of the Deep

Redfern, Nick (2020: Visible Ink Press, 366pp.)

Redfern is an indefatigable seeker of oddities, and his many interests leave the title topic obscured. He collects interesting reports on lake and sea monsters but goes much further afield, all the way to reporting claims of cannibals living underneath London and a giant snake killed in Bolivia by the CIA (I have to admit the latter story is fascinating).

There are two sections of cryptozoological value. One consists of long quotations from the work of Henry Lee (*Sea Monsters Unmasked*, William Clowes and Sons,1883). It's surprising how relevant Lee's work is to the still-quoted body of sea serpent evidence. The second useful aspect features the author's investigations of modern reports of creatures in small bodies of water in England.

Redfern writes that the classification schemes proposed for sea monsters aren't useful without more evidence, and I've no argument there. He thinks some cryptids are material animals and some are projections of ancient predator archetypes. There are no footnotes, chapter notes, or endnotes, only a 10-page bibliography. Some editing mistakes contribute to the book's hurried, disjointed feel. While the side trips reduce this book's impact on cryptozoology, there are a few things for the inquiring mind to take away.

There is not an a priori reason that I know of why snake-bodied reptiles, from fifty feet long and upwards, should not disport themselves in our seas as they did in those of the Cretaceous epoch which, geologically speaking, is a mere yesterday. – Thomas Henry Huxley, naturalist, 1893

MATT BILLE

Monsters & Marine Mysteries

Hawthorne, Max (2021: Far From The Tree Press, 342pp.)

Hawthorne, champion sport fisherman and author of the *Kronos Rising* novels about surviving prehistoric predators, here collects his writings about sea monsters and his arguments for large unknown predators. Hawthorne includes some personal encounters with the paranormal, but my focus here is the cryptozoology. He also includes many stories about big fish and the sometimes-bigger ones that got away. I love these sorts of stories: when he reports fish bigger than the official records, there's no reason to dismiss them. We rarely have *the* biggest one of anything.

Moving on to actual monsters, however, I have numerous disagreements. On the one flipper, he includes some interesting accounts, particularly of giant cephalopods I didn't know about. On the other, he includes the old *U-28* hoax as fact. He is certain that a video by Garry Liimatta is proof of a giant, shell-less turtle he calls the Super Predator. I still see a blobby shape that might be a sea elephant. He is open to conventional explanations in some cases: assuming the 1918 Port Stevens monster shark was not a hoax, I think he's right about it being a huge light-colored whale shark and not a Megalodon. Hawthorne's chapter on accounts of 10-meter (33-foot) great white sharks is interesting even if not (yet?) supported by sufficient evidence.

He devotes two chapters to a monstrous mosasaur-like creature reported by a cruise ship sailor in 2014, a tale that illustrates a common problem in cryptozoology. To the author, the case is buttressed by having several witnesses. However, we have only the single witness who claims those witnesses existed. That's not a "multiple-witness" sighting unless proof, in the form of actual testimony from those witnesses, surfaces. There are no photos and no other reports, so Hawthorne is basically going on the fact he thinks the witness was sincere.

Hawthorne spends a lot of time reconstructing predator attacks on whales and sharks. Some of the photographs of the damage are startling, but he is (as he knows) matching up bite shapes from photos and models and not the flexing, writhing, fighting animals. That he's matching them to hypothesized animals whose jaws and dentition have never been examined adds to the uncertainty.

Hawthorne's belief that giant squid get bigger than we've measured is reasonable. The idea that enormous ones attack adult whales by bludgeoning them with their tentacles, though, is hard to take seriously.

Hawthorne gives some sources in footnotes, although these are of varying quality. There's too much speculation here to prove the existence of sea monsters, though there's still a lot of fun in the angling tales.

The ocean is a wilderness reaching round the globe, wilder than a Bengal jungle, and fuller of monsters... – Henry David Thoreau

Others

Unless you expect the unexpected you will never find it, for it is hard to discover and hard to attain. – Heraclitus

Animal Legends

Burton, Maurice (1957: Coward-McCann, 318pp.)

Dr. Burton, one of the eminent zoologists of his century, discusses all sorts of odd stories and characteristics of animals, from blackbirds "anting" with lit cigarettes to cats fishing with their tail-tips. For the cryptozoologist, we have his description of conger eels swimming on their sides at the top of the water (he observed this firsthand), looking very un-eel-like and rather monster-like, an estimate that moray eels might grow to 16 feet (4.9 m) long, and the proposition that the Loch Ness monsters were huge eels. He believes one or more unknown animals, possibly even including a plesiosaur, could be involved in sea serpent sightings, while he feels the evidence concerning the Yeti doesn't point conclusively one way or the other.

Burton soon became more skeptical on all cryptozoological claims, as expressed in his 1961 book *The Elusive Monster: An Analysis of the Evidence from Loch Ness*, but *Animal Legends* remains a fascinating book in every way.

Mermaids and Mastodons

Carrington, Richard (1957: Rinehart & Company, 251pp.)

Another excellent book from the 1950s, like those of Willy Ley and Maurice Burton, containing information on a broad spectrum of topics of zoology and cryptozoology. Carrington reviews mermaids first and feels they are a charming myth but no more. However, "The age-long enigma of the great sea-serpent is still unsolved." He reviews dragons, birds of myth and legend, the discovery of dinosaurs, mastodons and mammoths, the finding of the coelacanth, and lastly, three terrible extinction stories: the quagga, the passenger pigeon, and Steller's sea cow (he thinks an 1834 sighting of the sea cow might be valid but has no hope the animal survived much past that). The book includes a very good bibliography.

The Mystery Monsters

Soule, Gardner (1965: Ace Books, 191pp.)

An example of the "monster" books popular in the 1960s and 70s, written for junior high school on up by people like Soule and Daniel Cohen. The cover copy of Soule's second book on the topic (1963's *The Maybe Monsters* was the first) is hilarious ("The two-ton sea monster that flies!" is how it presents the leaping giant manta), but the text is decent. Soule visits the Flathead Lake monster (a sturgeon, he thinks), then giant clams, electric eels, whales, and other known species: he throws the word "monster" around a lot when referring to maximum size. The giant leptocephalus, the Soay turtle-ish-monster, the Queensland marsupial tiger, and other classic cryptozoology items are described matter-of-factly. Informative and fun, even though skepticism rarely rears its head. The same can't quite be said for his update, *Mystery Monsters of the Deep* (1981), which has much good information but plumps for Megalodon survival without new evidence and also implies a carcass found by the Japanese fishing boat *Zuiyo Maru* has been widely accepted as a plesiosaur when it's actually been widely accepted as a rotting shark. Cohen's contribution can be typified by *Monsters, Giants, and Little Men from Mars: An Unnatural History of the Americas* (Dell, 1975). This was one of my favorites as a kid because of the attitude that most American monsters (hodags, anyone?) were good silly fun, but there were a few oddities suggesting that just maybe...)

The Empty Ark

Crowe, Philip (1967: Charles Scribner's Sons, 281pp.)

This book recounts Crowe's travels around the world as an ambassador for the World Wildlife Fund. Everywhere Crowe went, he asked local experts about rare and strange creatures. As a result, there are tidbits in this book on many cryptozoological subjects. Unknown species mentioned include giant anacondas, an unknown South American bear, Yeti, the *almas*, new species of bats, and a cat on the Japanese island of Iriomote. Crowe heard hints of survival concerning "lost" species, including the Fiji petrel, the moa, the takahe, wild specimens of Przewalski's horse, and the thylacine. [The cat, petrel, and takahe have since been found.] Crowe produced a first-rate book that is still valuable today.

A World Full of Animals

Hunt, John (1969: David McKay Publications, 378pp.)

Hunt, a conservationist and zookeeper, produced a now-dated but still highly enjoyable tour of the vertebrates, focusing mainly on mammals. For cryptozoologists, there's a good discussion of how the tarpan was "re-created," plus reports and rumors of African bears, wild Przewalski's horses, and surviving thylacines. Most intriguingly, Hunt reported (without giving a source) that "Russian reports" he took seriously indicated that not only was Steller's sea cow alive but that a surviving population was under official protection.

Matt's Musings: We all want Steller's sea cow back: not just because it's spectacular, but because it would mean that one of the most distressing human-caused extinctions never happened. Despite sighting reports in the 19th and 20th centuries, though, I don't expect we'll ever see one.

Field Guide of Whales and Dolphins

Morzer Bruyuns, Willem (1971: C.A. Mees, 258pp.)

Sea captain and naturalist Willem F. J. Morzer Bruyuns, in his four decades on the oceans, kept notes and made paintings of every cetacean he encountered. He had seen most of the species known by the time he wrote his book in 1971, plus some oddities. In Africa's Gulf of Aden, he saw what he thought were orcas of a new type—solid brown with small white markings or scars. (Some authorities suggest this was one of the since-classified beaked whales, but the illustration shows it with an orca's distinctive fin, so there's still some uncertainty.) Off Senegal, he reported large numbers of brown and white dolphins about six feet (1.8 m) long. They looked like the Atlantic spotted dolphin, but the spots were missing. Then there is his never-identified "Illigan dolphin," resembling the known melon-headed whale but brown with a pink underside and yellow flanks, seen off the Philippines in schools of up to 30 animals. There's more, but you get the idea. This is a beautiful book, with in-person observations and a few mysteries to go with the paintings.

Animal Fakes & Frauds

Dance, Peter (1976: Sampson Low, 128pp.)

Cryptozoologists often deal with manufactured or otherwise suspect specimens. This slender hardcover is a unique book with countless fascinating illustrations of such things. Dance was a conchologist at the British Museum and saw many such creations for himself. He discusses animals of myth and legend and includes old drawings with the histories of known fakes, such as "Jenny Haniver" mer-creatures, "feejee" mermaids, "dragons" made from skates or rays, fake Yeti scalps, and Dr. Albert Koch's elaborate 114-foot "sea serpent" skeleton. America's most enduring fake creatures, the jackalope and the fur-bearing trout get in here, too. (The "alligator man" does not, and I'm not sure why.) He tells us Jenny Hanivers were still being made in Mexico for tourists whose fascination with the deep exceeded their ichthyological acumen. Dance also presents little-known fakes like the grunk (head of a duck, body of a grouse), faked composite insects, taxidermied mammal crosses, a vole and a mole skeleton intermixed for a "new mouse," fake fossils, and much more. It's a smashing good read.

Arthur C. Clarke's Mysterious World

Welfare, Simon, and John Fairley, with Arthur C. Clarke (1980: A&W Publishers, 217pp.)

This well-illustrated, well-written book recaps the 1970s TV series of the same name. The authors' tone, reflecting the series, is balanced and rational compared to many works from this era and ours. Four of the 12 chapters focus on cryptozoology. Clarke, who comments at the end of each chapter, is intrigued by a Sri Lankan legend indicating "… we may have missed the Neanderthals, by a few centuries, not by millennia." He also thinks beyond doubt there are one or more real creatures behind sea serpent stories. Much of the information is dated, and hoaxes like the Surgeon's Photograph have since been exposed, but this is a nostalgic snapshot of a time when everyone was curious about oddities and science was taking notice.

Living Wonders: Mysteries and Curiosities of the Animal World

Michell, John, and Robert J.M. Rickard (1982: Thames and Hudson, 176pp.)

This is a book I've held onto for decades. Stuffed with information on everything from toads entombed in stone to tales of eagles carrying off children, this volume visits all the major cryptids of the time and many related "creature" stories. There's a distinctly English flavor to the tales of fairies and living curiosities. If you want to read about everything from a sudden "blizzard" of butterflies to unusual swimming feats by land animals (what was that kangaroo doing miles from the Australian coast, seemingly headed for New Zealand)? It includes a 1976 photograph of one of a "small pack of thylacines" being watched at a secret location, though sadly, they turned out to be dogs.

Mysterious America

Coleman, Loren (1983: Faber & Faber, 301pp.)

This is one of Coleman's most influential books. In it, he takes readers on a tour of the country's oddities, many of them dealing with animals or apparent animals. Everything interests him: unknown apes, out-of-place animals, possible prehistoric survivals, and what he calls "paraphysical" entities. His special interests include mystery cats and "phantom" kangaroos. He includes the documented 1974 kangaroo vs. Chicago police incident, fictionalized in 1996 on the TV drama *ER*. One of the highlights is the 1977 case of an oddity called the "Dover Demon," in which Coleman reprints an article by one Walter Webb, who followed the case and meticulously described the steps of Coleman's investigation. [No animal was ever found.] As a Fortean, Coleman is interested in waves, connections, synchronicities, and the like, but there are also many interesting entries on everything from black panthers to swamp apes to intrigue the cryptozoologist.

The Flight of the Iguana

Quammen, David (1988: Delacorte Press, 302pp.)

The Song of the Dodo

Quammen, David (1996: Charles Scribner's Sons, 702pp.)

The Boilerplate Rhino

Quammen, David (2000: Charles Scribner's Sons, 288pp.)

Natural Acts

Quammen, David (2008: W. W. Norton & Company, 352pp.)

The zoological writings of David Quammen are best dealt with as a group. Most of Quammen's books collect his articles from *Outside* and other publications, while *The Song of the Dodo* is original.

The Flight of the Iguana offers an essay entitled "Stranger than Truth: Cryptozoology and the Romantic Imagination." Quammen holds the common view that "cryptozoology is biased toward large unknown animals." He seems skeptical about the existence of such animals but thinks well of the scientists involved and describes the journal *Cryptozoology* as "intriguing, diverse, and mainly quite sane."

The Song of the Dodo is subtitled *Island Biogeography in an Age of Extinction*. Quammen deals not only with literal islands but with isolated areas on larger landmasses, which is definitely a topic of interest to cryptozoologists! Quammen examines what happens to island populations—how they change, how many individuals they need to remain viable as a species, and how they become extinct. Two sections cover the 1986 discovery of the golden bamboo lemur (*Hapalemur aereus*) and the disappearance of the thylacine.

The Boilerplate Rhino has the essay "Limelight," which covers the media circus concerning the 1994 sighting of two octopi of unknown species. The seemingly confused cephalopods, both male, were filmed while trying to mate. One species has been identified, while the other remains a mystery.

Natural Acts includes two essays of cryptozoological significance. "Avatars of the Soul in Malaya" concerns discoveries in the world of moths and butterflies, including some very odd new species. In "Rumors of a Snake," Quammen reviews stories of a giant anaconda in South America. Of the famous claim by Major Percy Fawcett to have shot a snake 62 feet (18.9 m) long, Quammen observes, "It might all be true, but most likely it isn't."

Mythical Monsters

Gould, Charles (1992: Studio Editions, 407pp.)

In this reprint of a book published in 1884, the reader will find many oddities of natural history. Some, not surprisingly, have been explained or disproved over the subsequent decades. Of most interest is the sea serpent section. Gould believes one or more species of unknown animals are involved in sea serpent reports. In this book, he includes many reports made before and around his time, including cases where Gould corresponded with the witnesses himself.

Drums Along the Congo

Nugent, Rory (1993: Houghton Mifflin Publishing, 248pp.)

This is a chronicle of Nugent's adventures in search of the alleged living dinosaur of the Congo, which the author believes that he spotted. He relates his adventures with humor, and at times they are hair-raising. While Nugent includes photographs, the object shown is much too distant for identification.

Biological Anomalies: Mammals I

Corliss, William (1995: Sourcebook Project, 286pp.)

This is the first of two valuable collections of zoological and cryptozoological material. Mammals I was followed by **Mammals II** (1996: Sourcebook Project. 318pp.) These volumes contain a wealth of reprinted articles from popular and scientific sources from all over the world on thylacines, Nandi bears, sea serpents, mystery whales, two sightings of what sound like pterodactyls, and many other subjects. Every item includes references. Some items are reprinted from *Strange Life: A Sourcebook on the Mysteries of Nature* (Sourcebook, 1976) which also includes stories about surprising animal intelligence, peculiar behavior, etc.

Mammals I concerns itself mostly with things like unexplained behavior, amazing senses, hybrids, and mutations. *Mammals II* serves up serious nutrition for cryptozoologists. Several chapters on possible late survivors include the mammoth, a claim of live mastodons in Russia (it's unclear how they wandered onto the wrong continent), the thylacine, a giant lemur, and others. The Unrecognized Mammals section includes MacFarlane's Bear, the onza, the Marozi, the Nandi bear, a mermaid, a fleet of possibly mammalian sea serpents, Francois de Loys' alleged South American ape, and other classics (though not the Yeti or Sasquatch). It's fascinating reading all the way through, and many of the sources are highly reputable. The footnotes and source index are superb: anyone interested in mammalian oddities will find these alone worth the price of the books.

In Search of Prehistoric Survivors

Shuker, Karl (1995: Blandford Press, 192pp.)

This book is subsumed and superseded by **Still in Search of Prehistoric Survivors**, but it still merits mention as an intriguing collection of reported animals from around the world. Shuker's tone is sometimes more credulous than I would like: it is, for instance, almost impossible to imagine that the world's largest flying bird is living undiscovered in the Ohio Valley of the United States. However, Shuker has done a massive amount of research and shown that in some cases (such as that of the Queensland tiger or *yarri*), the evidence is stronger than I'd thought.

. . .

The Queensland Tiger has always seemed to me to need further scrutiny: those reported fangs are suggestive of a specialized carnivorous marsupial. – Colin Groves, mammalogist

Bunyips & Bigfoots: In Search of Australia's Mystery Animals

Smith, Malcolm (1996: Millennium Books, 207pp.)

Smith, a zoologist, has written a terrific book: enjoyable, fact-filled, and skeptical but open-minded in tone. He doubts the existence of both the title animals but concludes there are some real mysteries to be solved. Smith believes Australia probably does house imported big cats, though he can't imagine how they arrived and is also impressed by some "sea serpent" reports from Australian waters.

Tales of Giant Snakes: A Historical Natural History of Anacondas and Pythons

Murphy, John, and Robert Henderson (1997: Krieger Publishing, 221pp.)

The authors here recount all that is known about the history, habits, and sizes of the world's largest snakes. They are skeptical of the idea of an unknown giant in the Amazon basin. Murphy and Henderson conclude that three species (the anaconda and the two largest pythons) "appear to approach, and possibly slightly exceed 30 feet (9.1 m) on occasion," although they include some credible-sounding reports of what may have been larger specimens. Mandatory reading for all those interested in the subject of giant snakes. An enjoyable companion is Chad Arment's *Boss Snakes: Stories and Sightings of Giant Snakes in North America* (Coachwhip Publications, 2008), an entertaining collection of claims and folklore.

. . .

Matt's Musings: Everyone has their "bigger snake" stories. Growing up in Florida, I remember claims of rattlesnakes that stretched "from one side of A1A (a two-lane paved road) to the other." I saw a rattler skin on the wall of a sporting goods shop that, even adjusting for a kid's imagination, was surely over the record of eight feet (perhaps artificially stretched?). When I checked years later, alas, the store had closed.

Cryptozoology A to Z

Coleman, Loren, and Jerome Clark (1999: Simon and Schuster, 267pp.)

For a book whose subtitle bills it as an "Encyclopedia," this is shorter than one might expect, but there's plenty of good material in here. The authors cover the major animals, publications, and personalities in cryptozoology, making this a first-rate introduction for the newcomer or a handy sourcebook for the experienced researcher. A quick browse takes us from Batatut (a small bipedal primate whose footprints were reported by no less an authority than Dr. John MacKinnon, who described the saola) to William Gibbons (pursuer of Mokele-mbembe) to MacFarlane's bear (an oddity I discussed on the TV series *MonsterQuest*) to the *Storsjoodjuret* (Sweden's most famous lake monster).

Two quibbles: I would have liked to see the references broken down by topic and a wording error in the Megalodon [*Carcharocles megalodon,* or most recently *Otodus megalodon*] entry gives the erroneous impression I think this extinct creature survives. The authors necessarily had to leave a lot of mysteries out, but the important ones are all here, and the writing is clear and balanced. The bottom line is this book is a very important and useful addition to the cryptozoologist's library.

Mysterious Creatures: A Guide to Cryptozoology

Eberhart, George (2002: ABC-CLIO, 722pp.)
This massive two-volume encyclopedia attempts to catalog every cryptid worth mentioning, from purely mythical animals to those recently confirmed and described. References are given in all cases, and several supplementary essays cover important aspects of cryptozoology. I have the hardcover original, which came out at a price of $185 in 2002 dollars, but there are more affordable paperback versions from CFZ press available new and used. It's a unique resource for any zoologist or cryptozoologist and easily one of the most valuable cryptozoology works ever.

Of course, we know little or nothing about the population densities or reproductive rates of so-called cryptids, but there seems to be little doubt that the largest ones must be among the rarest of living species. – Dmitri Bayanov, primate cryptozoologist

The Ghost with Trembling Wings: Science, Wishful Thinking, and the Search for Lost Species

Weidensaul, Scott (2002: North Point Press, 341pp.)
Weidensaul explores and participates in searches for missing species, from birds to thylacines. Successes like the rediscovery of Gilbert's potoroo and the Congo bay owl are here, as are sad failures like the search for the thylacine. The author also probes the human stories of people who spend their treasure, their time, and sometimes their lives in such pursuits. He looks at hints of new discoveries on land and sea, remarking that "If cryptozoology is ever going to hit pay dirt, the jackpot is most likely to be marine. Even inshore waters are a mystery, and it is the height of hubris to think we've uncovered all the big surprises." A very valuable book packed with information and insight. Weidensaul went on to write, among other things, a gorgeous

book titled *A World on the Wing: The Global Odyssey of Migratory Birds* (W.W. Norton & Company, 2021).

The Search for the Last Undiscovered Animals

Shuker, Karl (2003: Fall River Press, 338pp.)

This compilation and updating of various articles Shuker has done hopscotches around the world and includes many types of cryptids, some famous and some obscure (I'm pretty well-read, but the possible deep-sea arachnid caught me on the hop). Some, like the possible additional or presumed species among cassowaries, emus, and kiwis, are relatively traditional zoological mysteries. Giant killer otters and Mongolian death worms are definitely more cryptozoological, although the evidence isn't convincing in either case. Another edition is titled *The Beasts That Hide from Man* (Paraview Press, 2003).

Cryptozoology: Science and Speculation

Arment, Chad (2004: Coachwhip Publications, 393pp.)

The first half of this book is a good, indeed essential, exploration of the sources, methods, and scientific status of cryptozoology. Chad takes us through the history of cryptozoology, before and after the word was invented, and elucidates the principles of how it should be practiced. These won't entirely surprise anyone—they do arise from the basic scientific method—but Chad puts them together here with a good eye for what applies in the search for new animals. He talks about ethnology and logic as well as science, noting some of the fallacies in logic that he sees in cryptozoologists and in those who criticize them.

The second is an exploration of cryptid reports, many little-known but intriguing (like the long-tailed wildcat that used to be reported in Pennsylvania). He works into this a good discussion of cryptid-hunting. There's a lot of Sasquatch lore in this book, as would be expected for the dominant cryptid of North America, and some good material on his other interests, including snakes, oversize orangutans, dwarf seals (I never heard of this topic!) and a giant bird claim from West Virginia.

Arment is steadfast in his argument that cryptozoology is, or can be, a valid and valuable scientific endeavor. He also defines it, as I do, as excluding the paranormal phenomena that keep pushing their noses under a tent that's not fastened down as well as it should be. This is about zoology, and it's a landmark work of reasoning and information, with valuable appendices (one is "Suggestions for the Obtaining of Larger Zoological Specimens for Scientific Study," by the late Ivan T. Sanderson) and a good bibliography.

A Dictionary of Cryptozoology

Coghlan, Ronan (2004: Xiphos Books, 273pp.)

Consisting of hundreds of short entries, this comprehensive volume covers almost every cryptozoological or mythical animal from around the world. A handy reference, especially for the more obscure reports. I haven't seen the first sequel, *Cryptosup* (Xiphos, 2005), but I have his third, *Further Cryptozoology*, which came out in 2007. Some entries in this collection are add-ons to articles from the earlier books, which diminishes the value a bit. We go from the "Adiyaman creatures" (red-footed humanoids from Turkey) to *Zuzeca* ("Gigantic serpent in Sioux mythology.") There is a source given for each one, but some are just the names of websites while others are names of periodicals—but ascribing things to *Cryptomundo* or *Fortean Times* is almost useless. Some entries are as short as seven words, a few as long as two pages. The book is indeed useful as a dictionary, though. *Further Cryptozoology* is the same, with the most interesting entry to me being the *Kap Dwa*, a two-headed 12-foot fabricated creature (or gaff, as such things are called) allegedly from Patagonia.

In Search of the Ivory-Billed Woodpecker

Jackson, Jerome (2004: Smithsonian Books, 256pp.)

This is an important book on the life, death, and possible survival of the magnificent ivory-bill, America's largest woodpecker. Dr. Jackson, an eminent ornithologist who worked on the species for decades, describes his arduous multi-state search efforts and the stories he's tracked down. He thinks a few dozen of the hundreds of reports since the last unquestioned sighting in 1944 is impressive. One is the story from a newspaper editor in Kountze, Texas, who had a dead ivory-bill dropped on his desk in 1961 by a hunter who wanted him to know the woodpecker wasn't extinct. The editor pulled out pictures and descriptions of the ivory-bill and positively identified the bird. Then the hunter put the specimen in his pocket and disappeared. To Jackson, too many ornithologists dismiss ivory-bill reports and witnesses without proper examination. He concludes the species may still exist.

Cryptozoology and the Investigation of Lesser-Known Mystery Animals

Arment, Chad (editor) (2006: Coachwhip Publications, 228pp.)

A collection of essays on a variety of cryptozoology-related topics, including Paul Gauguin's mystery parrot, old silver coelacanth figures in churches, and claims of freshwater cephalopods, flying snakes, and those impossible but fun tales of living dinosaur-like critters in North America. It includes my article on new and cryptic species of wild pigs. Everything is well researched and written, and a reader can lose hours after picking this up.

Extreme Expeditions: Travel Adventures Stalking the World's Mystery Animals

Davies, Adam (2008: Anomalist Books, 164pp.)

The first book in a series by Davies, who has spent years poking around in the remote and uncomfortable locations described in his first-person adventure tales. In this one, he reports he found little at the traditional monster haunts of Lake Tele and Loch Ness, believes he saw a large unknown animal in Norway's Lake Seljord and collected reports, hair, and a footprint cast in pursuit of the bipedal Sumatran primate known as orang-pendek.

And no one has a right to say water-babies don't exist until they have seen no water-babies existing, which is quite a different thing, mind, from not seeing water-babies. – Charles Kingsley, author, *The Water-Babies*

Monsters of Texas

Gerhard, Ken, and Nick Redfern (2010: CFZ Press, 162pp.)

This is a fun read, setting down reports of giant birds, Sasquatch-type beasts, and other Texas oddities. The authors present people's claims in a straightforward fashion, leavened with humor though applying less skepticism than I would have used. Their most important contribution, I think, concerns the possible grain of truth hidden in the chupacabra myth. Coyotes and coyote hybrids with long hind legs, prominent fangs, and hair loss seem to turn up in Texas often enough to hint there may be some recurring genetic anomaly presenting itself. The authors do take with some seriousness stories of zoologically impossible or improbable things they think may be apparitions.

Orang Pendek: Sumatra's Forgotten Ape

Freeman, Richard (2011: CFZ Press, 332pp.)

In this, Richard Freeman's best book to date, he goes searching for the *orang-pendek* or "short man" reported from Sumatra and neighboring regions. He goes right to work in the first chapters, collecting and examining reports from a variety of witnesses, mainly Sumatrans but also including noted British conservationist Debbie Martyr, MBE, who is certain of her own sightings. Next, Freeman broadens the aperture to review similar reports from Africa, Southeast Asia, etc., to which he gives mixed reviews. Then he zooms back in on Sumatra to tell of his grueling personal experiences searching for the animal. He collected reports, prints, and what he hopes is a tuft of hair from an unknown primate. (Alas, it is inconclusive.)

Freeman rejects one popular suggestion, that the species is *Homo floresiensis*, in favor of a more slightly built, normally bipedal orangutan relative. In a field dotted with unsubstantiated claims, Freeman's embrace of a theory less exciting than surviving "hobbits" is a mark of sound thinking. He does not prove the *orang-pendek*'s existence in this book, but he cements its case as one of the most plausible cryptids.

Medusa's Gaze and Vampire's Bite: The Science of Monsters

Kaplan, Matt (2012: Charles Scribner's Sons, 256pp.)

Kaplan asks in this book where our current and past monster myths developed and how they've changed. Why have people all over the world believed in dragons? Which cultures have vampire stories? From the Minotaur to the Kraken, *Jaws*, and *Alien*, Kaplan explores how fossils, entertainment, folklore, and fear of the unknown have led us to believe in the monstrous.

American Monsters: A History of Monster Lore, Legends, and Sightings in America

Godfrey, Linda (2014: Tarcher Penguin, 367pp.)

It is an unfortunate truth that many American cryptids are based on a handful of sightings, sometimes spread over many years. That doesn't mean *none* of them exist, though, and it doesn't make them less interesting to read about. This is a tour of such reports and legends.

I never knew what to make of Godfrey's first cryptozoology book, *Real Wolfmen: True Encounters in Modern America* (TarcherPerigee, 2012). The author obviously did a lot of work, collecting creepy tales and experiences and talking to sincerely puzzled or scared witnesses. While not committing herself to a single explanation, she deals too lightly with the fact that the dogman is unlikely in the extreme. It would need a mammalian evolutionary line, stretching back hundreds of thousands of years, which has left no trace.

In *American Monsters*, Godfrey presents tales "of animal-like or humanoid" creatures from all over the New World, with the U.S. predominating. She is open to the possible existence of several types of giant birds, sea serpents, hairy humanoids, and so on, although she parks pig-people seen shopping for groceries firmly in the category of urban legend. At the end, she suggests that some monsters exist only in our minds, some as flesh and blood cryptids, and some as "things that live outside the range of our senses" and are only seen when conditions are right (Godfrey has also written books on the paranormal). Whether your interests lie in oversized eagles, water monsters, Native American predators, or alligator-men, reading this book will give you a good idea of the range of American monster folklore, and you'll have fun doing it. Godfrey includes good endnotes and a lengthy bibliography, although she uses only a few skeptical sources.

A Canadian Bestiary: A Collection of People, Places and Beasties from Canadian Folklore, Cryptozoology, Native Religion, and Mythology

Fisher, Todd (2014: Stonebunny Press, 218pp.)

The book contains hundreds of very brief entries about the title topics. It's handy if you come across the name of some creature and can't place it. There's a "revised and expanded" second edition, but I've not seen it.

A Menagerie of Mysterious Beasts

Gerhard, Ken (2016: Llewellyn Worldwide, 240pp.)

Ken Gerhard and I disagree on a lot concerning unexplained zoology, but everyone with an interest in folkloric beasts is going to love this book.

First, Gerhard avoids the common trap in which books about (mostly) American "monsters" are dominated by Sasquatch. Second, he edits the eyewitness stories with a light touch. The tales unroll as they were told to him or to others, and Gerhard saves his comments, most of which I agree with until he's explored the humans-and-creatures landscape of each beast. Gerhard means this as a tribute to classic books by Gould, Ley, and others. He's done good research in libraries and in the field. I'm something of a specialist in the Lake Iliamna mystery, but there are accounts here that are new to me.

Few, perhaps none, of the creatures in this book will be proven real. A washtub-sized spider, for example, doesn't work biomechanically (as Gerhard acknowledges) no matter how scary-cool it would be, and no one is going to find a live pterodactyl because there aren't any. (Just once, I'd like to read a flying reptile report that actually matches what we know they looked like.) Even if no creature in this book ever enters a scientific journal, though, Gerhard reminds us that the American affection for monsters is alive and well.

. . .

Calculatus eliminatus always helps an awful lot / The way to find a missing something is to find out where it's not. – Allan Sherman, songwriter for the TV special *The Cat in the Hat*, 1971

The Natural History of Hidden Animals

Heuvelmans, Bernard (edited by Peter Gwynvay Hopkins) (2016: Routledge, 145pp.) (First publication 2007)

In this work, somewhat patched-together but approved by the "Father of Cryptozoology" before his death in 2001, Hopkins presents Heuvelmans' summary of the history of cryptozoology. There's some general philosophy in the early chapters, including Heuvelmans' explanation of why he thought the insects and small tetrapods didn't fit in his vision of the field. (I still don't get it.) He has a chapter on the term "living fossil," which he finds to be useless. He spends another discussing what he considers "lost worlds" that may still hold spectacular discoveries, although he notes some, like Amazonia, are being reduced to fragments.

In the history chapters, Heuvelmans argues that zoology up until the 19th century "didn't need cryptozoology" because those scientists were more open-minded than their successors. He takes swipes at critics, from Sir Richard Owen to George Gaylord Simpson, and I think he scores some points. Heuvelmans mentions major writers and events in the chapters leading up to the beginning of cryptozoology, which he dates as the publication of Antoon Oudemans' *The Great Sea Serpent* (E. J. Brill,1892). He describes the methodology of Oudemans thus: gathering comprehensive information from all possible sources, deleting hoaxes and misidentifications, and creating an identikit of the creature being sought.

Heuvelmans credits four major discoveries to this method, although two predate Oudemans' book: the mountain tapir (*Tapirus pinchaque*, François Roulin, 1829) and the giant squid (*Architeuthis dux*, Johannes Steenstrup, 1857). The third was the okapi (*Okapia johnstoni*, found for science by Sir Harry Johnston and described by Philip Sclater in 1901). The fourth is his own find, which he stood by until his death, of living Neanderthals. He does not explain why others, like the giant panda, don't qualify. He credits himself not with inventing cryptozoology but with systematizing and thus "baptizing" it. Finally, he disputes the need, almost universally accepted in zoology, for physical type specimens: he says cryptozoology aims at "describing an animal scientifically before having to capture or kill it." The book is too short to be a full history, and it is a bit disjointed, but Heuvelmans' observations make it essential to understanding the field.

Scientifical Americans: The Culture of Amateur Paranormal Researchers

Hill, Sharon (2017: McFarland & Company, 248pp.)

This is a book stuffed with information and useful thinking for all those who seek a scientific approach to paranormal phenomena or have an interest in those who do. Hill, a geologist by training, has spent years researching oddities and oddity-seekers. (I've interviewed her before for my blog.) She reports here on her study of amateur research and investigation groups (ARIGs) concerned with UFOs, ghosts, and cryptozoology. Hill draws a distinction between paranormal phenomena (what might be proved/resolved by science) and supernatural (what cannot). She argues strongly that groups saying they are "scientific" usually are not doing good science. While Hill emphasizes that there is no simple definition for science or the scientific method, there are many sound principles scientific endeavors have in common. Her analysis of what is and is not scientific and why a lot of intelligent Americans have trouble with the distinction is worth the price of the book by itself. Hill suggests some science educators view the public too simplistically, as mere receivers of facts, while a good chunk of the public views science as a static collection of facts and rules.

Hill's chapters on cryptozoology are good but necessarily leave out a lot. The Bigfoot-focused chapter on cryptozoology doesn't mention the influential John Napier. I wish the book were longer: the brevity of these chapters and the book itself doesn't allow Hill to tell us much about individuals, aside from a short piece on two skunk ape hunters. (Hill mentions "uniforms," noting, "Cryptozoologists typically require a hat..." both humorous and true.) Hill does think amateurs have a role to play in scientific investigations. She cites the unknown-primate DNA study of Professor Bryan Sykes, in which amateurs worldwide contributed samples to an expert: the negative results don't invalidate the approach.

It all adds up to an excellent book, not only on the primary topic but on the definition and philosophy of science and the role science plays (and should play) in American society. When the main criticism comes down to wishing the book was longer, the author has done a great job.

Monsters die out when the collective imagination no longer needs them.– Glen Duncan, author

Cryptid Creatures: A Field Guide

Halls, Kelly Milner (2019: Little Bigfoot, 224pp.)

There needs to be a guide for younger readers in here, and this one for ages 7-12 is a most enjoyable excursion. Milner Halls, who also wrote a book called *In Search of Sasquatch* (Clarion, 2011), provides short overviews, with eyewitness reports, of 50 cryptids. Each is assigned a Reality Rating, a nice touch. She includes Bigfoot and Nessie, lesser-known cryptids, and a couple of facetious ones like the drop bear. She notably includes the spiny rat *Isothrix barbarabrownae* as a modern discovery that still has a bit of mystery since only one specimen (collected in 1999) exists. Some of the writeups ending with variations of "the search continues" are puzzling: the Canvey Island Monster (definitely explained as a frogfish) is one such. Rick Spears' illustrations are utterly charming. He offers rather cuddly drawings of adult cryptids, plus lots of adorable babies.

...cryptozoologists should go to great trouble to ensure that their writings are technically accurate and up to date with the rest of zoology. While some may regard this perspective as elitist, unsympathetic or simply arrogant, I remain dismayed that so many clumsy and misleading errors clutter the cryptozoological literature. ...Science proceeds by self-correction. – Darren Naish, paleontologist

Matt's Musings: Dr. Naish and I have one collaboration, as he contributed heavily to the chapters on mystery whales in my 2006 book Shadows of Existence: Discoveries and Speculations in Zoology. *The aforementioned Dr. Shuker has a less fortunate (for him) connection in that we share a slight physical resemblance.*

Florida's Unexpected Wildlife

Newton, Michael (2007: University Press of Florida, 208pp.)

This is an enjoyable and always-interesting zoological tour of the state I grew up in. Newton covers Florida's introduced wildlife: snakes, parrots, monkeys, more parrots, etc., along with some uncertain residents and outright cryptids. He isn't convinced by the explanations of the famous cases of Old Three-Toes and the Saint Augustine globster. He makes the valid point that prosaic explanations, not just sightings, should receive media scrutiny. Newton considers some "water monster" reports to be mysteries but points out the lack of evidence that the McCleary killer sea-serpent story ever happened. The author thinks the Skunk Ape may be out there and writes, accurately, that this populous state still has major chunks of wilderness. He offers a decent list of endnotes, a good bibliography, and a 45-page list of Skunk Ape sightings.

Newton adds an illustration of a problem in cryptozoological (and other) writing: the addition of details not contained in the source material. In Florida's 1948 "giant penguin tracks" case, an author named Mike Dash wrote in his book *Borderlands: The Ultimate Exploration of the Surrounding Unknown* (Overlook,1999) that the tracks came out of the sea, extended two miles along the beach, and reentered the sea. No contemporary source records that.

As to the media, Newton cites the confession of one Ray Wallace to making the hoax tracks that "started" the Bigfoot legend in 1958. Newton points out no one in the initial wave of reporting did any investigation past talking to the Wallace family or asked for evidence beyond a picture of Wallace's wooden feet.

One skilled, knowledgeable, and experienced investigator working in the home range of the Florida panther may obtain copious proof of its presence, but 20 enthusiastic amateurs searching the same range will probably only result in the panther departing without leaving a fresh trace. – James D. Lazell Jr., mammalogist

Things and More Things: Myths, Mysteries and Marvels!

Sanderson, Ivan (2007: Adventures Unlimited Press, 364pp.)

This is a combination of two of the prolific Ivan T. Sanderson's earlier books, *Things* and *More Things*. Sanderson is a colorful and controversial figure, and some of his reports of strange animals and incidents are exaggerated or unsupported. However, he writes entertainingly and with a field zoologist's experience of creatures, including living dinosaurs (one of which he claims to have seen), Bigfoot, the Yeti, lake and sea monsters, and so on. He includes a wild tale—although he doesn't vouch for its accuracy—of gigantic human-like skulls claimed by a correspondent to have been recovered from the Aleutians. "Globsters" washed up on beaches fascinate him, too. As I write this, numerous used copies of this compilation appear on online booksellers. I have the two originals, too, but it took me a long time to find them.

Karl Shuker's Alien Zoo

Shuker, Karl (2010: CFZ Press, 390pp.)

This book is a compilation of Shuker's regular columns in *Fortean Times* magazine, with some updates and "bonus features" thrown in. I read it twice through as soon as I received it. Hundreds of entries in this fascinating book cover everything from surviving thylacines to new lizards to alleged pterodactyl-type creatures. Shuker's interests in folklore, culture, and art lead him down many interesting pathways. He looks at everything from an unknown bird shown in a Gauguin painting to the mix of exotic feathers, fakes, and the occasional palm frond that have been passed off as feathers from the wings of angels.

Some items that could have been updated were not: the weird horizontal-tailed fish from California is a mystery I'd solved years ago by talking to a state fishery biologist who identified it as a bizarrely mutated channel catfish.

I would be more skeptical than Shuker at times. I would have great trouble being open-minded about the man who saw a sauropod dinosaur step across a fence—in New Mexico! Shuker, ever curious, posts it without editorializing and asks readers for further information.

Shuker shows the complexity involved in tracking down, or even defining, animals mentioned in local reports: Indonesia's *orang bati* is variously reported to be a bat, a flying human, and a member of a small, primitive semihuman tribe.

Shuker's collection, like all good crypto books, leaves us with some solutions and some more mysteries. We now know a famous sketch of a lake monster in Russia was just support for a tall tale. We wonder what became of animals once presumed to exist, such as Washington's eagle, a giant bird that was shot and described by John James Audubon himself but hardly reported since.

Shuker provides references with each entry and an index at the end. The book sometimes leaves you wanting more, but it will not disappoint you. It's very well worth your money.

Matt's Musings: Alas, Audubon's description of Washington's eagle was too amazing to be true. The famous naturalist appears to have deliberately turned a large normal eagle into something unique. Evan "alaser," it was far from the only time he embellished.

The Species Seekers: Heroes, Fools, and the Mad Pursuit of Life on Earth

Conniff, Richard (2010: W. W. Norton & Company, 464pp.)

In this excellent book, Richard Conniff introduces us to the scientists, naturalists, dilettantes, and others (from the brilliant to the crazy) who contributed so much to the natural history we know. While the focus is on zoology as developed by European and American seekers, this also works as a history of the natural sciences in the 18th and 19th centuries. This period saw hunting for new species raised to a manic level it had never attained before and hasn't since. When professional naturalists were few and the term "scientist" nonexistent, species-hunters came from every walk of life —doctors, sea captains, hunters, and some inquisitive women who didn't get their due then and don't really get it now. (I had no idea that Beatrix Potter, creator of Peter Rabbit, was a bona fide expert on fungi.) Conniff creates an especially vivid portrait of Mary Kingsley, who died young in 1900 and who was as daring a field collector as anyone.

I've often thought a book could be written strictly on the scientific contributions of missionaries, and Conniff does recount Father Armand David's many daring discoveries in China. The famous names like Darwin are here, but we also meet such men as Walter Rothschild, an incompetent banker largely erased from family history but a keen naturalist and a funder of major collecting expeditions; Paul Du Chaillu, who made countless contributions but also created the myth of the ferocious gorilla; and the men and women who supported naturalists (Sir Richard Owens' wife wrote in her diary about coming home to find a dead rhinoceros in her previously immaculate front hall).

Some of the naturalists here may have hastened the demise of species by overcollection, but others foresaw the need to start protecting the natural world. Their discoveries also contributed greatly to the development of the idea of natural selection. Conniff gives us these people as they lived, not ducking the racism, sexism, and imperialism that plagued even the greatest minds of the day but not letting it obscure the rest of the story. This thoroughly researched and superbly written book is a time machine to the great era of species-hunting, and I imagine any student of the natural sciences will enjoy the ride immensely.

The term 'scientist' was coined in 1834 by Rev. William Whewell. He combined 'scientia' [Latin=knowledge] with 'artist,' which I think more people should know. Because there is an art to doing good science. – Anne Larsen, Life Sciences Historian

Tetrapod Zoology

Naish, Darren (2010: CFZ Books, 316pp.)

Dr. Naish, a British paleontologist, runs *the* most fascinating blog on the internet, *Tetrapod Zoology*. Naish is an expert on dinosaurs, but his curiosity embraces everything from what happens when an animal dies while grasping a branch to what's so cool about the amphibians called slow-worms. Naish's collection of zoology, cryptozoology, and paleontology in this book will hold any reader's attention. When it comes to cryptozoology, Naish is skeptical in the best sense of the word: he is sure there are important undiscovered animals out there, and he is open-minded but insists on scientific standards of evidence.

Mirabilis: A Carnival of Cryptozoology and Natural History

Shuker, Karl (2013: Anomalist Books, 194pp.)

This collection of animal oddities and legends overlaps some other Shuker books, but it's a short, fun read with a lot of tidbits. Shuker has assembled here some of the most enduring legends about animals (Can toads live centuries enclosed in stone? Alas, no) and some most people have never heard of. We find wonderful headlines like "Giant Crocodile-Frogs of Borneo" and "Giant Spiders in Suburbia." The most substantive item for cryptozoologists is the sleuthing by Shuker and others that reduced "Trunko," one of the biggest, weirdest creatures ever reported, from amazing cryptid to dead whale. Shuker's curiosity embraces everything from flying turtles (unfortunately real only in Japanese movies) to flying mice, which are neither flighted nor mice but are really cute gliding mammals. Good bibliography.

Hunting Monsters: Cryptozoology and the Reality Behind the Myths

Naish, Darren (2017: Sirius, 242pp.)

As a cryptozoological reader of some 45 years and a correspondent of Naish, I looked forward to this book, and I was not disappointed. Naish offers a very good skeptical analysis of the whole cryptozoology business, even if I think it could have been a little better.

One point a reader will notice early on is that there is so much ground to cover that the author can only touch on many points in passing. Skipping over the Great New England Sea Serpent, a touchstone of the sea monster topic is an example.

Naish starts with whether cryptozoology is, or can be, scientific and decides it can be but that it often is not. He begins and ends with the point that cryptozoology exists in a cultural milieu and is influenced by folklore, tradition, etc., as well as modern innovations like the internet. This is true, if not entirely original. He credits influences including Dr. Charles Paxton, whose work I greatly admire, and folklorist Michel Meurger.

Naish isn't closed-minded. He has suggested new species to explain cryptozoological sightings, including a cryptid seal and a giant orangutan, but in his blog, *Tetrapod Zoology* and elsewhere reports, he's uncovered new information and has come to conclude the "star" cryptid animals are not there. This book explains his reasoning well.

When he offers an explanation, I'm not always convinced. The "finning" seal (a seal waving one flipper in the air for cooling) for the *Valhalla* sighting, for example, is clever, but I can't look at the first-hand original drawing and get a seal out of it. The opposite is true of the HMS *Daedalus* sighting, which Naish convinces me we can put to rest.

The subject is vast, so the bibliography is essential. It's pretty good but could have been more extensive. Lest anyone think that's damning with faint praise, this is an excellent and important book. If it doesn't hunt down every major cryptid, it will make the veteran cryptozoology reader think hard and give the new reader a starting point grounded in good science.

Mystery Creatures of China

Xu, David (2018: Coachwhip Publications, 263pp.)

This is the first book ever written on the cryptids of China, and it's lovely. David Xu, a Beijing-based writer, pulls together story threads from ancient legend to modern sightings from all over China. Here he provides a sumptuously illustrated compendium of creatures from the famous (e.g., the Yeti) to creatures virtually unheard of in the West (e.g., the *tuoniao*, a large bird reported from Sichuan province). The book offers short-to-medium-length accounts split into aquatic, humanoid, carnivorous, herbivorous, reptilian, and winged cryptids. Even as a longtime reader of cryptozoology, I found surprises on every page, with probably two-thirds of these creatures new to me. China, even in the 21st century, offers many unknown-animal reports, and it would be surprising if none of them pointed us to new species in that vast land.

The author is careful to note that explanations include rumor, folklore, and so on. This is easy to apply to a bull with a fin on its back, but some cases are genuinely puzzling. What to make of a large hoofed animal a bit like a deer or goat, but sometimes reported as scaled and with a single horn? Just a unicorn-ish legend? Maybe, but it's been reported for over 2,500 years, and we know of animals whose two horns are well aligned to be seen as one from the side. The author displays his knowledge of paleontology here by suggesting presumed-extinct mammals that might match the sometimes-inconsistent descriptions. For a more plausible animal, take the *hengziniao*, a very large owl that makes a startling "heng-heng" call: there are not many reports, but nothing about it seems unrealistic. The illustrations range from ancient woodcuts and sculptures to modern photographs. A special addition, most useful for those of us who do not know Chinese geography well, is the outstanding map section.

There are two flaws, both concerning lake-dwelling cryptids. One is that I wish the author had managed to get permission to publish even one image from the numerous photographs and videos he writes that have been taken of famous lake creatures. The other is that, in introducing us to particular lakes, the author gives only general descriptions like "large" and does not mention numbers for the area, volume, or depth of the lake.

These are small deficiencies in a book that is beautiful, intriguing, and most definitely fun. There is plenty here for the zoologist, the folklorist, and the historian alike.

Shuker Nature Book 1: Antlered Elephants, Locust Dragons, and other Cryptic Blog Beasts

Shuker, Karl (2019: Coachwhip Publications, 412pp.)

Shuker's curiosity about all things zoological is boundless. In this volume, based on entries in his blog of the same name, the British zoologist plumbs the depth and breadth of the animal world, in fact, myth, and art. Some topics will be familiar to most readers of cryptozoology, but what makes this such an enjoyable cabinet of curiosities is that many of the items are not familiar. Shuker wonders about humans as much as beasts: why we put flying elephants in art, why monks put creatures half cat, half snail in the margins of illuminated manuscripts, and why stories of gigantic spiders drinking from whale-oil lamps popped up in cathedrals. We've all seen the silly postcards of a claimed half-man, half-alligator taxidermy fake (Shuker loves "gaffs," as these are called). Shuker explores his childhood fascination with creatures such as Sea Monkeys™, tales of giant bunny rabbits, and Trunko, the bizarre "seagoing polar bear-elephant" that, alas, was just another dead whale. And what was the story behind the poisonous "fury worm," classified first-hand by Carl Linnaeus himself but apparently nonexistent?

Shuker also revisits the famous ape, Oliver. While he agrees Oliver was just a chimp, he thinks the animal's bipedal gait was too natural to be the result of training and there is still a bit of a mystery. [I knew the man who gave Oliver sanctuary, Wallace Swett of Primarily Primates, and helped him out a bit, but I didn't know Oliver had been cremated and is thus unavailable for further study.] Concerning primates of another sort, the author explores legends and folklore about miniature humans from several Native American tribes and whether they are linked to Pedro, the mystery mummy from Wyoming, who has vanished despite serious attempts to track him down.

Shuker closes with a mystery of his own, a dog-size, bounding mammal he met on a dark road in 2014. He concludes this was likely a coypu, a South American rodent that escaped captivity in Britain and must have survived the government's extermination campaign. This is a book that lovers of animals, oddities, and cryptids will wade into with gusto.

The Natural History of Unicorns

Laver, Chris (2020: Harper Perennial, 272pp.)

This book offers a unique approach to a three-part zoological riddle: Where did our concept of the unicorn come from, what real animals might have been involved, and why has the idea persisted? We can, as the author puts it, hopscotch from one historical stone to another and trace the idea from the earliest writing by Ctesias, a Greek living in Persia who wrote a book on India, to the divergent unicorns of legend, myth, and alleged reality to the modern-day. Various animals lent part of their personality or anatomy to the unicorn, although it was around for centuries before anyone described it as looking like a horse. The unicorn belongs to everyone, with variations all over Eurasia and Africa.

While some touchstones are uncertain (it's not clear Biblical writers ever thought the Hebrew word *re'em* concerned a one-horned beast), the unicorn kept popping up in everything from travelers' tales to tapestries to heraldry to fine art. It became a symbol of whatever people wanted it to be: secular, sacred, spiritual, or sexual. The animal had a particularly long and chameleonic career in Christian imagery, where it could be fierce but (of course) became docile around virgins. When the narwhal started providing actual tusks far more impressive than the countless other types of horns and tusks that had been marketed as a unicorn, the animal was permanently locked into the European imagination.

Laver closes with two interesting episodes. Writers including Henry Morton Stanley mentioned an odd hoofed animal in the Congo, and some people speculated this was the unicorn. The finding of the okapi, spectacular in itself, was about the last gasp of the "wild unicorn" idea. Then came Dr. Franklin Dove's 1933 experiment with transplanting horn buds and producing a one-horned bull. We don't know whether ancient cultures hit on this trick, but they may have, and it could explain a lot.

The intricacies of translating and comparing ancient terms sometimes slow the pace of this work, but it's a rewarding journey with a lot for cryptozoologists to think about.

Matt's Musings: Laver doesn't cite Willy Ley, who in Exotic Zoology *wrote about a common European description of the horn: "... what is white, dark at the base and tipped with red, and loses its power in the lap of a virgin? Maybe a symbolism can be so obvious that it is not recognized, but I harbor considerable doubts about it."*

Monsters of the Last Frontier: Cryptids and Legends of Alaska

Weatherly, David (2020: Eerie Lights, 236pp.)

For a lover of monster legend and lore, this is a delightful read. There's something interesting on almost every page. Sam Shearon's cover artwork, front and back, is gorgeous. The book has a major weakness (below), but I read it avidly and was sorry when it ended. Weatherly does not accept all the creatures here as real, but he doesn't throw everything into the "hoax or myth" bucket, either. Weatherly is always respectful of the First Nations/Alaska Native traditions but does not insist they have to be literally true.

The book is comprehensive, covering everything from Sasquatch to otter-men to thunderbirds (always a fun topic). It deals, of course, with the Iliamna Lake "monster." Weatherly includes a very good collection of stories, although I wish there was more reason to believe the wilder "it snapped the fishing line" tales. There are other water creatures of lake and ocean, as you'd expect in the state with the longest seacoast and the most lakes in the U.S. I'd thought the biggest reported creature that was seen on a sonar trace from the fishing vessel MV *Mylark* in 1969, was universally discounted these days, but it still intrigues Weatherly.

I've read some stories of large wolf-like canines, known as waheela and other terms, and I agree with Weatherly that matter still merits some thought. As to other critters, did you know an "African lion" has been reported from Alaska?

Hairy Man, Sasquatch, call it what you will, there are plenty of hairy primates in modern reports and the stories from Native cultures. Weatherly mentions an old incident at Lake Iliamna, which I've learned separately is likely a hoax, but there are newer stories here, too, and they come from all over the state.

Weatherly, an Alaskan himself, has collected a lot of material, and his writing is good. My disappointment lies with the documentation. While many sources are mentioned in the text, they are not listed or detailed in any way that would enable readers to look them up. Indeed, the book has no footnotes, no endnotes, no bibliography by topic or chapter, and no index. A couple of dozen books and three websites are listed, but that's it.

So, to cryptozoologists and other readers: you'll find some good campfire stories whether you believe them or not. To the author: please consider a future edition with thorough citations. I'd buy a few of those.

SECTION 2
RELATED SCIENCES

In a single stroke, the Linnaean classification system wiped monsters off the face of the map. There might still be unknown beasts and fearsome creatures out there, but now they each would have a family, a genus, a species... the medieval world's monsters and wonders were, one by one, either incorporated into this taxonomy or excluded as myth. – Colin Dickey, *The Unidentified: Mythical Monsters, Alien Encounters, and Our Obsession with the Unexplained*

There are things a cryptozoology researcher must know outside of the cryptozoological literature. Whether they do fieldwork or stick to academic approaches, any researcher wanting to understand why a certain cryptid does or does not make sense in the reported habitat has a logical evolutionary ancestor, resembles some fossil or living species, etc., needs a grounding outside the often-repetitive and unevenly scientific literature of cryptozoology.

Books will not give anyone all the answers, but reading them and having them around will certainly help researchers ask the right questions.

What follows are reviews of books I've found useful and

accessible. The usual disclaimers apply. This isn't remotely comprehensive. The science here is inevitably tied to the year the books were written, although I threw out books where the science had changed completely. I don't apologize for including books meant for children: if you're new to a particular science, they can help. And cryptozoologists should be bringing their kids up with a good dose of science anyway.

Paleontology and Evolution

Amidst the vicissitudes of the earth's surface, species cannot be immortal, but must perish, one after another, like the individuals which compose them. There is no possibility of escaping from this conclusion. – Charles Lyell, *Principles of Geology*, 1830

Natural selection, the survival of the fittest, does not necessarily include progressive development... if there were no advantage, these forms would be left, by natural selection, unimproved or but little improved and might remain for indefinite ages in their present lowly condition. – Charles Darwin, *The Origin of Species*, Fifth edition, 1869

Old Fourlegs: The Story of the Coelacanth

Smith, J. L. B. (1958: Pan Books, 284pp.)

Professor Smith here describes in great detail the discovery, study, and importance of the coelacanth and all the adventures, snafus, bureaucracy, and hindrances dealt with in its discovery. He has the highest praise for Marjorie Courtenay-Latimer, who spotted the fish in a trawler's trash-fish pile. He conveys the astonishment ("a bomb had burst in my brain") of seeing her sketch of the fish and of the frantic efforts to see the specimen for himself and then to study it and publish on it. After his first meeting with the fish in 1938, he repeatedly woke up his wife (Margaret was also a degreed scientist, working as his assistant) to ask if he'd only dreamed they'd seen a coelacanth. As a chemist, he had a hard time with the few genuine South African ichthyologists of his day, but once the paper was published in *Nature*, all doubt disappeared. Then it was on to the 14-year quest for another specimen. This posed significant hardships, not least because the first specimen was hundreds of miles from the main population in Comoros. (A British officer stationed in those islands during the war wrote that he'd seen specimens but didn't know that they were important: they had drifted up when his unit went fishing using depth charges.) The British Museum wanted the fish, a desire blocked only by Courtenay-Latimer's threat to resign from the East London Museum, which could not afford to lose both its famous fish and its famous curator. Smith became famous too, doing interviews, receiving foreign scientists, and writing books and papers with Margaret's help.

Smith was proud to be South African, so I should mention he comes across as focused on his work and apparently accepts the apartheid system as normal. While he is grateful for the assistance of "three young colored men" with zoological education, he writes that "natives" tell you what you want to hear. (This, of course, is often true when said "natives" are speaking to people who took over their lives at gunpoint.)

Smith is sometimes a bit hyperbolic, but he also displays a dry sense of humor, and the book ably conveys the flavor of the times and the excitement of the discovery.

There is an updated version of this book, with new information and photographs, revised by Mark Bruton, who studied ichthyology under the Smiths. See *The Annotated Old Fourlegs: The Updated Story of the Coelacanth* (University of Florida, 2018).

Matt's Musings: J. L. B. Smith didn't stop with the coelacanth. He authored 500 papers and named 370 fishes. He received correspondence about coelacanths in such places as South Korea and the Bermudas, none of which panned out. He also received information on "flying reptiles" near Mount

Of Books and Beasts

Kilimanjaro and (understandably, with a coelacanth in front of him) did not rule out the possibility.

Prehistoric Animals

Augusta, Joseph, with illustrations by Zdenek Burian, translated from the Czech by Greta Hort (1963: Spring Books, 47pp. plus extensive plate section, numerous editions exist.)

While much of the knowledge in this book is outdated, it enthralled a generation of professional, student, and public readers. Dr. Augusta's text, in Dr. Hort's translation, is clear and informative. Augusta considers my favorites, the placoderms, "the oldest and most important" of the fishes of the Devonian: he thinks all other fishes descended from placoderms. After the text, we get to 60 of Burian's illustrations. Starting with dazzling color plates on the Cambrian and Silurian Seas, we press on through vivid depictions of early fishes, dinosaurs, mammals like the early horses (a high point in a section that's nearly all high points) and finally, the cave bear *Ursus spelaeus*. This is a fading snapshot of the science, but it's a gorgeous snapshot.

Matt's Musings: Burian's work makes me think about the intrinsic value of books themselves. My copy, obtained online, is a very fragile one, browning at the edges and damaged at the spine. I don't expect to use it as a reference, but now I know it will be preserved and no one will break it up to sell the plates. It's a book a paleontology devotee will want to have for its own sake.

Other Origins: The Search for the Giant Ape in Human Prehistory

Ciochon, Russell, with John Olsen and Jamie James (1990: Bantam Books, 262pp.)

This tale of scientific discovery presents what we know about *Gigantopithecus* and recounts expeditions to Vietnam in an unfortunately vain quest for more fossils. The known fossil record of the biggest ape that ever lived left consists of teeth and three partial jawbones, so there's a great deal we have yet to learn. The authors dismiss the idea of the species' continued survival. They mention cryptid primates like Sasquatch and Yeti but don't give any the idea any credibility. Required reading for anyone interested in "unknown primate" questions.

Quest for the African Dinosaurs

Jacobs, Lewis (1993: Villard Books, 314pp.)

This book mainly recounts Dr. Jacobs' pioneering fieldwork on African dinosaur fossils. He takes readers through his own discovery of three new species and explores the Mesozoic era in a continent often overlooked in popular works focused on spectacular New World species. He also provides a thorough discussion of dinosaurs themselves. Jacobs spends one chapter on allegations of living dinosaurs in the Congo. He considers the idea absurd: while his tone is overly harsh, his doubts are logically based on the lack of fossil or current evidence and the fact that the area involved has changed since the Mesozoic and is not a "lost world" where relict species are likely.

The Beak of the Finch

Weiner, Jonathan (1994: Alfred A. Knopf, 332pp.)

Another "must-read" when exploring evolution is Weiner's award-winning study on the finches of the Galapagos Islands. The book includes valuable explanations about DNA, hybrids, natural selection, and the dynamics of small, isolated animal populations.

Dinosaur in a Haystack: Reflections in Natural History

Gould, Stephen J. (1995: Harmony Books, 480pp.)

All the works of this prolific writer, evolutionary biologist, and paleontologist contain information cryptozoologists can apply, and I picked this one almost at random as an example. Stephen J. Gould's curiosity extends from early human evolution to overlooked women in science to fascinations with beetles, snails, and the "lesser phyla" of tiny or obscure animals that even biologists tend to overlook. This book contains his essay on "Dinosaurmania" and *Jurassic Park*. He writes that dinosaurs were just as big and exciting when he was a kid: what made them a cultural force was the rising power of commercialization. He greatly admires the arsenal of special effects Spielberg and company used to create believable creatures, although he deplores the departures from the superior science and deeper characterization offered in the book. One essay explores the saga of the South African antelope known as the *blaauwbuck*. In 1799, it became the first large territorial mammal to be shot out of existence by human hunters. Gould tracks the few surviving specimens and the ones that have been lost or destroyed. Everything here is interesting at the least and vital at the most. I do hope someone will issue collections of Gould's work by subject, for example, all the essays on living tetrapods, but there's no movement toward that.

During the Cretaceous Period, many of the inland seas dried up, leaving the Plesiosaurs stranded without any fish. Just about that time Mother Nature scrapped the whole Age of Reptiles and called for a new deal. – Will Cuppy, American humorist

Big Cats and Their Fossil Relatives

Turner, Alan (1997: Columbia University Press, 234pp.)

In this appealing book, Turner discusses the current big cats and all known fossil forms, putting his subjects in context. Opening chapters tackle the taxonomy and evolution of felids and topics explained, in addition to looking at the cats themselves, including behavior, ecology, specialization, and more. Turner does not address any cryptozoological subjects but provides a great deal of knowledge useful in evaluating "unknown cat" claims. Mauricio Anton's illustrations are gorgeous.

In Search of Deep Time: Beyond the Fossil Record to a New History of Life

Gee, Henry (1999: Free Press, 272pp.)

Gee's book is the first I read that gave me a good grasp of the cladistics revolution in taxonomy, the science of classifying species. While some scientists found him unfairly dismissive about the traditional approach to fossil classification, looking for connections through "last common ancestor" as determined by shared characteristics is now a major component of paleontology and evolutionary studies. Gee believes "looking at the world in terms of the pattern rather than the process that creates the pattern" allows more objective analysis than focusing on likely "trees." Gee was life sciences editor of *Nature* when the hobbit (*Homo floresiensis*) discovery erupted and said at the time the find encouraged him to think "stories of other human-like creatures might be founded on grains of truth," and "Now, cryptozoology, the study of such fabulous creatures, can come in from the cold." My apologies to Dr. Gee about his much-praised new book, *A (Very) Short History of Life on Earth: 4.6 Billion Years in 12 Pithy Chapters* (St. Martin's Press, 2021): it just missed my deadline for adding new book reviews.

Sea Dragons

Ellis, Richard (2003: University Press of Kansas, 326pp.)

A great introduction to some of the candidates put forward for sea monster reports. Ellis describes the history of marine reptile discoveries, the major groups, and dozens of species. All there are illustrated with his usual excellent drawings. He includes the controversies about how plesiosaurs swam and how flexible their necks were, quoting experts from all sides. He also discusses the oddities like Eurhinosaurus, a swordfish-like ichthyosaur with seemingly useless teeth in the overhanging upper jaw that never would have touched anything.

Evolution: The Triumph of an Idea

Zimmer, Carl (2006: Harper Perennial, 487pp.)

For a highly readable one-volume story of evolution and the development of evolutionary biology, you can't do better than this. Zimmer is a good writer who knows how to balance technical information with explorations of animal behavior (plants don't get equal time here) and human stories. (Trivia: Zimmer has a species of tapeworm named after him.) One seminal thought is that "Because evolution can only tinker, it cannot produce the best of all possible designs." Everything can change, every species can be dethroned. The human eye works very well, but there are numerous possible improvements that may or may not happen over time. Zimmer takes us through all aspects, from the explosion of cichlid fish species in Lake Victoria to the origins of language, the land excursions of the "walking fish," and the role of extinction in the chapter he titles, "The Accidental Toolkit: Chance and Constraints in Animal Evolution." He goes on to explore the evolution of whales (*Basilosaurus*, he notes, had "a slender serpent body"), the role of disease, coevolution, etc. He writes clearly about what happened and how we know that it happened that way. The last third is on human evolution, a complex business affected by everything from disease to the development of culture. The reader will finish with a solid grounding from which to study the possible (and impossible) evolution of an ecosystem or species of interest.

In science, it often happens that scientists say, 'You know that's a really good argument; my position is mistaken,' and then they would actually change their minds ...It doesn't happen as often as it should, because scientists are human and change is sometimes painful. But it happens every day. – Carl Sagan, astronomer and author

Fossil Legends of the First Americans

Mayor, Adrienne (2008: Princeton University Press, 488pp.)

Mayor is a scholar of the overlooked chapters of history and prehistory, such as historical Amazons and early automata. Here she asks what Native Americans thought of their finds in fossil-rich North America and uncovers a treasure trove of anecdotes, myths, and fossils.

Native contributions to fossil lore were long overlooked, and most have been lost or forgotten. Early fossil hunters sometimes paid Indians to lead them to fossils, but few thought the locals had any sound information to offer, generally dismissing them as mere curiosity collectors or object-worshipers. Mayor, though, finds interest in fossils that existed across the continent. Many Native American tribes considered fossils important. They gathered fossils, traded them, incorporated them in sacred and everyday art, and speculated about what kind of beasts had left them. They understood these bones came from many types of animals, which various tribes thought included the great thunderbirds and both land and water monsters.

Fossils are kept even today in medicine bundles and other Native-held artifacts. Many more (some obtained from tribes by purchase or barter, but most simply taken) went to museums.

A longtime point of contention is that bones eroding away in the air had to be removed for preservation, while some Native Americans objected this was interfering with a natural cycle. The controversies continue into the present, with the battles over Tyrannosaurus Sue and other specimens. Mayor takes time to deconstruct such frauds and myths as the red-haired mummified giants in Nevada that some cryptozoologists still believe existed. There are a few Native stories of unfossilized dinosaur bones, although these may arise from linguistic difficulties.

While Mayor provides maps of each region, it would help the reader to see some of the crucial small areas mapped in more detail. There are many photographs and drawings here, but I found myself wanting more: perhaps a companion volume of art and photography would be an interesting future project.

If the book is not perfect, it is a (literally) groundbreaking work that shows how much we've overlooked that is still accessible. Mayor knows how to document a book: the Index and Notes take up 100 pages. Hopefully, this book creates more respect for Native Americans and for the fossils they saw and gathered. Much has been lost, but much remains to be learned.

Take nothing on its looks: Take everything on evidence. There's no better rule. – "Mr. Jaggers," Charles Dickens, *Great Expectations*

When Fish Got Feet, Sharks Got Teeth, and Bugs Began to Swarm: A Cartoon Prehistory of Life Long Before Dinosaurs

Bonner, Hannah (2009: National Geographic Children's Books, 48pp.)

A unique and delightful look at the Silurian and Devonian periods, suitable for students but including some funny bits and cool facts that will help adults learn or recall the main events of this pivotal time in our planet's history. It's also the first book I've seen for kids that provides some information on my favorite predator, *Dunkleosteus terrelli*. There are short, clear explanations of everything from the creation of soil to the adaptations needed for plants and animals to invade the dry land environment. Recommended to me by no less than Dr. Robert Bakker, this is just a terrific book: order one for your kid's library and another for yourself. Another book with clear explanations for young readers is *Fossils for Kids* (Rockridge Press, 2020) by my friend Ashley Hall at the Museum of the Rockies. A new book on Dunkleosteus for kids is out, too, Professor Ben Garrod's *Dunkleosteus* (Zephyr, 2021).

Your Inner Fish: A Journey into the 3.5-Billion-Year History of the Human Body

Shubin, Neil (2009: Vintage Books, 256pp.)

This book takes us all through the title subject, but the centerpiece is the leap from water to land. Dr. Shubin and colleagues traveled to Canada's Ellesmere Island in 2004 to unearth fossils of the 375-million-year-old *Tiktaalik roseae*. The nine-foot (2.8 m) Tiktaalik made Shubin write, "We were staring at the origin of a piece of our own bodies inside this 375-million-year-old fish. We had a fish with a wrist." It was, so far as we know at this point, the earliest "anatomical link between fish and a land-living animal." Shubin's writing is clear, engaging, and sometimes humorous, so the facts and dates and scientific methods will go down with a spoonful of sugar for even casually interested readers.

Living things do not inherit skulls, backbones, or cell layers from their ancestors—they inherit the processes to build them. – Neil Shubin, evolutionary biologist

In the Shadow of Man

Goodall, Jane (2010: Mariner Books, 400pp.)

It's been a long time since I read this one (I think in the original 1971 edition), but I turned back to it because so many cryptozoologists are hunting unknown primates. Well, this book shows how it's done: months of patient, sometimes grueling field study to get the first glimpses (Dian Fossey was luckier in finding her gorillas than Goodall was with her chimps) and years to really understand your subjects. Goodall was, among other things, the first to document chimp family structures and learn how varied the personalities of wild chimps are. Goodall has encouraged the search for Sasquatch and other mystery primates: "I guess I'm romantic. I don't want to disbelieve," is one of her quotes, although she also said, "It's bizarre we've never found any remains." There's a lot in this book and her other writings to teach those who hunt for such creatures.

A field scientist needs patience—or maybe an ability to deal creatively with impatience. One of my strengths as a field researcher is a tolerance for boredom. – Eva Saulitis, marine biologist

Horseshoe Crabs and Velvet Worms: The Story of the Animals and Plants That Time Has Left Behind

Fortney, Richard (2011: Vintage Books, 332pp.)

Cryptozoologists still like the appealing phrase "living fossil," which has become unpopular with scientists even though it was coined by Darwin himself. The living fossils we hear about are splashy ones like the coelacanth. Dr. Fortney, a paleontologist, here examines creatures from horseshoe crabs to ginkgo trees to single-celled archaea living under extreme environmental conditions. He takes the reader on his travels to see cycads, platypuses, musk oxen, lungfishes, and more, explaining how far back each creature's ancestry goes and why it survived. He does, of course, treat the coelacanth as well. Along the way, he discusses extinction events, island populations, and how science and its tools evolve (he recounts an early use of DNA fecal analysis on a sample purportedly from an "extinct" thylacine). He writes there are "time havens" where species may linger after the world has moved on, but evolution never stands entirely still, and thus "living fossil" isn't a useful term. This book is a superb education for cryptozoologists on how some creatures evolve greatly, some evolve slowly and minimally, and some get thrown under the paleontological bus and vanish forever.

All Yesterdays - Unique and Speculative Views of Dinosaurs and Other Prehistoric Animals

Naish, Darren, with C.M. Kosemen and John Conway (2012: Lulu.com, 100pp.)

This slender book will show you dinosaurs in a way you never thought of before. The authors have explored the ways in which current reconstructions of dinosaurs may vary from the real thing. Along the way, they post some unique questions, like "How did stegosaurs have sex?" (Your first thought might be that it wasn't possible, only it obviously was.) Uniquely colored and shaped dinos are presented to make the point that many reconstructions, with muscles "shrink-wrapped" about the skeleton, don't reflect the way most animals really appear. A dinosaur we think of as sleek could have been pudgy, or one we think of as dull could have been garish. For added fun, the authors wonder how future paleontologists might reconstruct a baboon (all legs and teeth) or a cow (a svelte, fast-moving animal). This is the kind of book that not only shows you something new but makes you think about things that you considered settled and familiar. Scott Hartman's illustrations are terrific.

. . .

Differing interpretations will always abound, even when good minds come to bear. The kernel of indisputable information is a dot in space; interpretations grow out of the desire to make this point a line, to give it direction. The directions in which it can be sent, the uses to which it can be put by a culturally, professionally, and geographically diverse society are almost without limit. The possibilities make good scientists chary. – Barry Lopez, *Arctic Dreams: Imagination and Desire in a Northern Landscape*

Prehistoric Life: The Definitive Visual History of Life on Earth

DK Publishing (multiple authors) (2012: Doring Kindersley, 512pp.)

If you're a non-paleontologist like me, sometimes you just want an at-a-glance reference to see where some creature evolved, where the shorelines were during the Devonian period, or what a Neanderthal jaw looked like, and this book provides that. It's stuffed with illustrations of all kinds, and the text is clear. Knowledge and theories about the history of life change all the time, but this is a good guide to the basic framework and a lot of the plants and animals as they evolved over the eons.

The Walking Whales

Thewissen, Hans (2014: University of California Press, 256pp.)

Cryptozoologists are fond of whales. Not only are they amazing, but there are several mysterious sightings still unexplained, and we are adding more beaked whales and dolphins every decade. Dr. G. M. "Hans" Thewissen's book is the best I've read on whale evolution.

A veteran paleontologist and specialist in whale ancestry, Thewissen offers clear and well-illustrated information on the whales and their ancestors. He also relates his own adventures as a paleontologist in India and Pakistan, including the risks, the tedium, and the thrill of discovery. Science is, after all, a human story. One crucial discovery was made when a bone was accidentally broken in the lab: despite all our modern tools, science still depends partly on luck.

The author leads us, with very good explanations, through the complicated business of how evolution transformed land animals into aquatic ones. Just twenty years or so ago, whales were often used by young-Earth creationists as an example of huge changes in a relatively short time with no transitional forms. Now we know that whales offer one of the most complete evolutionary records of any modern group, with many transitional forms. The author compares the way evolution works with what's available, not always successfully, by asking readers to imagine the Batmobile being given to an engineer ordered to use its parts to build the Beatles' Yellow Submarine. I want a little more explanation of how whales became carnivores, given that their closest living relatives are vegetarians, but I was fascinated to learn that teeth are, in fact, present in fetal baleen whales, and traces sometimes show up in adults. Excellent book in every way.

Species evolve exactly as if they were adapting as best they could to a changing world, and not at all as if they were moving toward a set goal. – George Gaylord Simpson

The Story of Life in 25 Fossils: Tales of Intrepid Fossil-Hunters and the Wonders of Evolution

Prothero, Donald (2015: Columbia University Books, 408pp.)

This is an excellent book, focusing mostly on the key transition fossils between groups but also including some crowd-pleasers like *T. rex*. Prothero includes well-written accounts of human beings, like Mary Anning, who did so much to bring the past to life. For the cryptozoologists, he takes a swipe at Loch Ness (harshly, but his scientific points are valid) and another at the supposed African sauropod mokele-mbembe (again, he's right about the science). He visits the endlessly interesting question of how big certain animals, like *C. megalodon*, got to be. He protests about how creature sizes in popular media are exaggerated, sometimes hugely. Examples include marine reptiles (except for the long-necked elasmosaurs, he doubts any species exceeded 13 m) and fishes like *Leedsichthys*, which was once accorded a length over 25 m but now about a third that size. There's plenty in this book for the paleontologist, the cryptozoologist, and the general enthusiast of all things zoological. The fossils, presented in timeline order, show how each major group we know today evolved and how strong the transitional fossil record is—half-snakes, half-plesiosaurs, etc., abound.

I have a few nitpicks. The ichthyosaurs certainly did not have a speed limit of 1.2 km an hour, so there's some kind of misprint there. And Loch Ness was searched by sonar, not radar—a very different thing. But this is a great birthday gift present for any natural-history lover on your list.

The most important scientific tool is the eraser. – Luna Leopold, geomorphologist

Matt's Musings: Now we come to dinosaur books: it's impossible to deal with paleontology or evolution, let alone both, without them. The Age of Reptiles doesn't just provide fodder for (extremely unlikely) survival theories: it illustrates how a group of vertebrates can explode from an assortment of unimpressive ancestors to radiate into every niche of land, air, and sea. Plus, anyone who doesn't love dinosaurs is sadly deprived. Two great recent books are reviewed here.

Dinosaurs: How They Lived and Evolved

Naish, Darren, and Paul Barrett (2016: Smithsonian Books, 224pp.)
    Paleontologists Naish and Barrett offer here an altogether

splendid treatment of what, as of 2016 (this business changes quickly, especially regarding feathers) we know about dinosaurs. Where Steve Brussate's 2018 *The Rise and Fall of the Dinosaurs* presents a highly readable story, beginning to end, Naish and Barrett dig (literally) into the meat and bones of dinosaur evolution. Naish and Barrett chronicle what happened, mixed with discovery stories and asides on the science. *Dinosaurs* starts with an overview chapter, then goes into the complexities of the family trees, then chapters on anatomy and on biology, ecology, and behavior. The authors provide a fascinating chapter on the origin of birds and how they survived and thrived, showing what we know of Mesozoic-era birds and what features survived. Birds also offer clues we can trace back to look at dinosaurs. These two scientists make it clear how countless dinosaur features, from feathers to femurs, evolved and worked. The book is sumptuously illustrated with photos and artistic depictions, plus line drawings that explain anatomical features. They close with a thorough examination of the K-Pg extinction event and its aftermath.

The text gets a little dry in spots for the nonscientist, and the structure of the book lends itself to too many "we will look in detail at this later" statements. These are quibbles, though.

Evolution in Minutes

Naish, Darren (2017: Quercus Publishing, 415pp.)

Very handy "pocket guide" to the topic. Naish, an accomplished vertebrate paleontologist, packs hundreds of mini-essays on everything from Bergmann's Rule to Hox genes into 13 sections. You can read it through, dip into it from time to time, or look up something specific via the index. Convergent evolution, incipient species, DNA, molecular clocks, and many other topics important for the cryptozoologist are here in one-page essays, each with an illustration. Compromises made to keep this mini-book (about 13 centimeters square) from being too thick include a bare-bones Table of Contents and, unfortunately, no bibliography or endnotes.

. . .

Take the platypus—that is not a finished product. It is clearly still in beta. – Stephen Colbert, humorist

The Dinosaur Artist

Williams, Paige (2018: Hatchette Book Group, 410pp.)

This much-praised book opens a window into the trade with illegally or quasi-legally trafficked fossils. While the focus here is dinosaurs, the events and issues apply to all types of fossils which have commercial value. (A small *T. rex* tooth on eBay was $2,499.00 when I wrote this review.) Williams explains how this situation arose, including the effect of movie stars bidding huge sums for theropod skulls.

Williams' centerpiece is the famous case in which American fossil hunter/dealer Eric Prokopi went to jail for selling a *Tarbosaurus bataar* (a close relation to *T. rex*) shipped out of Mongolia with deceptive documents. She takes us on long treks through the Mongolian desert, including the famed Flaming Cliffs site, where Roy Chapman Andrews obtained the first confirmed dinosaur eggs almost a hundred years ago. She also takes us through changing Mongolian politics and the lives of Propokpi and his associates. We also meet the pioneering Mongolian paleontologist Bolortsetseg Minjin, a woman who did more than anyone to make her nation's fossils a national resource rather than an easily plundered source of treasures.

The book explores the tension in fossil hunting between paleontologists, who prize documenting fossils in place, and the private fossil hunters, who are accused of taking fossils out of the vital context of location and strata but argue they save many fossils that would otherwise be destroyed by weathering or development. It's all exhaustively researched and documented. Don't forget to read the endnotes: like post-credits scenes in Marvel movies, they hold some fascinating nuggets. On balance, it's a terrific book. So, safari hats off to Williams for taking us on this journey and giving us plenty of reference material: the endnotes, index, etc., run 128 pages.

End of the Megafauna: The Fate of the World's Hugest, Fiercest, and Strangest Animals

MacPhee, Ross (2018: W. W. Norton & Company, 256pp.)

Extinction is an important topic for cryptozoology, and this book offers a look at some seemingly mysterious extinctions. Why would giant mammals that dominated the world so recently, many well into the age of modern humans, vanish? MacPhee estimates 750-1,000 species of large animals died out in the last 50,000 years, a span he calls Near Time. (Among other side notes, the author doubts anyone has actually eaten mammoth meat, aka Pleistocene roadkill.)

MacPhee runs down the world's major features and ecosystems of the Quaternary period to set the stage for Near Time. He also offers a sampling of the more spectacular inhabitants. Then it's on to the history of human efforts to explain extinctions, from Biblically-dominated times to the present. The contenders (with many variations) are overkill by humans, ecosystem change, or both: the author considers and discards hyperdisease and impact events. After discussing the evidence from major islands and continents where extinctions have taken place, MacPhee writes that neither overkill nor climate change is satisfactory as the single driver of extinction. Some extinction waves came after human presence, some not: in Africa and Eurasia, there were no sudden waves of extinction at all. Moreover, very few of the many kill sites and dumps we'd expect from Near Time overkill episodes have been found. In the end, he writes there were cofactors in each extinction event, and we don't yet know what contributed most to each one. The study must go on.

There are 38 pages of back matter, including notes, references, a glossary, and a guide for additional reading. The illustrations—maps, graphs, photos, and Peter Schouten's artwork—are magnificent.

This is a fascinating book: no matter what causes are involved in which settings, MacPhee has explained in one lovely volume much of the science involved in Near Time extinctions. Bravo!

The Rise and Fall of the Dinosaurs: A New History of a Lost World

Brusatte, Steve (2018: William Morrow and Company, 404pp.)

In *Rise and Fall*, the latest in dinosaur science is presented in a highly readable book doubling as a rip-roaring adventure tale. The story of dinosaurs, not just as fossils but as real animals, is masterfully presented here. The first thing Brusatte does, superbly, is to put the dinosaurs into context. From the end-Permian extinction through the first phase of the Triassic period, the dinosaur-to-be lineage was one of several vying for dominance, and it was not particularly favored to win that contest. Dinosaurs ascended through adaptability and luck, radiating into niches all over Pangea. As the world transformed several times over the next 150 million years, the dinos changed with it. They developed thousands of species (a new one is described, on average, every week). In China and elsewhere, they also produced the tiny forms that adapted to flight and endured as birds. Brusatte interweaves his science with dramatic tales of the great adventures and colorful lives of both professional and amateur paleontologists that unfolded along with the expanding science.

T. rex is the only dinosaur that gets its own chapter. Brusatte weighs in on the controversies over whether *T. rex* had feathers and whether it hunted in packs, arguing for "yes" and "yes." (Also, did you know young rexes grew at the rate of five pounds per day?) At the end, he takes us on a harrowing journey with the last dinosaurs as they watch death bloom from the sky.

The author reminds us repeatedly that dinosaurs are not merely skeletons or film stars (taking several shots at *Jurassic Park* along the way). They were dynamic, living, breathing animals that ruled the Earth for a thousand times as long as modern humans have been dominant. The science will continue to evolve, but it's hard to imagine that a better treatment of dinosaurs in a mere 350 pages of text is on the horizon.

Three Stones Make a Wall: The Story of Archaeology

Cline, Eric (2018: Princeton University Press, 480pp.)

The human past is a fascinating subject, and it pops up often in cryptozoology, where pictures, statues, and descriptions of interesting and sometimes unidentified animals are cited as evidence. Accordingly, it's worth the effort to develop an understanding of how such things are found, dated, and interpreted.

The author, an archaeologist of note, takes the reader through a history of archaeology (as opposed to mere grave robbery, although they certainly overlapped). After a teaser about King Tut, he begins with the discovery of Troy. While people have explored ancient habitations and tombs all over the world, organized, methodical archaeology, as we understand it, was established by European efforts in the 18th century. As Cline proceeds by areas or specific locations (Central America, Egypt, Mesopotamia, Greece, Masada, Jamestown, etc.), he explains the tools and methods, from hand-held brush to ground-penetrating radar, and what each can add to the knowledge of the past.

That past, he notes, does not simply lie buried. Stratigraphy can be anything from a simple new-over-old layering to a complete mess. When Troy was repeatedly rebuilt after earthquakes and conquest, the construction would start by leveling off the ground on which the new city would be built, destroying anything left standing and jumbling up the artifacts and their time periods. Interpretation of such places is never straightforward, and archaeologists may offer very different scenarios. Associations with famous figures and legends can begin in local custom and may or may not be borne out by science. Words of old historians can be challenged, too: Cline accepts most of Flavius Josephus' account of Masada but doubts the Jews committed mass suicide (the Romans wouldn't have given them time). Another point of contention is credit. Most famously, Heinrich Schliemann didn't pick the spot to look for Troy. Local people had already pointed Frank Calvert to it, but Schliemann provided the money and appropriated full credit.

Cline also introduces us to many famous (and some important but non-famous) archaeologists. He takes the time, necessarily, I think, to reject the TV/internet world of alien construction companies and New Age mysticism as he defines what archaeology is and what it isn't. Cline discusses the question of ownership and makes a point in several places about the damage done to archaeology by the trade in terms of stolen and/or looted artifacts. He also explains the basics of dating and reconstruction and touches on the ever-thornier questions of who has the right to look where and what should be repatriated to its original homeland.

I've mentioned many instances of good writing in this section, and Cline's is near the top of the list, making this book perfect for everyone. It's weird that the Flores "hobbits" rate exactly four words given that other human finds, like Lucy, get detailed treatment. I also wanted more illustrations, like something showing how the many levels of Troy or Megiddo (21 layers!) collapsed on each other and what that "layer cake" looks like now. Nonetheless, this is an extremely valuable introduction to the topic. It's also a great starting point for further research: the endnotes and bibliography fill over a hundred pages.

Human Evolution: A Very Short Introduction

Wood, Bernard (2019: Oxford University Press, 160pp., 2nd edition)

The prominent Dr. Wood, a Professor of Human Origins, has written a cogent and authoritative introduction to how we emerged. He opens with the development of the science through the discovery of evolution and then genetics. He explains where and under what circumstances hominid remains can be found, how they are dated, and how we reconstruct past ecosystems. He moves on through how we reconstruct hominins from fossils and classify them using tools from human inspection to DNA. Wood spends a third of the book giving the reader the tools to understand the last two-thirds, where he gets into the major discoveries, disputes, and debates that produced our modern view of human ancestry. His tables and charts are so simple, clean, and useful that they'd be immediately rejected by every corporate organization I've ever worked for. He discusses four contenders for the title of "earliest hominin," then archaic and transitional forms, and finally modern humans. His overall time chart shows 31 known and proposed species. The item that will startle some readers is his depiction of Neanderthals as a species separate from *H. sapiens*. He offers a chart of 17 morphological and behavioral differences to support this. Wood explores diffusion and interspecies relations, then closes by speculating on how our views will evolve as new sites, new fossils, and new tools transform our current understanding. To someone who took their last anthropology class 40 years ago, this was a painless and informative read.

Environment and Exploration

The sea in all its vastness is its own, real world. Man is nature's sci-fi. – Criss Jami, *Killosophy*

Green Laurels: The Lives and Achievements of the Great Naturalists

Peattie, Donald (1936: Literary Guild, 368pp.)

In this memorable book, Peattie, an accomplished naturalist and an excellent writer, traces the efforts of men, not all of them famous, who shaped European and American understanding of the natural world. (They are all men: he excluded such accomplished naturalists as Mary Anning, Maria Sibylla Merian, and Beatrix Potter, who made lasting contributions to paleontology, entomology, and mycology, respectively.) He begins in the Middle Ages when Europe still relied on oft-unreliable copies of the work of Aristotle ("a half-god lost in clouds") and Pliny. He describes the opening of the miniature zoological world by Galileo and others. Then it's on to the naturalists like Georges-Louis Leclerc Buffon, Baron Jean Frédéric Cuvier, Sir Richard Owen, and Alexander von Humboldt, who, spurred on after 1735 by Linnaeus' system of taxonomy, basically ransacked the entire world for specimens. "Every Linnean species was turning out to be, in fact, two, three, fifty, or a hundred species." This resulted in enormous backlogs in museums, as many naturalists focused on describing vertebrate animals over all else. One of the men who brought order to the "lower" animals was Jean-Baptiste de Monet Lamarck, remembered now for his theory of the inheritance of acquired characteristics, but who also did indispensable studies of arthropods. Incidentally, Peattie considers Lamarck an unfairly despised genius whose theory was crucial to the way Darwinian evolution occurred. Peattie carries on through John Bartram, the first great American-born field naturalist and the man who discovered *Franklinia*, a tree never again seen in the wild. The book visits John J. Audubon, Alfred R. Wallace, Charles Darwin, and many others, closing with entomologist John Henry Fabre. It's a classic introduction to the people who brought to the Western world the wonders of nature.

Under the Sea: A Treasury of Great Writing About the Ocean Depths

Soule, Gardner (editor) (1969: Meredith Press, 347pp.)

I'm going to ask some indulgence here because I think it highlights the value of older books to reprint this item from my blog just as I wrote it in 2013.

I'm browsing a book from 1968 I used as a source on marine life when writing my previous books. Tucked inside, I find photocopies from another book and little notes like "Copeia no.3, p.584, 1989 (2 new dogsharks)." I love having the wisdom (and stupidity) of the world at my fingertips on the internet, but I also miss the days of prowling musty stacks of magazines and scientific journals, going back a century or more, at whatever university I was near (Purdue, Utah State, University of North Dakota, University of Arkansas, and so on), which led to little nuggets of information no one had previously stitched into a pattern.

Also inside this book, I find a photocopied page from the 1989 Smithsonian book Sharks in Question, which says a great white shark definitely over 24 feet (7.3 m) long has recently been caught in Australia and the jaws saved. This one seems to have been forgotten or disproved, I'm not sure which.

Back to *Under the Sea*. In this book, we learn that a dolphin named Keiki trained to swim fast to get fish rewards never exceeded 14.5 knots, although much higher speeds are reported in the wild. There is a geophysicist's argument that continental drift isn't possible. There is an account of a ship called the *Oceaneer* trying to catch a sea monster (or a monstrous sleeper shark) and a report that the whale shark has "credibly" been reported at 60 feet (18.3 m) long. (Modern authorities knock off 10 or 15 feet.)

There is an article about recent pioneering work in bioacoustics and the discovery that not just whales but fish make a variety of noises. There is research on kelp by William Beebe and later a writer gushing over how the Great Barrier Reef is primeval, unchanging, a permanent source of delight. There is a study of how the carcasses of long-dead fish in the Antarctic could have worked their way to the TOP of the ice in one spot.

Here we learn about a new phylum, *Pogonophora*, consisting of worms that had been tossed overboard as annoying "fibers." The discoveries roll on: the pygmy angelfish, the living fossil *Neopilina*. There is another of my handwritten notes: "1960 new sawshark *Pristiophorus schroederi*." Named for the pianist in Peanuts? Probably not.

The rousing (and inaccurate) giant squid scene written by Verne in *20,000 Leagues Under the Sea* is here. Then there's Sir Arthur Grimble's first-hand tale of having a reef octopus fasten itself to his face and neck. There are accounts of octopuses using stones or shells as tools, an ability that seemed to be largely forgotten in popular literature until recent reports documenting tool use.

The book moves on to submarines and then to waves, with an account of the U.S.S. *Ramapo's* triangulation of a wave 112 feet (31.4 m) from trough to crest. The *Ramapo* was in the conjunction of three low-pressure centers with a barometer down to 28.4 inches. The method of triangulation and why it was reasonably accurate even in terrible conditions is well explained. Following items note waves splashing over 133 feet (40.5 m) on lighthouses, being measured by a weather ship at 80 feet (24.4 m), and smashing up the liner *Michelangelo*, breaking bridge windows 81 feet (24.7 m) above the waterline.

There's a folded scrap from an ancient email to my AOL address, in the prehistoric days of the 1990s, from British zoologist Karl Shuker, telling me I had crossed up the names of two exotic birds in the *Exotic Zoology* newsletter I used to write. He was right, of course.

Soule's book contains a plan for a glass diving bell able to descend to 35,000 feet (10, 670 m) and a submarine to track ocean fish for the Bureau of Fisheries. The designer was Bill McLean of what is now the China Lake Naval Weapons Center, who I communicated with and wrote about in conjunction with the Project Pilot air-launched satellite program of 1958. Another scientist from the same institution describes a manned station to be built under a rock on the seafloor.

A satisfying sampler indeed, even 50 years after its writing!

Matt's Musings: If you're interested in monster waves, read Susan Casey's book The Wave (Doubleday, 2010.) The Ramapo wave is the highest ever measured but not the highest reported, and waves in the region of 100 feet / 30 m are more common than anyone thought until the present century: they've even been surfed.

The High Frontier

Moffett, Mark (1993: Harvard University Press, 192pp.)

Moffett describes Earth's least-known land environment—the tropical rainforest canopy. He also describes Terry Erwin's studies of canopy arthropods which have netted (literally) new species beyond count, and his predictions of the total number of species yet to be found. Good bibliography and excellent photographs.

Scientific facts, more often than is known, are learned by accident. – William Beebe, naturalist and undersea explorer

Lost Wild America

McClung, Robert (1993: Linnet Books, 277pp.)

This is a first-rate work covering the history of extinctions and endangered species in and around the United States. A wealth of data includes profiles of lost, rediscovered, and rare animals of all types, woven into a very readable narrative and illustrated with drawings. Thorough bibliography.

. . .

Mary and Thatcher had lived in enviable times when biologists were discovering new species right and left, not watching them go extinct. – Barbara Kingsolver, author, *Unsheltered*

The New York Times Book of Science Literacy, Volume II: The Environment from your Backyard to the Ocean Floor

Wade, Nicholas, with Cornelia Dean and William A. Dicke (editors) (1994: Times Books, 480pp.)

There are many good collections of science writing, both themed and general, in any given year. This imposingly titled example has several articles of interest. These include "A Cornucopia of Life," describing the diversity of the seafloor and how little we know of its denizens: "The Aye-Aye," an update on the bizarre little primate once feared extinct: and "To Conserve or Catalog Rare Species," concerning the discovery of Somalia's boubou shrike and the controversial decision to release the first specimen back into the wild. (There is no newer edition.)

Explorations

Ballard, Robert (1995: Hyperion Books, 407pp.)

In this fascinating account of Ballard's undersea discoveries, the explorer and geographer tells us about the discovery of a totally new ecosystem—the deep-sea hydrothermal vent colonies. Ballard recounts how biologists simply did not believe the first report of life surrounding a vent. The myriad of animals discovered at these vents has contributed to our understanding of the origin and development of life, particularly life that does not use the sun to store energy through photosynthesis, instead of using the heat and minerals of the Earth's mantle to store energy through chemosynthesis.

Deep Atlantic: Life, Death, and Exploration in the Abyss

Ellis, Richard (1996: Alfred A. Knopf, 395pp.)

Few authors could write a readable first-class book solely about the environment deep under the Atlantic Ocean, but Ellis has managed it. Meticulously researched (the bibliography covers 47 pages), this highly readable work includes many tidbits for the cryptozoologist. Examples are Ellis' favorite creatures, the giant squids; the weird fish reported by pioneer undersea explorer William Beebe; and the now-famous hydrothermal vent colonies with their otherworldly inhabitants. Also valuable is a discussion of the six-foot larva once known as *Leptocephalus giganteus*.

The Octopus's Garden: Hydrothermal Vents and Other Mysteries of the Deep Sea

Van Dover, Cindy Lee (1996: Helix Books, 183pp.)

In this fascinating account of exploratory probes of the ocean depths, Van Dover shows the reader the variety of bizarre environments recently discovered under the sea and their even more bizarre inhabitants: the famous tubeworms, "spaghetti worms," and a shrimp named (by another researcher) *Chorocaris vandoverae* after the author. She even explores whether deep-sea vent shrimp are edible (emphatically not). She also describes the topography and geology of the seafloor, both subject to rapid change from lava flows, vent fields, etc., and believes that camera views don't entirely replace the intuitive discoveries that come in seeing the deep with human eyes. Finally, she writes about what she calls "the Trilobite Factor," the belief that there are still major discoveries (if not actual trilobites) ahead. A paperback edition released the same year is titled *Ocean Journeys: Discovering New Life at the Bottom of the Sea*. The writing is of the charming sort that invites the reader to come along, and the book is packed with well-explained science.

The Universe Below

Broad, William (1997: Simon and Schuster, 432pp.)

Broad's book on discoveries under the sea covers oceanography, warfare, and other matters not directly related to marine zoology, but there's enough about new denizens of the deep to keep any cryptozoologist turning the pages. Broad includes a comment from Dr. Robison of the Monterey Bay Aquarium Research Institute, who says we have so far missed classifying at least one-third of the large species in the sea. "We may find that's conservative," he adds. "It could be half."

Coral Seas

Steene, Roger (1998: Firefly Books, 272pp.)

This stunning photographic tour of coral reefs and other marine landscapes includes photographs of the Mimic Octopus and several undescribed marine invertebrates, including a foot-wide sea star that looks exactly like what you'd get if you sewed it from cloth and overstuffed it. I believe this is the first book with color photos of the mimic. It also includes the first photograph I, and no doubt many people, ever saw of an albino humpback whale.

Throwim Way Leg

Flannery, Tim (1998: Atlantic Monthly Press, 326pp.)

Dr. Flannery has written a captivating book about his adventures seeking new species in New Guinea (the title is a pidgin expression for starting on a long journey). Flannery has described two new species of kangaroos and over twenty other species and subspecies of mammals. This book is part zoology lesson and part travelogue. Flannery makes it very clear New Guinea still has large tracts of untrodden and almost inaccessible terrain where there are doubtless more species to look for. Must reading for those interested in New Guinea's fauna or in the challenges of penetrating Earth's last unsurveyed regions for the sake of zoology.

Life in the Treetops: Adventures of a Woman in Field Biology

Lowman, Margaret (1999: Yale University Press, 219pp.)

The arboreal environment doesn't get much attention from cryptozoologists or from people in general, but it's a fascinating place. Lowman recounts her pioneering work in exploring forest canopy environments on four continents. In the course of telling about her experiences, she provides information on forest ecology, botany, and the unusual creatures of the upper story. Lowman has just released a memoir, *The Arbornaut: A Life Discovering the Eighth Continent in the Trees Above Us* (2021: Allen & Unwin; 368pp.)

Swift as a Shadow: Extinct and Endangered Animals

Purcell, Rosamond Wolff (1999: Houghton Mifflin Publishing, 160pp.)

A haunting collection of superb photographs of museum specimens of endangered and extinct animals. Specimens depicted include the thylacine, passenger pigeon, quagga, and Javan tiger. A touching, memorable book.

The Eighth Continent: Life, Death, and Rediscovery in the Lost World of Madagascar

Tyson, Peter (2000: William Morrow and Company, 374pp.)

This excellent book explores Madagascar, an island of zoological discovery and mystery. Tyson takes the reader to meet such pioneers as herpetologist Chris Raxworthy, who has a backlog of 150 new species to describe, and primatologist Patricia Wright, discoverer of a new lemur. Along the way, he describes the biodiversity of this endangered land and probes reports indicating two species of Madagascar's supposedly extinct megafauna—a pygmy hippo and a giant lemur—just might still exist. Tyson later wrote a travel guide entitled *Madagascar: The Eighth Continent* (2013: Bradt Guides, 384pp.)

The Empty Ocean

Ellis, Richard (2003: Island Press, 384pp.)

If seeking new creatures in the oceans, it's worthwhile to understand how the food web works and what prey (and predators) may interact with your target species. As Ellis warns in this outright terrifying book, that the food web has, in many places, been ripped apart. One need only see how fisherfolk celebrate catches they would have thrown away as worthlessly small a few decades ago. From coral reefs to sea horses to sea turtles and (especially) major game and food fish, the damage we've done means the oceans will never be the same despite our best efforts. However, Ellis also highlights successful strategies for protection and restoration, including the effects of protected areas. As of the date of publication, the state of the oceans might be called (in my words) "extremely critical, but not yet entirely hopeless." (It has, sadly, only gotten more dire as the years have passed).

Fathoming the Ocean: The Discovery and Exploration of the Deep Sea

Rozwadowski, Helen, with Foreword by Sylvia Earle (2005: Belknap Press, 276pp.)

We all know modern tools are allowing us to get a better view of the deep seas than we've ever had, but how did that kind of exploration get started? How did humans first get interested in the word below the first few sunlit meters of the sea, and how did we start probing that world? Helen M. Rozwadowski, in the first book I've read devoted to the early ocean surveyors, shows us how the Age of Sail fostered the age of deep-sea exploration. As commerce, whaling, fishing, and travel grew in economic importance and matured from coastal to trans-oceanic pursuits, naturalists, professional and amateur, grew more interested in the depths. These men (and women) tried a number of modifications of fishing nets and trawls for this work, then added purpose-built, often very ingenious tools like water samplers and recording thermometers. They were followed increasingly by government-sponsored professionals, most notably in the epic 1872-76 voyage of the HMS *Challenger*, the beginning of the modern age of ocean exploration. (While we think of Charles Darwin as the official naturalist on the HMS *Beagle*, Rozwadowski reminds us he wasn't: he was added as a "Gentleman's Dinner Companion" to Captain Robert FitzRoy, and his work as a naturalist was done on his own initiative with no official support or recompense.) In this superbly documented and referenced book, the author includes the views of governments, ordinary sailors, and the Western public, along with those of scientists. This is an essential book for the understanding of deep-sea exploration, both historical and modern.

I remember when we found the first population of living Cerion agassizi *[a land snail] in central Eleuthera... But who can I tell; who cares? And I answered myself, I don't have to tell anyone. We have just seen and understood something that no one has ever seen and understood before. What more does a man need?* — Stephen Jay Gould, *The Flamingo's Smile: Reflections in Natural History*

Where the Wild Things Were: Life, Death, and Ecological Wreckage in a Land of Vanishing Predators

Stolzenburg, William (2008: Bloomsbury Publishing, 304pp.)
    The author looks at cases, both experimental and real-life, where the top predators in an ecosystem have been wiped out and show us

what happens next. It turns out that a lot of things happen, none of them good. One result is an explosion of "mesopredators" (the second-tier carnivores, ranging from coyotes to raccoons to feral domestic cats) which wreak havoc on ecosystems without the larger predators to compete with (or eat) them. Who knew that bringing in a new apex predator (whalers) and wiping out the northern Pacific great whales drove the former apex predator (killer whales) to decimate some seal and sea otter populations, resulting in kelp forests being replaced by barren seafloor overrun with the urchins? One of Stolzenburg's important points is that, ecologically, human hunters don't replace the predators: they hunt in specific seasons rather than all year round and pick off the largest animals. This book is important for anyone interested in wildlife conservation and in learning what happens when an ecosystem is disrupted.

Nature's Ghosts: Confronting Extinction from the Age of Jefferson to the Age of Ecology

Barrow, Mark (2009: University of Chicago Press, 512pp.)

Early Europeans viewed North America as a place of incredibly diverse and seemingly inexhaustible natural riches. Settlers couldn't believe the abundance of birds and fish and useful furry animals. How that view slowly—very slowly, in fits and starts and with many advances and retreats—changed to a modern view of conservation, losing many key species along the way, is the subject of Barrows' well-written and thorough treatment. I've not come across another book like this, which introduces people both famous and forgotten, organizations that evolved into modern conservation forces, and the contradictions of naturalists who worried about extinction even as they shot and collected every specimen in sight. I knew of the work of John James Audubon and Aldo Leopold, but Victor Shelford? John C. Phillips? The American Committee for International Wildlife Protection? Concerning some other people, like biologist Archie Carr, I knew of them but hadn't realized how influential they were. I found information new to me on every page, and there are 82 pages of endnotes to reinforce the 360-page main story. This truly is a landmark work.

The World is Blue: How Our Fate and the Ocean's Are One

Earle, Sylvia (2010: National Geographic Society, 319pp.)

Earle, Explorer in Residence at the National Geographic Society, provides a readable and compelling "state of the oceans" report. The facts and figures are all here, but they are mixed with anecdotes and vivid descriptions of marine life to keep the reader in the right context. Earle argues for more protected marine reserves (noting that American hunters can take millions of ducks every year because there are enough protected marshlands and flyways to keep the duck population healthy.) She touches on all the major groups of marine life and describes the latest in submersibles and other technology. One of my heroes of exploration and conservation, "Her Deepness," has here made a contribution that should be read by everyone interested in marine life and conservation—which essentially means *everyone*.

Pink Boots and a Machete

Mayor, Mireya (2011: National Geographic Society, 304pp.)

Mayer has written a terrific book about science and adventure. A well-known anthropologist and TV personality and discoverer of a new species of mouse lemur, Mayor tells gritty stories of her adventures around the world, leavened with humor and self-reflection. (I wrote about her in my 2006 book *Shadows of Existence*, although I accidentally called her a Rhodes scholar instead of a Fulbright scholar: I'm sure both schools were offended.) Most of this book is taken up with field expeditions, and the strongest message is that finding and conserving wildlife in remote regions of the world is still hard. As in "very hard," as in "you can die," which she almost did on more than one occasion. Radios and modern gear and even rescue helicopters can't insulate you. Mayor includes in her gear a little black dress and isn't above using the attention it draws. I don't think that demeans or diminishes her: her point is that social skills matter no matter where you are. Her book is superb.

We must teach our children to smell the earth, to taste the rain, to touch the wind, to see things grow, to hear the sun rise and night fall – to care. – John Cleal, poet and painter

The Ocean of Life: The Fate of Man and the Sea

Roberts, Callum (2012: Viking Press, 416pp.)

Conservation biologist Roberts is interested, not just in the creatures of the sea, but in humanity's relationship with said creatures and with the ocean itself. Everything from the origin of water to the modern practices that threaten to make the oceans unlivable is within his net, and he weaves it skillfully, engagingly, and with an urgency that will make readers think, "What can I do?" Roberts offers his vision of a new regime where fishing is done sustainably and the environment is at least partially restored. Great reading for those who want to understand the ocean ecosystem and how it's changing.

The Sixth Extinction: An Unnatural History

Kolbert, Elizabeth (2015: Picador, 336pp.)

Extinction—how it happens, when it happens, and whether it's for good—occupies a lot of space in the minds of cryptozoologists. I can't say enough about this book: Kolbert is authoritative, engaging, and memorable in her assessment of the science and her first-person reports on her trips to see the threats and the threatened species for herself. There have been five mass extinctions in known geological history, the most recent being the impact that ended the Mesozoic, and Kolbert documents the way human beings have brought about yet another mass extinction. Some of the extinctions are unwitting (early Native Americans certainly didn't intend to wipe out the mastodon) and some shockingly deliberate, as when a scrounger stomped on the last viable Great Auk egg ever to exist. Kolbert recounts her own journeys, ranging from the depressing to the amusing, to pull us in and give the science a human dimension, but she never lets herself overpower the story. Rarely has an author provided us with such a compelling account of an ongoing crisis that demands global action before we lose yet more irreplaceable creatures and their habitats.

The rarer they get, the fewer meanings animals can have. Eventually, rarity is all they are made of. The condor is an icon of extinction. There's little else to it now but being the last of its kind. And in this lies the diminution of the world. How can you love something, how can you fight to protect it, if all it means is loss? – Helen Macdonald, naturalist, in *H is for Hawk*

Vaquita: Science, Politics, and Crime in the Sea of Cortez

Bessensen, Brooke (2018: Island Press, 320pp.)

The vaquita, the world's smallest cetacean, once numbered thousands of animals in the Sea of Cortez. Then it was hundreds. And then it was a dozen—at best. In addition to the vital story of its near-elimination in the nets of totoaba fish poachers (which Bessensen risks her life to document), there are two things here of interest to cryptozoologists.

One is the challenge of getting a good count of a decent-sized animal (1.5 m [5 feet] for an adult female) despite it having a limited range. Vaquitas are boat-shy, and there are so few that searchers rarely see them. Lucky photos by tourists and amateurs are very important.

The other thing is that some local fishermen have convinced themselves the animal does not exist, being only a prop for some government or corporate plot to disrupt their livelihoods. While some younger fishermen have never seen one, others refuse to believe the creature exists because the restrictions meant to save it make life very hard for them. This book will move you, anger you, and make you think.

Matt's Musings: There is a dire warning in Vaquita *for any species with a restricted range. As of December 2021, there are probably between eight and 10 vaquitas. They are hard to study: they are never on the surface near a boat long enough to attach tags. The efforts of the Mexican government, Sea Shepherd, and others have not stopped the slide toward extinction. Totoaba poaching is so lucrative that drug gangs are involved and even police boats are fired on. Anyone who gets hard proof of a new species needs to get the authorities involved as fast as possible, ridicule be damned.*

There is a word, sad and resonant, for the last member of a dying species. The word is endling. – Sy Montgomery, *The Best American Science and Nature Writing 2019*

Endless Novelties of Extraordinary Interest: The Voyage of HMS Challenger and the Birth of Modern Oceanography

MacDougall, Doug (2019: Yale University Press, 257pp.)

The epic three-year voyage of the *Challenger* lasted 1000 days from 1872-1876 and covered 68,000 nautical miles. The ship was the first fully-equipped oceanic research ship dedicated solely to discovery. The voyage multiplied our knowledge of the oceans, their creatures, and the environment, laying the foundation for the modern sciences dedicated to those topics. MacDougall eschews a day-to-day account (although he gives us a good picture of life on the ship) for themed chapters like one on deep-sea discoveries. The ship visited every ocean but the Arctic and took countless thousands of samples and specimens. Some naturalists hoped for the rediscovery of "living fossils," but although that didn't happen, they gathered an enormous trove of information on corals, islands, minerals, and life of every kind. It took 19 years to publish all the reports. This is a fascinating book that has much to tell us about the development of modern science and the ocean world.

The folly of mistaking a paradox for a discovery, a metaphor for a proof, a torrent of verbiage for a spring of capital truths, and oneself for an oracle, is inborn in us. – Paul Valéry, philosopher

In Oceans Deep: Courage, Innovation, and Adventure Beneath the Waves

Streever, Bill (2019: Little, Brown, and Company, 303pp.)

This is a very good, if somewhat, episodic account of humanity's exploration beneath the sea by every means we know of: diving suits, free-diving, submarines, submersibles, self-contained habitats, and remotely operated vehicles (ROVs). Streever is well-qualified to write this book. He is not just a science writer but a biologist and a diver of vast and varied experience.

There are fascinating facts and stories throughout this book. Some topics like the evolution of collecting devices from dredges towed by surface vessels to remotely operated vehicles (ROVs) that can explore, photograph, and gather specimens. Streever explains how divers experienced and learned to prevent and treat "the bends" caused by gas bubbles created when divers return to the surface too rapidly. (It was originally called "caisson disease," named for the workers building caissons in pressurized chambers underwater to support major bridges like the Brooklyn and Golden Gate.) He recounts a very interesting talk with Don Walsh, one of two men on the submersible *Trieste* when it dove to the bottom of the Mariana Trench. I didn't realize what a shoestring operation that was. (Walsh still thinks the flatfish he reported, generally believed to be a sea cucumber, might have been a fish.) Streever is fascinated by new technology, like the latest nuclear submarines and ROVs.

Somehow, I didn't like the book as a whole quite as much as I liked the parts. Maybe it needed just a bit more context on how the various segments of marine-exploration history affected the big picture of how we see and use the oceans. There are 21 pages of fascinating chapter notes, although no bibliography. Streever obviously loves the ocean, and he knows it better than most of us ever will. All quibbles aside, this book is a voyage worth taking.

The Brilliant Abyss: Exploring the Majestic Hidden Life of the Deep Ocean, and the Looming Threat That Imperils It

Scales, Helen (2021: Atlantic Monthly Press, 288pp.)

Scales spends the opening chapters of this excellent book explaining the geology and topography of the underwater world. She presents the vertical journey by dropping a marble from a ship and describing the changes of light and life until it hits the bottom of a deep trench six hours later. She highlights a three-year study that photographed 347,000 animals in the Pacific, only one-fifth of which were assignable to known species and genera. She mentions the origins and legends of the abyss (from *abyssus*, "bottomless pit," in Latin) and its monsters. The book goes on to describe the history of seafloor exploration from sampling lines through modern robots and submersibles. Then the author takes us to the seas, where she describes being on a research cruise where sperm whales breach around the ship while the scientists haul up samples from over 2,000 m (6,560 feet) down. She spends a chapter on introducing the sperm whale and its marvelous adaptations, how humans have studied it, and the bizarre bone-eating zombie worms that gather on sunken whale skeletons. On the same voyage, scientists dropped dead alligators to the seafloor and watched how the predators moved in. We learn about Ernst Haeckel, whose 19th-century work on jellyfishes formed the basis of modern efforts to study the bewildering variety of undersea invertebrates. She includes the discovery of a whole new ecosystem, the geothermal vent community. The total of species living in vent communities worldwide is over 700 and climbing. The book includes other discoveries, like octopus nurseries and the Mariana snailfish (documented at 26,500 feet [8,080m] down).

Next, Scales considers what the oceans mean to us and what we're doing to them. She explains the function of the oceans in sequestering carbon, the role of photosynthetic algae in generating oxygen, the pharmacological value of marine life, and other benefits. Then she explores the threats: overfishing (notably the rise and fall of the orange roughy population), the destructive trawling of seamount ecosystems, the rise in twilight-zone fishing, pollution by everything from microplastics to nerve agents, and seabed mining. She argues that the deep sea needs to be protected completely by something akin to the International Antarctic Treaty.

It's a book with a lot of science on fascinating animals, plus thought-provoking arguments and even a couple of cryptozoological lines. "When Yeti crabs were discovered, it would have been poetic if they were found to eat marine snow." (They don't.) She writes that plesiosaurs were "extinct oceangoing reptiles that looked like Loch Ness monsters" instead of the other way around. The copious source notes are an excellent resource.

Gone: A Search for What Remains of The World's Extinct Creatures

Blencowe, Michael (2021: Leaping Hare Press, 192pp.)

What remains of a species after it has gone extinct? In this moving book, Blencowe introduces us to 11 extinct species. He offers a history of how each one became extinct and travels to see for himself what remains have been preserved. Most memorably, he goes to a Danish museum to look in the eyes—just the eyes, preserved in a jar—of the last two Great Auks ever to live. In another museum (there's a list and map in the backmatter), Blencowe looks at the head and foot that comprise the only soft tissue remains of the dodo.

Most of the extinctions are famous ones, like the dodo and Steller's sea cow, but at the end, he adds Ivell's sea anemone, an almost-transparent invertebrate only 20mm long. It lived on one English lagoon, where Blencowe searched for it while perched on a child's inflatable alligator. Fieldwork is not always dignified.

Blencowe spares no words in describing exactly what humans did to make each species vanish. Sometimes it was development (California's Xerxes blue butterfly, killed off when the plant necessary to its diet was bulldozed), sometimes thoughtless overhunting (surely no sailor harpooning a sea cow thought they were limitless, but he faced hunger in the moment), and sometimes pragmatic (releasing goats on Pinta Island—handy for visiting sailors but death to the island's tortoises.)

Some of these cases are understandable because of the eras in which they happened, but understanding why sailors valued a permanent food supply over tortoises doesn't make Blencowe's visit to Lonesome George's grave any less poignant.

Blencowe drives home, not in speeches but simply with poignant words, that every one of these species is a warning because they didn't have to be extinct, and the ruins of their once-vibrant bodies should remind us we can allow no more such losses. Get the hardcover edition for its wonderful illustrations by Jade They.

Zoology of Land, Sea, and Air

This section is light on birds, reptiles, and amphibians since its starting point was the books I'd read based on my own interests. There's a lot on marine creatures, especially whales because I created a whale-tracking project in 2018 and devoured a lot of the literature.

The Immense Journey

Eisley, Loren (1959: Vintage Books, 210pp.)

The well-known anthropologist/naturalist Loren Eisley here collects some of his essays on life on the planet Earth. He ponders the initial steps in the discovery of the deep sea, the first animal to crawl ashore, and the evolution of early humans. He includes the Piltdown hoax and the oddly modern-looking "Boskop Man" from South Africa, which fascinated him but has since been identified as a mirage based on selective sampling. Eisley muses on Ice Ages, birds, flowers, and the ground beneath us. Cryptozoologists know Eisley as the first scientist ever to see the miniature mummy from Wyoming, which he considered "an anomalous mummified stillbirth with an undeveloped brain." Eisley's lyrical writing transports the readers, not only around the world but into past ages. The science has become outdated, but the human element of this journey survives.

Catch Me a Colobus

Durrell, Gerald (1972: Viking Press, 221pp.)

Durrell's many books introduced a generation to wildlife. Here he describes new and strange animals, their behavior and idiosyncrasies, and his collecting trips to Africa and Mexico. He includes some challenges I hadn't thought of: how do you accustom a wild animal to different food before you have to load it on a ship? How do you explain your needs to the cook? He also discusses the challenges of running a zoo dedicated to helping endangered species as well as entertaining visitors.

There's a great deal of humor in Durrell's work, and the heartbreak of losing a lioness giving birth is balanced by the tale of a chimp who learned to unravel a chainlink fence and led his companion on an adventure that involved trashing a bedroom. Durrell notes individual personalities: a baboon who made her mate work his way up gradually to being trusted to touch the new baby, or an orangutan who is "the most mechanically minded" of all the zoo's apes and watches construction crews all day.

Durrell closes the book with a plea for conservation: animals "have no Member of Parliament they can write to; they can't perform sit-down strikes; they have nobody to speak for them except us." The kind of open-ended collecting-and-shipping-home trip Durrell routinely got permits for isn't done anymore, which is a good thing, but opening up Durrell's books was always an adventure and is still fun and informative.

Animals of East Africa

Leakey, Louis (1969: National Geographic Society, 199pp.)

This was my favorite animal book as a kid: I borrowed it from the library over and over, and as an adult, I hunted down a used one. Despite all the knowledge we've gained since 1969, it remains an engaging, informative, well-illustrated tour of the title subject. Louis S.B. Leakey (yes, the *famous* Louis Leakey) tells of surviving a rhino charge and various other adventures along the way. In addition to existing animals, there is a chapter devoted to vanished ones like the quagga. Among other delights, it has the earliest photo I've ever seen of a black zebra with broken-up white markings. It's suitable for teen and adult readers. Don't let the date dissuade you.

Shadows in the Sea: the Sharks, Skates, and Rays

McCormick, Harold, et al. (1978: Scarborough, 415pp.)

This was an important reference for me for a long time. Peter Benchley called it "One of the best books about sharks ever written." In addition to sections on many of the 600-odd species covered (there are about 1100 species now, including over 400 sharks), there are chapters on shark attacks, anti-shark efforts, sharks in folklore, the commercial value of sharks, shark evolution, and even an appendix page devoted to how to cook shark. There's an interesting section on the bull sharks appearing in a freshwater lake in Nicaragua: the authors find it interesting no other ocean fish makes the "commute" to the lake and that the locals say they have two species of sharks there. The book describes the great white as "the most voracious fish in the open sea" and gives its maximum length as at least 36 feet (11 m) and maybe 40 (12 m), figures since attributed to mistakes involving basking sharks. The authors quote a shark authority, Dr. E.W. Gudger, as estimating there could be 75-foot (22.8-m) whale sharks. There are tons of shark anecdotes from fishermen, sailors, and scientists. An example: in 1959, a swimming elephant off Kenya was reportedly killed in a frenzy of shark attacks. Much of the science became obsolete in succeeding decades, and we no longer think of sharks as mindless eating machines, but this is still a book to have around.

We do not just fear our predators, we are transfixed by them. We are prone to weave stories and fables and chat endlessly about them. – Peter Benchley, author of *Jaws*

Birds at Risk

Whitlock, Ralph (1981: Moonraker Press, 159pp.)

Whitlock compiles a large amount of data on the world's rarest birds, including a surprising number of species whose status (i.e., living or extinct) was unknown at the time of writing. This book also includes information on many recent discoveries.

The Collins Guide to the Rare Mammals of the World

Burton, John, and Bruce Pearson (1987: The Stephen Greene Press, 240pp.)

Authoritative handbook of the world's rarest mammals, with copious color illustrations and range maps. Despite its date, this remains an invaluable reference. (The book was last reprinted in 1992, but I still pull it off the shelf.)

Bears of the World

Domico, Terry, and Mark Newman (1988: Facts on File, 189pp.)

In this handsome book on the title subject, the authors discuss Bergman's bear, a reported variant of the Kamchatkan brown bear. Zoologist Sten Bergman described this animal from a pelt seen in 1920 as enormous and entirely black. They write that much of the Kamchatka Peninsula has long been closed off for military reasons and that a former Soviet official who had access said the giant bears were still reported.

Rare Birds of the World

Mountfort, Guy (1988: Collins Publishing, 256pp.)

Similar to Burton and Pearson's **Rare Mammals**, this is a wonderfully useful guide to the 1,000 most threatened species of birds at the time of writing. Anyone with an interest in new, rediscovered, or vanishing birds should still, decades later, have this around. There is a 1991 edition.

MATT BILLE

Vanished Species

Day, David (1989: Gallery Books, 288pp.)
Superb artwork and well-researched text grace this large-format book on animals known or believed to have gone extinct within historical times. An entertaining and thought-provoking work.

Last Chance to See

Adams, Douglas, and Mark Carwardine (1990: Harmony Books, 220pp.)
Writer Adams and zoologist Carwardine describe their travels to see the most endangered animals in the world, including the Komodo dragon ("ten feet long and a yard high is entirely the wrong size for a lizard to be") and the Yangtze River dolphin. A well-written, often humorous, and moving account.

A Parrot Without a Name

Stap, Don (1990: Alfred A. Knopf, 239pp.)
An enthralling account of adventures with ornithologists John O'Neill and the late Ted Parker in search of rare and new species of birds in Peru. The book focuses mainly on O'Neill's expedition, a long and difficult one. The climax comes when a colleague hands him a small, green, newly-shot bird and asks, "What is it?" O'Neill turns the bird over in his hands for a minute, then responds calmly: "It's nothing. It's something new." And it was.

Wild Echoes

Bergman, Charles (1990: Alaska Northwest Books, 322pp.)
Bergman, an environmentalist, recounts his efforts in search of

North America's most endangered animals, including the probably-extinct ivory-billed woodpecker, the Florida panther, and the black-footed ferret. Bergman manages the difficult trick of writing a very personal, often poignant, book that is also informative and highly educational.

Great White Shark

Ellis, Richard, and John E. McCosker (1991, HarperCollins Publishers, 270pp.)

Ellis, along with marine biologist McCosker, collected every known fact about the sea's most feared predator in this thoroughly illustrated, referenced, and readable book. The authors discuss the truth about the largest documented white shark ever caught. Setting aside unverifiable accounts or photographs with nothing for scale, the authors believe the record is about 22 feet (6.7m) long. Another chapter is devoted to the claims that *C. megalodon* might still be alive, something the authors reject. Fascinating reading.

The Call of the Siren

Dietz, Tim (1992: Fulcrum Publishing, 216pp.)

This is a well-written and affectionate book on the manatee and its relatives. Dietz pays special attention to the Florida manatee, an animal I loved to see when I lived in that state: it is basically Nature's imitation of a floating leather sofa. He includes a good discussion of Steller's sea cow and its possible survival.

The Diversity of Life

Wilson, Edmund (1992: Harvard University Press, 440pp.)

It's a reflection of the pre-internet era that I bought this book almost entirely for a short discussion of new mammal species I knew from no other source. Of course, I was immediately drawn into Wilson's scholarly, yet lively, exploration of life. He writes masterfully of the evolution, adaptation, radiation, speciation, interdependence, extinction, and endangerment of the world's plants and animals. A second edition published in 2010 included a new preface.

Finders, Keepers: Treasures and Oddities of Natural History

Purcell, Rosamond, and Stephen Jay Gould (1992: W. W. Norton & Company, 155pp.)

Paleontologist Gould and photographer Purcell offer a fascinating look at the natural history collections of eight collectors from different nations whose work spanned three centuries. The photographs are beautiful and often haunting.

Everyone knows of Louis Agassiz, but I'd not heard of Philip Franz von Siebold, the only Western naturalist allowed to do research in the closed Japan of the 1800s. Mary Anning is here, and so is her lesser-known collaborator Tom Hawkins, described as "unpleasant, litigious, and probably insane." Here we meet Peter the Great, who bought entire collections from leading naturalists and institutions, and Walter Rothschild, who collected birds of paradise wherever they lived while some species were being wiped out by the hat trade. The wasteful collecting methods of naturalists who wanted every specimen they could get and wealthy men who wanted one of everything to stock a *wunderkammer* (cabinet of wonders) are decried today. Gould only touches on this and quotes Ernst Mayr about how such mass collections did yield some benefits, the example being how Rothschild's bird blitz provided later scientists with specimens of all ages, sexes, stages of molt, etc.

Another famous name is Eugen Dubois. He is remembered for describing *Homo erectus* and then keeping the remains locked up for a quarter-century. His often-overlooked life's work, though, was the study of primate brains of all species and eras. An even stranger figure is Frederik Ruysch, Peter the Great's preparator, a man of astonishing skill but disturbing if not depraved sensibilities. Purcell's photographs of everything from ammonites to foxes to brain casts display the enduring results of this phase of natural history.

This is a book about remarkable, often obsessed people and what they gathered from the natural world. The famously agnostic Gould quotes the Bible in describing how men thought themselves on a holy quest in a sacred occupation. As bizarre as that seems to us, it was a very real motivation. Gould touches on the colonial aspect of collecting, but only briefly: his interest is in the thinking of the people involved and the massive collections they made, the foundations of many modern museums.

A Shadow and a Song: The Struggle to Save an Endangered Species

Walters, Mark Jerome (1992: Chelsea Green Publishing, 238pp.)

A poignant chronicle of the decline and extinction of the dusky seaside sparrow. Walters also explores the controversial and still somewhat mysterious events that brought an end to the efforts to save the dusky.

Dolphins and Porpoises: A Worldwide Guide

Sylvestre, Jean-Pierre (1993: Sterling Publishing, 159pp.)

Thorough treatment of the world's small cetaceans. Included are such cryptozoological tidbits as a possible dwarf spinner dolphin, anomalous killer whales, and species whose identity is in dispute. (There is no newer edition.)

Kingdom of Might: The World's Big Cats

Brakefield, Tom (1993: Voyageur Press, 154pp.)

A fascinating and sumptuously illustrated tour of the great cats. Brakefield also discusses feline hybrids and the color variations of each species. Cryptozoologists will be disappointed by what's missing: there is nothing on the marozi (spotted lion), onza, or other problematical cats. There's a new book by José R. Castelló called *Felids and Hyenas of the World: Wildcats, Panthers, Lynx, Pumas, Ocelots, Caracals, and Relatives* (2020: Princeton, 280pp.) that looks good, but I've not yet gotten my paws on it.

The Lizard Man Speaks

Pianka, Eric (1994: University of Texas Press, 179pp.)

The search for small animals, including insects, is sometimes referred to as "microcryptozoolgy." Whatever animals most interest the reader, this book is worthwhile, detailing the entertaining and informative adventures of a herpetologist on his collecting trips. The reader will learn a great deal about lizards, and Pianka includes the stories of his discovery and classification of several new species.

The Tribe of Tiger

Thomas, Elizabeth Marshall (1994: Simon and Schuster, 240pp.)

Thomas' fascinating, if sometimes speculative, look at the world's variety of cats contains information about the "extinct" Eastern cougar, including Thomas' personal sighting. Also: you'll never look at your domestic tabby the same way again.

Mammals of New Guinea

Flannery, Tim (1995: Cornell University Press, 538pp.)

Flannery collects all the known mammals of the New Guinea region, including many recent finds. Of special interest is Flannery's account of his search for the newest tree kangaroo, the *dingiso*. This sizable mammal was not confirmed by science until Flannery collected the first specimens in 1994. Flannery also includes sections describing the region's geography, ecology, and paleontology.

Rarest of the Rare: Vanishing Animals, Timeless Worlds

Ackerman, Diane (1995: Random House, 184pp.)

In this beautifully written travelogue, Ackerman goes in search of some of the rarest animals in the world. Of special interest is her voyage to the island of Torishima to see the short-tailed albatross (*Diomedea albatrus*), which was declared extinct in 1949 but clung to an extremely precarious existence on this speck of volcanic rock. Ackerman (who is also a published poet: try *Jaguar of Sweet Laughter* [Vintage, 1993]) displays a vivid, magical writing style that brings the reader irresistibly along on her adventures.

From the deserts of Namibia to the razor-backed Himalayas, there are wonderful creatures that have roamed the Earth much longer than we, creatures that not only are worthy of our respect but could teach us about ourselves. – Diane Ackerman, *Rarest of the Rare*

Whales, Dolphins, and Porpoises: The Visual Guide to All the World's Cetaceans

Carwardine, Mark (1995: Doring Kindersley, 256pp.)

A well-written and superbly illustrated guide, including two cryptic species. Martin Camm's illustrations include a speculative drawing of *Mesoplodon* (or *Indopacetus*) *pacificus*, at the time of publication known only from two skulls and a few unconfirmed sightings, and one of "Species A," the mysterious beaked whale of the Eastern Tropical Pacific [originally thought a new species but later determined, in another example of successful scientific detective work, to be the adult of *M. peruvianus*]. A quarter-century later, Carwardine followed this up with a new book, reviewed separately.

Mammals of Australia

Strahan, Ronald (editor) (1996: Smithsonian Institution Press, 756pp.)

This massive reference work is indispensable to those seeking crypto-marsupials. It provides a good portrait of the "extinct" thylacine and offers an authoritative compendium of the animals recently discovered or rediscovered in Australia. [There is a still larger 2008 edition.]

The Pictorial Guide to the Living Primates

Rowe, Noel (1996: Pogonias Press, 263pp.)

This handbook offers brief, well-written descriptions of all known primate species, good illustrations, and range maps, plus an explanation of the taxonomic issues concerning each species—it's surprising how many species' taxonomy remains unsettled. Accurate but not too technical for the lay reader, this is a first-rate addition to anyone's reference shelf. (There have been no new editions since 1997.)

The Science Times Book of Fish

Wade, Nicholas (editor) (1997: Lyons Press, 288pp.)

This collection of New York *Times* articles on aquatic life offers several items of interest to the cryptozoologist. They include articles on our favorite fish, the coelacanth, the many bizarre new species brought up from the Amazon, and new freshwater fishes from Brazil. This last article introduces biologist Michael Goulding, who has described 400 new species. (There is no newer edition.)

The Search for the Giant Squid

Ellis, Richard (1998: Lyons Press, 322pp.)

Cryptozoologists love the giant squid because it's a huge, weird, seemingly impossible monster that persisted in being real. Ellis has searched exhaustively through the literature and lore of the squid, and the result is a highly readable and informative work. Looking at the favorite question of how big *Architeuthis dux* gets, he concludes, "we don't know." He can't vouch for any squid reaching over 60 feet (8.3 m), including the long tentacles, but he includes an intriguing sighting report at the end that makes him wonder. As always with an Ellis book, the bibliography is worth the price of the entire work: this one is 38 pages. A superb contribution.

The Great Auk

Fuller, Errol (1999: Harry N. Abrams, 420pp.)

Beautifully written, sumptuously illustrated homage to the Great Auk (*Alca impennis*), one of the world's most famous extinct birds. Fuller believes a few birds probably survived the species' presumed demise in 1844, but the scattered sightings after that date provide no real hope the bird still lives.

Mammals of Madagascar

Garbutt, Nick (1999: Yale University Press, 320pp.)

A thorough, well-illustrated guidebook that includes everything from taxonomy to viewing opportunities for every known species of living mammal on the island. Garbutt also covers extinct species but does not mention any of the reports concerning "extinct" mammals which might possibly survive.

The Private Life of Sharks

Bright, Michael (1999: Robson Books, 285pp.)

Bright has three books in this collection, and this is his best. It's a fascinating look at the animals everyone living near the ocean fears and wonders about. If the book doesn't allow for examination of every species (there are other catalog-type books for that), it presents all the largest and best-known types with a sprinkling of the wee ones. Shark history, behavior, and physiology is covered, and a major section explores the vagaries of shark attacks on humans. This is a great addition to your marine zoology bookshelf.

The Science Times Book of Mammals

Wade, Nicholas (editor) (1999: Lyons Press, 288pp.)

This entry in the valuable *New York Times* series includes 47 articles on mammals. Of special interest are pieces on David Oren's search for the reported ground sloth of the Amazon and the rediscovery of the woolly flying squirrel. (There is no newer edition.)

Walker's Primates of the World

Nowak, Ronald (1999: Johns Hopkins University Press, 224pp.)

A fact-packed reference from one of the world's leading authorities, this book provides information on 282 living and recently extinct species. Nowak is also the author of the broader reference book, *Walker's Mammals of the World*, which is widely considered the Bible of mammalogy. (There is no newer edition of *Primates*.)

Antelopes, Deer, and Relatives: Fossil Record, Behavioral Ecology, Systematics, and Conservation

Vrba, Elisabeth, and George Schaller (editors) (2000: Yale University Press, 341pp.)

A scholarly collection of papers and essays on all aspects of the title subject. The book includes two papers covering the new and rediscovered species in Southeast Asia.

The Astonishing Elephant

Alexander, Shana (2000: Random House, 320pp.)

What will stick me from this book is not so much the elephants themselves (fascinating as they are) but the story of how humans and elephants interacted and how science uncovered the mysteries of this great beast. Alexander traces the human use of captive elephants, from wars through circuses to more humane environments like Disney's open-space Animal Kingdom. Most startling here are the horrid events in the post-Reconstruction United States, when oft-mistreated circus elephants killed dozens of people. Humans disproportionately killed "problem" elephants, often in inhumane ways, until almost all circus elephants were Asian females.

On the positive side, Alexander describes the slow, patient research that told us how elephants really live and how intelligent they are. She includes the 1984 discovery made when acoustic biologist Katherine Payne, used to the study of whales, noticed the vibrations from low-frequency vocalization by a captive elephant. The ensuing research showed elephants can communicate by infrasound even when miles apart. She also describes the work of how to induce elephant breeding, natural and artificial, and the poaching she felt might make it more necessary despite hopeful protective steps. The takeaway for me is how, for millennia, humans kept, used, hunted, and studied elephants without learning some of the most important things about them.

If elephants didn't exist, you couldn't invent one. They belong to a small group of living things, so unlikely they challenge credulity and common sense. – Lyall Watson, naturalist and biologist

Hope is the Thing with Feathers: A Personal Chronicle of Vanished Birds

Cokinos, Christopher (2000: J.P. Tarcher, 352pp.)

Eloquent story of Cokinos' investigation of the disappearance of six North American birds, including the heath hen, the Labrador duck, and the passenger pigeon. He also explores the not-quite-confirmed extinction of the ivory-billed woodpecker. Cokinos, a nature writer and poet, hopes the woodpecker has not vanished forever and recounts sighting reports of ivory-bills as recent as 1999.

The Sibley Guide to Birds

Sibley, David (2000: Alfred A. Knopf, 544pp.)

This time focused on the birds of North America (U.S. and Canada) has a mind-numbing 7,000 drawings, paintings, and maps by Sibley. The mind reels even as the eye feasts on concise depictions and descriptions of birds, including field marks and other suggestions to help birders identify them.

Matt's Musings: I bought Sibley's books as a pair when I had some freelance assignments for a nature encyclopedia to create entries and range maps for auks and storks. It's surprising to think that, only 20 years ago, I colored in the range maps for a reference book by hand (although an artist reworked them later). I worked with my bird-biologist friend Dr. Cherie McCollough in writing the descriptions. Cherie, now Chair of the Department of Life Sciences, Texas A&M University-Corpus Christi, has provided vital advice on much of my zoology-related work.

Beyond the Last Village: A Journey of Discovery in Asia's Forbidden Wilderness

Rabinowitz, Alan (2001: Island Press, 336pp.)

Dr. Rabinowitz, one of the great conservationists of the past half-century, here recounts his travels and discoveries in Myanmar. His effort to study animal life, especially in the northern rainforest region, not only found many rare species but gave him an understanding of the area's ecosystems and people he writes about with equal passion. Cryptozoologists most often think of him as the scientific discoverer of the leaf muntjac, *Muntiacus putaoensis*. It was a complete surprise to Rabinowitz when, in 1997, he saw very small muntjac skulls kept as trophies and then met a hunter with a freshly-killed specimen.

There's a lot in here for us armchair types who wonder how arduous exploration of this kind really is. Rabinowitz tells how his party spent two months tramping 250 miles into unsurveyed territory, where most of them got pneumonia and Rabinowitz limped along with a serious knee injury. His team documented the presence of many rare species, and their work helped create the vast Hkakabo Razi National Park. Rabinowitz had many other accomplishments, including leading efforts to conserve his beloved jaguars and leopards, and this book is a perfect introduction to the man and his mission.

It is very rare, once you've been told about an animal and its habits, to then never find anything tangible. – Alan Rabinowitz, zoologist, on Sasquatch

A Gap in Nature: Discovering the World's Extinct Animals

Flannery, Tim, and Peter Schouten (2001: Atlantic Monthly Press, 184pp.)

A well-written and thought-provoking look at some of the mammals, birds, and reptiles definitely (or almost definitely) lost to the world since 1500. Beautifully illustrated with paintings by Schouten.

The Sibley Guide to Bird Life and Behavior

Sibley, David, *et al.* (editors) (2001: Alfred A. Knopf, 608pp.)

This book, assembled with many contributing ornithologists or other experts, describes 80 families of birds found in the U.S. and Canada. The value for those just starting to understand birds (as I was) is the 100-page exploration of birds as a group—anatomy, flight, behavior, intelligence, hybridization, classification, evolution, and much more. More such information is provided on each family discussed.

A Certain Curve of Horn: The Hundred-Year Quest for the Giant Sable Antelope of Angola

Walker, John (2002: Atlantic Monthly Press, 320pp.)

John Frederick Walker, an accomplished journalist, explores conservation, politics, hunting ethics, and other topics in the course of telling the story of the giant sable antelope. This distinctive subspecies of the sable antelope, instantly identifiable by its curving five-foot horns, was thought possibly extinct before its rediscovery in 2002.

National Audubon Society Guide to Marine Mammals of the World

Reeves, Randall, *et al.* (2002: Alfred A. Knopf, 528pp.)

This is a thorough, sumptuously illustrated work covering all the marine mammals. Includes interesting recent developments on the classification of the cetaceans. The lack of a bibliography is the only shortcoming. [There is a 2009 edition.]

The New Zoo

Shuker, Karl (2002: House of Stratus, 304pp.)

An updated and expanded revision of Shuker's 1993 *The Lost Ark*, this book brought the story of new and rediscovered animals up to date but adds much cryptozoological material and a large collection of illustrations. Very hard to find in hardcopy.

Search for the Golden Moon Bear: Science and Adventure in Pursuit of a New Species

Montgomery, Sy (2002: Simon and Schuster, 336pp.)

Naturalist/writer Montgomery recounts her adventurous travels with biologist Gary Galbreath through Southeast Asia in search of a rare bruin with a stunning golden coat. The animal is an occasional variant of the Asian black bear, and individuals show a variety of colors. Both authors think the mix of reports and descriptions of the region's bears may include evidence of a new species. A beautifully written travelogue as well as a book full of zoological information and discoveries, it also makes heartbreakingly clear there may be few further discoveries in Laos itself. Every animal of value in the country, they write, is being poached toward extinction.

Wild Cats of the World

Alderton, David (2003: Facts on File, 192pp.)
A thorough compendium of cat lore and cat taxonomy for the general reader. All known species are here, along with a good discussion of the peculiar hybrid called the Kellas cat. Excellent photographs, range maps, etc.

No Turning Back: The Life and Death of Animal Species

Ellis, Richard (2004: HarperCollins, 428pp.)
Ellis' book on animal extinctions is readable, thought-provoking, and thoroughly researched, with some interesting tidbits for the cryptozoologist. It's quite a challenge to cover the whole topic of extinction, and some things are necessarily left out, but Ellis traces the modern cascade of extinctions and also finds space for a discussion of "back-breeding" efforts like those in the 1930s involving the Heck brothers' recreation of the auroch. Ellis holds out no hope for species like the ivory-bill woodpecker and the Tasmanian tiger (thylacine). He explains what has been going on with cetaceans, where new species pop up while at least three plunge toward the extinction horizon. He discusses some other recent discoveries and rediscoveries as well. Ellis includes 41 pages of references and adds

some footnotes throughout the book. Naturalists, cryptozoologists, and zoologists will all want to read this one.

The Carolina Parakeet: Glimpses of a Vanished Bird

Snyder, Noel (2004: Princeton University Press, 176pp.)
   The first detailed account of the only native parrot of the United States. Snyder challenges the conventional wisdom that the bird was wiped out by hunting (disease may have played a bigger role) and presents sighting reports and other evidence indicating the species lingered for decades beyond its official 1914 extinction.

Crocodiles and Alligators of the World

Alderton, David, and Bruce Tanner (Photographer) (2004: Facts on File, 192pp.)
   This book is an approachable, very well-illustrated guide to all the known types, including modern finds such as the 2000 rediscovery of the Siamese crocodile (*Crocodylus siamensis*). The past ten years have included a rush of new discoveries, and these are covered in a well-reviewed book I've not yet read, Colin Stevenson's *Crocodiles of the World: The Alligators, Caimans, Crocodiles, and Gharials of the World* (2019: New Holland Publishers, 176pp.)

Matt's Musings: Crocodile finds have continued at a surprising pace for such large animals. Examples include the Central African slender-snouted crocodile, Mecistops leptorhynchus (described 2018) and Crocodylus suchus, described in 1807 but synonymized with the Nile Crocodile C. niloticus until 2011 when it was reconfirmed as a unique species. Then came Crocodylus halli from New Guinea (2019), first diagnosed from a museum specimen and confirmed by examples already in captivity, living in Florida's St. Augustine Alligator Farm Zoological Park.

Seals and Sea Lions of the World

Bonner, Nigel (2004: Facts on File, 224pp.)

Bonner has written an authoritative guide to the known pinnipeds for junior high school students on up. Items of special interest include two species thought extinct but rediscovered, the Juan Fernandez and Guadeloupe fur seals; two in imminent danger, the Hawaiian and Mediterranean monk seals; and two which appear extinct, the Japanese sea lion and the Caribbean monk seal. (There is no newer edition.)

Tasmanian Tiger: The Tragic Tale of How the World Lost Its Most Mysterious Predator

Owen, David (2004: Johns Hopkins, 228pp.)

Owen presents a comprehensive account of what we know about the thylacine's biology, behavior, and so on, weaving in the tale of its unfortunate interaction with human beings. He discusses the animal's two extinctions: the first on the Australian mainland, the second on Tasmania. Owen includes a discussion of recent sightings and the proposals to bring back the tiger via cloning.

Singing Whales and Flying Squid: The Discovery of Marine Life

Ellis, Richard (2006: Lyons Press, 288pp.)

In some ways, this book feels more like two short books with some overlap. The first book is a history of marine exploration, with an emphasis on marine biology. The second focuses more on how fragile and endangered marine life is. Both halves are good, but in a work of 288 pages, they leave the reader wanting more of both subjects.

What is here is first-rate. Ellis is a good writer, able to explain fairly technical concepts in friendly language, and he's very knowledgeable about his subjects. His excellent drawings and paintings bring his subjects to life. Even the reader well-versed in marine literature will learn something: one eye-opener, for example, is how the old stories of swordfish attacking whales turned out to be true, although the reasons for such pointless (or pointed, from the whale's point of view) attacks are still a complete mystery. Ellis does not focus just on the charismatic animals: he gives the clearest explanation of the food web at the bottom of the ocean that I have read in a popular book.

Not surprisingly, there are sections in here on Ellis' favorite creatures, the giant squid and the cetaceans. I had hoped for a bit more on the beaked whales, particularly the Mesoplodon Species A and Species B mysteries. (The Species A mystery has since been solved.)

Of interest to cryptozoologists, Ellis notes that the bizarre seven-meter (23-foot) "elbow squid" has not yet been formally described, despite several videos, because no holotype was in hand. Ellis opts not to visit the subject of "sea serpents," which he has done in other books. He tosses off cryptozoology with a misstated aside on negative evidence, saying cryptozoologists point out that "because no one has ever seen a Sasquatch doesn't mean there aren't any." I wonder if "seen" is an editing mistake and he meant "caught." Overall, this is a very valuable book, something which will draw more people into the splendor of the oceans while painlessly introducing the science. I think it's clear that is precisely Ellis' purpose, and he accomplishes it in an exemplary fashion.

Whales, Dolphins, and Other Marine Mammals of the World

Shirihai, Hadoram, and Brett Jarrett (2006: Princeton Field Guides, 384pp.)

A lovely book packed with details and excellent illustrations. I'm always fascinated by the gaps remaining in our knowledge of marine mammals—who is related to who, what varieties (possibly species) are not yet clarified, where ranges might extend, etc. —and this book provides food for thought in almost every entry. It's not the kind of book you'd sit down and read straight through, but it's the kind you definitely want close at hand when doing any kind of research or writing on cetaceans, pinnipeds, and the rest.

A New Human: The Startling Discovery and Strange Story of the "Hobbits" of Flores, Indonesia

Morwood, Mike, and Penny van Oosterzee (2007: Smithsonian, 272pp.)

The Indonesian island of Flores was just another spot in a vast archipelago until it became the locus of a scientific earthquake. Lead discoverer Mike Morwood here tells the story of *Homo floresiensis* from his point of view. The Ling Bua cave and the diminutive LB1, a woman who apparently died only 18,000 years ago [a date since moved back to at least 60,000], is a fascinating tale of intuition, research, scientific and academic rivalry, and grinding hard work. In 2003, the team was elated to find the lower jaw of a "child" and then dumbfounded when they saw worn adult teeth.

The archaeology and paleontology involved are well described. Morwood explains why this area was interesting, geographically and geologically, as a place to look for the first Asians to island-hop to Australia. He also takes us through the customs and cultures of this vast archipelago, from a ritual bullwhip contest to minibuses that vie to be the loudest means of transportation on Earth.

Morwood's team's claim of a new human species, one that looks like none other and challenges not just our history but what it means to be human, set off an international carnival. LB1's brain size is mid-range for a chimpanzee. It wasn't considered possible for primates with 380 cubic centimeters (cc) of grey matter (one later paper says 417 ccs) to build fires, make stone tools, and undertake cooperative hunting of large animals. But they did. An apparent example of "island dwarfing," which once gave the world pony-sized elephants, apparently reshaped a species more closely related to its African ancestor than to the only known early hominid of Indonesia, *Homo erectus*.

One of the interesting post-discovery episodes here is the path to publication. It can take months to run the peer-review gauntlet and well over a year to publish in a journal like *Nature*. But as whispers curl around the edges of their closely-held story, threatening to ignite it and let someone else name the species first, Morwood and the editors at *Nature* do things on an unprecedented schedule, ramming the paper through peer review and publishing it in October 2004, seven months from the time Morwood first approached them. (Morwood's team considered naming the species *Homo hobbitus*, chortling about academic conferences discussing hobbits, but were eventually dissuaded.)

LB1 (there were bits of 12-13 individuals found, but LB1 had the only cranium, and there was only one other lower jaw) lived a hard life, but nothing could have prepared her for this. Unconvinced, scientists describe her as a *Homo sapiens* with microcephaly or one of three other suggested maladies. As nationalist and academic feelings clash, bones are taken without authorization for dating; an Indonesian institute lets underskilled preparers take latex molds, damaging the priceless bones; Morwood's US-British-Australian-Indonesian team is accused of "neocolonial" fossil-hunting; and Morwood hears intriguing tales of the *ebu gogo*, the little people who supposedly inhabit Flores to this day.

By the end of the book, the reader will, along with Morwood, experience relief when the species is established and the intellectual arguments won, even though the bones remain contested and locked away. Morwood died in 2013, having seen his species widely accepted after much controversy. The search for more "hobbits" goes on. (There is an updated edition of this book, which came out in 2009.)

. . .

Matt's Musings: At a 2015 cryptozoology conference, biologist/TV host Pat Spain told us Morwood had evidence the species survived into the 1920s. At this writing, Morwood's papers are still locked up in Indonesia, science held hostage to disputes about ownership and jurisdiction.

Every Living Thing: Man's Obsessive Quest to Catalog Life, from Nanobacteria to New Monkeys

Dunn, Rob (2008: Smithsonian, 288pp.)

This is a book that does what great science writing is supposed to do—explain the universe while enthralling the reader. In exploring how the definitions and scope of the living world have been expanded over and over again by dedicated researchers, Rob Dunn gives us compelling portraits of biological scientists who have proposed "crazy" theories, made inconvenient observations, and otherwise risked their reputations and sometimes their lives in the pursuit of knowledge. Dunn shows that, while being laughed at by a majority of one's scientific colleagues is no guarantee of being right, it's far from a surefire indicator of being wrong.

We don't know all the animals in the world, not by a long shot, and it's not just the little arthropods that are still being discovered. Dunn explores this theme and many related ones here. He anchors the book in his own experiences in the Amazon, where no one has any idea of the number of animal and plant species present, let alone what to name them. He also passes along the intriguing story of what may be an unknown and very large type of spider monkey, which is intriguing because cryptozoologists have collected numerous reports of something with the same description.

Dunn closes with the fascinating discoveries being made in the "deep biosphere"—the microbes that live miles beneath the Earth. Life on the surface, he notes, may in some ways be the exception. This is a profound work, not just concerning the biological sciences but concerning science as an enterprise.

Wild Blue: A Natural History of the World's Largest Animal

Bortolotti, Dan (2008: Thomas Dunne Books, 336pp.)

Cryptozoologists who investigate reports of truly enormous marine creatures would do well to look at the largest one we know, and *Wild Blue* is simply a great book in every way. It introduces us to a mammal we know surprisingly little about, despite said mammal's status as the largest creature ever to live on Earth. The author is outstanding at explaining cetacean biology, scientific principles, technology, and so on without ever losing his sense of wonder. He also introduces us to the key figures in blue whale research and lets us know what motivates them.

Bortolotti tackles the always-present question: how big do they get? While 33m and up has been claimed, he reports that about 30m is the longest validated measurement, with the largest whales approaching 182 metric tons. He also looks into taxonomy: the once-controversial pygmy blue whale has largely been accepted as a subspecies, but there's plenty of debate about how many subspecies there are, what populations intermix, etc.

Wild Blue is scientifically exacting yet always accessible to the nonspecialist reader. This will stand for a long time as the definitive work on its subject.

Naming Nature: The Clash Between Instinct and Science

Yoon, Carol Kaesuk (2009: W.W. Norton & Company, 341pp.)

Cryptozoologists have a strong interest in how different cultures label and group animals. Biologist and top-flight science writer Carol Kaesuk Yoon embraces the concept of a near-universal human way of perceiving nature, the *umwelt*, originating from our ancient hunter-gatherer experience. The Linnaean approach is a bedrock technique for imposing order on the *umwelt* by deciding what animal goes where, and she gives a lively history of the major figures while foreshadowing the advent of cladistics. Darwin thought natural selection would perfect taxonomy and end disputes.

We are, Yoon thinks, hard-wired to think about animals and nature a great deal, even as small children, and to notice types of animals. A toddler who has seen only a few dogs of very different breeds can still tell that a dog new to them is a dog and not a cat. Animals, too, can distinguish between types of other animals: witness the fact that monkeys have different cries to warn of different predators.

Yoon goes on to describe the birth of molecular taxonomy based on the chemistry of each organism, and then RNA and DNA, then to cladistics. All of them, Yoon thinks, are valid but also move us further from the *umwelt* and the human experience of animals.

The biggest impact of cladistics, to the lay reader, is the seemingly irrational claim that there's no such thing as "a fish:" rather, there are superficially similar tetrapods that may have had very different ancestries. The lungfish (her example) may be closer to the cow than the salmon. She offers the radical notion that this technique should move us to throw out existing taxonomy except where it aligns with cladistics.

The abandonment of the *umwelt*, Yoon writes, brings precision but loses the connection between humans and the natural world. She accepts the importance of taxonomy but argues the now-dominant science of comparing molecules or DNA "has left us blind to our own view of the living world." If animals are reduced to molecules and proteins, how much will we care to protect them?

She discusses as an example the way people once thought of whales as fish (one need only consult Melville for an example). This view, while scientifically inaccurate, has value in understanding the *umwelt* and should not be forgotten. Yoon also defends actual fish and considers that species are, to human senses, "the things we cannot help but see."

For cryptozoologists, the book contributes to the longstanding debate about how well local cultures know their animal neighbors. There are published examples of indigenous people, especially farming-centered as opposed to hunting-centered cultures, whose members don't know all the local fauna. Yoon offers numerous examples to the contrary, although she recognizes that need is a major driver of delineation. Indigenous cultures in Indonesia and the Philippines have some 600 groups of animals and plants. A striking example from the botany side is that, for the Tzeltal Mayans, it's not unusual for four-year-olds to be able to name almost a hundred plants. In this book, Yoon does not just describe a science: she makes us think about what science is and how it affects us. Her 295 endnotes provide a good basis for further research on the topic.

Nature! ... She is ever shaping new forms: what is, has never yet been; what has been, comes not again. Everything is new, and yet nought but the old.
Johann Wolfgang von Goethe

100 Heartbeats: The Race to Save Earth's Most Endangered Species

Corwin, Jeff (2009: Rodale Press, 336pp.)

I thought of Corwin as a good TV host and knowledgeable biologist. It turns out he's also a good writer. This book presents his experiences with some of the world's rarest wildlife. The title refers to the "100 Heartbeats Club," made up of species with fewer than 100 known survivors.

Corwin recounts here his own stories and some scary reports and statistics. He covers some causes and effects we might not always think of, like what the popularity of plastic wine corks means for the Spanish lynx.

One anecdote that stands out is his almost spiritual chance encounter with a Florida panther. "It broke through the leaves and, seemingly in slow motion, floated to the ground. It was darker than the panthers I'd seen in photos, more charcoal than sage."

There are stories of hope here, too. I knew the Mauritius kestrel had just barely been saved from extinction. I did not know the

International Council for Bird Preservation actually sent a scientist to shut down the rescue effort, but he found a way to revive it instead.

Corwin is sure the thylacine is extinct, although he allows himself a bit of hope about someday resurrecting it from DNA. He ends the book by asking everyone to look around for ways they can contribute to conservation. "Most things start small," he writes.

This is a book presenting good science to a broad audience. Corwin can occasionally be a little condescending (we know what an icebreaker is, Jeff), but that's minor. A glossary, thorough endnotes, and a bibliography complete a book that appeals to both reason and emotion.

World Ocean Census

Crist, Darlene Trew, with Gail Scowcroft, James Harding Jr., and Sylvia Earle (2009: Firefly Books, 256pp.).

World Ocean Census may be a dull title for a book, but this volume on the findings of the ongoing (as of the publication date) Census of Marine Life is just wonderful. Clearly and skillfully written, the text conveys both the science and the wonder of undersea exploration. Sections on everything from ancient fisheries to how new species are named (and how many new ones we are finding) flesh out the basic narrative.

There is a trove of material here about newly-discovered species and the way they are being discovered. When one contributor to the Census, Richard Pyle, dives to the "twilight zone" where the last surface light is fading out, "he finds new fish species at the rate of about *seven per hour* of observation." (Italics mine). The project estimates that while three-fourths of the world's marine fishes have been described, that leaves 5,000 still unknown. We also know very little about most ocean dwellers—their habits, migrations, and numbers. The estimate here is that we have good data on only the 200 or so fish, whales, and mollusks which are commercially important. The project is a shining example of international cooperation and the use of new tools like the ability to sequence DNA on board a research ship.

Then we get to the photos. I simply run out of superlatives in trying to describe the photographs in this book. It's not too strong to say the book reminded me, in this age of video and CGI, how evocative still photographs could be. I smiled at one (p.206) of a Hawaiian monk seal in exactly the classic "mistaken mermaid" posture, with flippers held across its chest at the waterline.

The book is a visual feast and a superb collection of information. New and weird species, photographed with astonishing clarity, pop out from almost every page. It's hard to imagine how this book could have been better. It's also hard to imagine a better book for introducing people to the fascination, diversity, and fragility of the ocean world.

Deep Blue Home: An Intimate Ecology of Our Wild Ocean

Whitty, Julia (2010: Houghton Mifflin Publishing, 246pp.)

Whitty, an environmentalist, is a wonderful writer in a class with Diane Ackerman when it comes to vivid descriptions and you-are-there evocations of time and place.

Whitty starts on Isla Rasa in the Sea of Cortez, a global center of seabird nesting and an example of difficult but successful conservation efforts. Later trips venture into the Pacific, the North Atlantic, and even the high desert of Mexico.

Whitty has a lot to tell us about the creatures of the great waters. Did you know hermit crabs are the basis for a moving community of other invertebrates totaling over 500 species? Or that some Pacific rockfish live over 200 years, a span more than doubled by the quahog *Artica islandia*?

The language will stay with you. Hordes of spawning capelin at the Newfoundland shore are "turning the waves into polished silver purses that roll ashore and spill their wriggling treasure onto the beach." At a Pacific cold seep called Hydrate Ridge, "the mud on the bottom of the sea is more alive than dead," with an amazing density of invertebrates. Working on a marine research ship, she learns that calling a specimen "interesting" is a cautious yet excited way of saying "possible new species."

Whitty deals with rough waters, drunken sailors, and a sperm whale that comes right at her while she's swimming until she has to look up and down to see the whole head. *Deep Blue Home* is a voyage home, and you'll remember the journey.

Eels: An Exploration, from New Zealand to the Sargasso, of the World's Most Mysterious Fish

Prosek, James (2010: HarperCollins, 310pp.)

Eels are endlessly interesting to cryptozoologists. There are still mysteries about them, and it's possible known or unknown species have grown large enough to be reported as "monsters." Prosek takes us around the world, meeting several types of eels and the people who catch, study, or revere them. He thinks the longfin eel of New Zealand approaches 3 meters (10 feet) and is startled by a huge one whose head looks ancient, gnarled, and evil. The book is as much about cultural connections and environmental threats to eels as it is to the animals, but it's a fascinating trip.

Fishes of the Open Ocean: A Natural History and Illustrated Guide

Pepperell, Julian (2010: University of Chicago, 272pp.)

Cryptozoology doesn't pay much attention to fish unless they are very large and unusual. I wonder what might be missing as a result of this oversight. No one thinks we've found them all. While most new species come from freshwater, a reference to pelagic fishes is a useful thing. This is a good one, authoritative, beautifully illustrated, and with good explanations of the oceanic food web and ecology. Pepperell, a marine biologist, spends the most time on the gamefishes and large fishes in general, but 160 species from the unicorn leatherjacket to the puffers get in. On the oarfish, he says the largest he's seen in photos look to be only 6.5 meters (21 feet) or so and the accounts of 11 meters (36 feet) and up are dubious. It's a great book if fishes draw your interest.

If you need a superb visual dictionary with excellent photos of hundreds of species, add:

Fishes: A Guide to Their Diversity

Hastings, Philip, with Harold Walker Jr. and Grantly Galland (2015: University of California, 336pp.) There are some 33,000 known species of fish, so no one book can capture them, but this is an excellent starting point if you need to figure out what a caught, stranded, or reported fish might be.

Kingdom Under Glass: A Tale of Obsession, Adventure, and One Man's Quest to Preserve the World's Great Animals

Kirk, Jay (2010: Henry Holt, 387pp.)

    I wanted to like this book more than I did. The subject is fascinating: Carl Akeley, the pioneering taxidermist/conservationist who mounted Jumbo the elephant and created the museum diorama. He also found time to lobby successfully for the world's first gorilla sanctuary when not hunting with Theodore Roosevelt or strangling a leopard with his bare hands. The strength of the book is the characters. Kirk re-creates a colorful cast of men and women who supported, opposed or exploited Akeley throughout his amazing life. Along the way, the reader will learn much about taxidermy and the safari culture of the early 20th century. Kirk succeeds, quite skillfully, in making the reader see, hear, and smell the world of colonial Africa.

    The negative here is the author's use of a "creative nonfiction" approach for "narrative flow." I doubt any author can give us the innermost thoughts of people from another era, and countless biographers have produced compelling narratives without needing that gimmick. Also, this is a book that demands a good photo section, something that is peculiarly absent.

Bottom line: not what I hoped for, but still an informative picture of hunters and wildlife on what was then called the Dark Continent.

Octopus: The Ocean's Intelligent Invertebrate

Mather, Jennifer, with Roland Anderson and James Wood (2010: Timber Press, 240pp.)

I included more than one octopus book because the animals are of great interest to cryptozoologists. The authors, all experts, repeatedly mention unknown species: no one thinks we're anywhere close to describing all the octopuses. These cephalopods are also adaptive, cosmopolitan, and uncannily smart. To answer everyone's favorite question, Roland Anderson once found a Pacific giant he estimated at 45 kilograms (110 pounds) with suckers three inches across and believes the species gets to 180 kilograms (400 pounds). That's intimidating, given that a 60-pound (27-kilogram) specimen in an aquarium killed meter-long dogfish sharks. Octopuses can "pinch" their suckers with such dexterity they can untie knots in surgical silk thread or employ their suckers to resist a pull of 100 times their body weight. Their camouflage is too complex to describe, complicating the "what species was that?" question. The authors mention an "undescribed Hawaiian species" that uses the same shapeshifting tricks as the famous mimic octopus. There are fascinating facts on every page here.

Demon Fish: Travels Through the Hidden World of Sharks

Eilperin, Juliet (2011: Pantheon, 320pp.)

Nature books with a lot of first-hand reporting in them can get chatty, preachy, or precious. Juliet Eilperin avoids these traps in her engrossing exploration of sharks and humans. She recounts her visits with shark callers, shark hunters, and many others, weaving them into a book that's both a natural history and a meditation on the changing ways humans think of, and alter, the natural world. This is not a book that goes into great detail about the history of sharks and the hundreds of species. Instead, Eilperin presents her facts judiciously, walking the fine line between too much and too little detail to enrich her narrative. I thought I was well-read on sharks, but I learned a lot here, especially about the challenges of shark conservation and the incredibly wasteful shark fin soup trade. Eilperin hits hard on the fact that taking the apex predators out of any ecosystem has long-lasting, broad, and maybe irreversible effects. I would have liked a little more information on how frequently this happens with sharks and how. (Humans kill well over half a million sharks per day.) That's a quibble, though. This is an excellent book that should, as the author clearly intends, add momentum to recent efforts to better understand and protect these ancient predators.

The Great Sperm Whale: A Natural History of the Ocean's Most Magnificent and Mysterious Creature

Ellis, Richard (2011: University of Kansas, 384pp.)

Herman Melville said of the sperm whale, "Of all the great whales, his is an unwritten life." Not anymore. I'm a fan of Ellis' writing, so it was no surprise that I loved this book. Yet I had no idea just how bizarre *Physeter macrocephalus* really is. It has countless features (like the single forward spout) that don't appear in other whales and a nose/spermaceti organ so weird it belongs on a creature from another planet. It wasn't until the present century that scientists really explored the startling way sperm whales hunt squid in darkness by finding and then stunning them with sound. The sperm's evolution is well-traced, showing many transitional forms (including the fearsome *Livyatan melvillei*), but there is still a lot we don't know.

As always with an Ellis book, this one is a mini-reference library, with a bibliography running 23 pages. Also, as always, Ellis' own drawings and paintings bring the whale to life in a way the photographic record can't quite capture. Everyone is curious about how big the whale gets. Ellis rejects the idea that bull sperms were historically larger than the 62-foot modern record, but he admits that a pair of 11-inch teeth in a museum (8 inches is big) make one wonder just what the all-time record was. Ellis does not mention one oddity, the old reports of aberrant sperm whales with true dorsal fins.

The occasional wrong word and repetitive paragraph slipped through the editing of this book. Ellis gives Charles Townsend's estimate of the casualties of New England Yankee whaling on page 238 but doesn't point out that it's drastically wrong until page 291. This is unfortunately true of some other Ellis books, like *Swordfish* (University of Chicago Press, 2013).

The sperm whale really is, as Ellis says, "The ocean's most magnificent and mysterious creature." Pick up this remarkable book and meet the monarch of the seas.

Kraken: The Curious, Exciting, and Slightly Disturbing Science of Squid

Williams, Wendy (2011: Abrams Image, 224pp.)

Williams, a science and environmental writer, has presented a fun, engaging, and generally fascinating look at the cephalopods. Squid get most of the ink, but she spends time with the octopuses, especially the giant Pacific octopus and the cuttlefishes as well. Cephalopods, it seems, have been with us for a half-billion years, thumbing their noses at extinction events (if they had thumbs or noses) while evolving some alien and remarkable features. These include skins capable of amazing changes of hue—though cephalopods cannot see color—and brains that are, in essence, distributed through the arms as well as the central gray matter.

One topic that fascinates Williams is the question of intelligence. Cephalopods are the smartest invertebrates on Earth, but how do they compare with mammals, and how can we even figure that out with a creature whose intelligence is so different from ours? There are even passing mentions of some tidbits for the cryptozoologists: she notes a claim of a Pacific octopus weighing 600 pounds (272kg) and a hotly-disputed theory that there may have been an octopus with a 150-foot arm spread (shades of *Octopus giganteus*.) This book will hold your attention like a tentacle holds a fish.

Barefoot Through the Amazon - On the Path of Evolution

Van Roosmalen, Marc (2013: CreateSpace Independent Publishing, 500pp.)

Dr. Marc van Roosmalen has lived a life you might think obsolete: that of an explorer of remote lands who has discovered numerous animal species and believes he has several more in the queue. From a 1976 study of monkeys in Suriname through his long labors in Brazil, van Roosmalen has worked with a minimum of support from the "civilized world." Staying in the brush many times until the local animals and local peoples became used to him, he discovered things no aerial survey or quick river trip could have uncovered. He's an expert in the plants of the rainforest as well as the animals. This book, taking us chronologically through his adventures in a sumptuously illustrated fashion, includes not just stories of species but explanations of how the rainforest ecology works. The highlights, though, are the new species. It was 1996 when a man brought him an undescribed pygmy marmoset that became the first of many species—some of which were given to him with no clue about where they originally came from. He also kept a dwarf porcupine as a pet, uncertain for a while whether it was a new species (it was). He had to rewrite the monkey genus *Callicebus* to accommodate some of the new forms. You'll meet his new spider monkey, giant peccary, and his dwarf manatee (most specialists reject it, but van Roosmalen doesn't retreat). Then there's the new brocket deer and a subspecies or color morph that van Roosmalen feels he's very close to proving: the white-throated solid black jaguar. His is a fascinating journey.

The Natural History Museum Book of Animal Records

Carwardine, Mark (2013: Firefly, 256pp.)

The book is colorful, readable, and has an intriguing collection of odd records (the fastest-digging monotreme is the echidna, just in case someone asks) along with the usual biggest, heaviest, smallest, and so on. It adds up to some 900 records from all over the animal kingdom. Carwardine is a veteran of wildlife books (I have his *Whales, Dolphins and Porpoises* and the touching *Last Chance to See*, with Douglas Adams) and is qualified to undertake this endeavor. Most of the time, his details are accurate, and they are certainly interesting.

Since I have a special interest in marine animals, it was cool to spend some time with the largest pinniped (a southern elephant seal caught in 1913 weighed an estimated 4,000 kg) and the fastest of the seals (the leopard seal's ability to leap onto a floe 2 m (6.5 feet) above the water indicates a launch speed of 22 km/hr.). On the sirenian side, did you know the Florida manatee has been known to migrate 850 km?

When it gets to records, the whales, of course, grab most of the superlatives. The biggest sperm whale brain weighed was 9.2 kilograms. A blue whale caught in 1931 was weighed in pieces: with an estimate added for lost blood [6.5 metric tons(mt)], the whole whale weighed a stupendous 199 mt. The dominant ocean vertebrates, in numbers, are the fishes, and we learn plenty of nuggets about them. The top location for shark bites in the years 2000-2011 is Florida (281). There is the occasional moment of clunky writing: e.g., coelacanths "have been dubbed as 'living fossils.'" There is also the occasional mistake. The claim marine biologists in 1963 saw an oarfish 15m long is flat wrong: the animal was a nearly-transparent invertebrate. The author gives a maximum weight of 272kg for the Pacific giant octopus, a number disputed in other references, though he adds a cautious note disputing the monster *Octopus giganteus* once believed to have been stranded in 1896. Also, speaking of the invertebrates, they get short-changed a bit here: there are only 41 pages on them, despite their vastly outnumbering the vertebrates.

This book has no sources. No footnotes, no endnotes, no bibliography. With them, the book could have been terrific: instead, it's always interesting but not as authoritative as it should be.

The Extreme Life of the Sea

Palumbi, Stephen, and Anthony Palumbi (2014: Princeton University Press, 240pp.)

The sea's most fascinating creatures and their habits are on full display in this exploration of recent discoveries about everything from the great whales to the tiniest invertebrates. I read a lot in this genre, and yet I learned something on almost every page. Worked into this narrative is a great deal of information on ocean conservation and the threats to marine life. Finally, the style works perfectly: the authors make it fun and sometimes humorous without losing the respect and awe due to the creatures of the sea. It's hard to imagine how this book could be much better.

The Rarest Bird in the World: The Search for the Nechisar Nightjar

Head, Vernon (2015: Pegasus Books, 242pp.)

Head, a leading South African bird conservationist, takes three companions into Ethiopia looking for a bird known only by one wing found in 1990. That's it: there were no sightings. The species was described, and the wing lay in a drawer for years until ornithologist Ian Sinclair happened across it. No one knew what the whole bird looked like or how its call sounded. All they had was a starting location. The expedition did get its sightings, but they didn't get the bird, and Head discusses what constitutes evidence in birding and in biology in general. He also discusses distribution, hybrids, ring species, and many other topics vital to a basic understanding of these dinosaur descendants.

Head goes on to ask what rarity means and what species might hold the always-temporary title of "world's rarest bird." One example, New Zealand's black stilt, has begun mating with other species, which Head describes as "selling its genes into oblivion." There are species not seen in decades, species known, like the nightjar, from one specimen, and in the end, no one can say. Head himself has gone in search of the white-chested tinkerbird, collected in Zambia in 1964 and never reported again, but come up empty. Head also discusses conservation successes that have taken some birds out of contention for "rarest." Head's writing is memorable, if sometimes too flowery, and this book will be read for a long time.

Whales, Dolphins, and Porpoises: A Natural History and Species Guide

Berta, Annalisa, editor (2015: University of Chicago Press, 288pp.)

In this overview of the cetacean world, Professor Berta and her colleagues provide all kinds of solid, up-to-date information, from whale biology and evolution to feeding behaviors to range maps and field marks, with at least a page devoted to each of the 89 then-known species. Recent entrants like Daraniyagala's beaked whale, Omura's whale, the Australian snubfin dolphin, and the narrow-ridged finless porpoise are all here. An interesting line in the long-finned pilot whale (*Globicephala melas*) entry (by Jessica Aschettino, one of 37 named contributors) is "*G. m. un-named subspecies.*" The killer whale section (by Robert Pitman) lists the animal as a single species with "at least six distinct ecotypes that may, in fact, represent different species or subspecies." I have two quibbles here: killer whales deserve more than two pages, and there should be illustrations, at least silhouettes, of the differences between ecotypes. Uncertainty about the exact delineations of minke whales, Bryde's whale, and others are also mentioned. For you beaked whale fans, there are 22 species described in a section written by Randall Reeves.

The oversize hardcover book is beautiful as well as informative. Photographs and other illustrations are plentiful and well-labeled. The text is authoritative but highly readable to the nonexpert. The only caution I offer is about the physical book. The binding feels flimsy and the pages don't lie flat, so handle it with care. This book is a magnificent achievement and a very useful reference.

The Lives of Hawai'i's Dolphins and Whales: Natural History and Conservation

Baird, Robin (2016: University of Hawaii Press, 352pp.)

This is the only regional cetacean book I included, and I did so because it gives a good idea of how cetacean research is done and how (and what) we learn.

This look at the cetaceans that live around the Hawai'ian chain is well organized, well written, and stunningly illustrated. Dr. Baird includes contact maps that show which species are likely to be where according to location and depth, and which ones are residents and which only transit the area.

We landlubbers sometimes think of the ocean as a single entity and an island as a big rock. Not so. This area of the Pacific is a kind of desert and the island chain an oasis that alters currents, temperatures, phytoplankton populations, etc., influencing the suitability of the area to seven species of baleen whales and eighteen toothed whales (including dolphins). The species descriptions are fascinating. I had no idea that killer whales not only engage in a game of "pass the dead fish" but include visiting humans in the game, or that a sperm whale once rammed and sunk a 40-foot (18-m) yacht for reasons completely unknown. The descriptions of the enigmatic beaked whales are especially informative.

Sex in the Sea: Our Intimate Connection with Sex-Changing Fish, Romantic Lobsters, Kinky Squid, and Other Salty Erotica of the Deep

Hardt, Marah (St. Martin's Press, 2016: 288pp.)

To understand the ocean ecosystem and its countless living components, it's important to understand how marine creatures reproduce. Ecologist Marah Hardt takes us on a trip from fish orgies right to whale threesomes, from species whose organs are practically invisible to the whale penis that chased researchers around inside a boat (I am not making that up).

Some species need precise conditions that human actions increasingly interfere with. Some synchronize their activities based on cues we've been unable to identify. Some produce one offspring at a time, others many thousands.

A lobster courting a female will spread his claws as if bowing until the female taps him on each shoulder: it's weirdly like being knighted. Meanwhile, our smiling friends, the dolphins, may go in for gang rape. Bone worm males are so tiny they live in the females' bodies: in proportion, a male human would shrink to the size of an aspirin tablet.

All these details are fun and fascinating, but Hardt never lets us forget they are part of a story: of the endless inventiveness of evolution, of the ever-present drive to survive, and of the interconnectedness of life in great oceans, from the microbes to the monsters. A terrific and thought-provoking book.

The Soul of an Octopus: A Surprising Exploration into the Wonder of Consciousness

Montgomery, Sy (2016: Atria Books, 261pp.)

Montgomery, a lyrically beautiful writer, recounts her personal efforts to study and connect with octopuses. The level of connection and the intelligence and emotional range displayed by the octopuses is startling. (I didn't know octopuses liked to watch cartoons.

Montgomery does not say whether they preferred, say, SpongeBob to Mickey Mouse.) If you want to understand how these creatures think, this is the book.

The Lost Species: Great Expeditions in the Collections of Natural History Museums

Kemp, Christopher (2017: University of Chicago Press, 250pp.)

Early in this fascinating book, Kemp writes that "Taxonomists and biologists describe about eighteen thousand new species each year." He mentions later that over 1,000 species were named from New Guinea *in a decade*.

Many of these (most, for some orders) are discovered in museum collections, not in the field. As Kemp shows, those aren't just obscure frogs or small invertebrates. Stories of museum discoveries (some supplemented by fieldwork once the specimens were uncovered) include all types. For mammals, we have the impossibly cute *olinguito* (*Bassaricyon neblina*), a raccoon relative from Colombia and Ecuador), the little black tapir, the Arfak pygmy bandicoot, frogs, turtles, tarantulas. It gets crazy when we get to the beetles: American institutions alone hold some one billion specimens, with thousands of species yet to be described.

Kemp opens this superb book with an explanation of why fleshing out the taxonomy of museum specimens is so important. Whether a frog lives on both sides of a river or the frogs on the other side have developed into a new species provides a great deal of information on speciation, the environment, and the actions needed to preserve them.

In the case of the little black tapir, a student in a Brazilian institution came to her supervising scientist with a tapir skull, telling him this one looked different from its drawer-mates. It was. It was eventually matched to a tapir skull Theodore Roosevelt had collected in 1903 (T.R. had also noticed it was odd) and led to research in the wild to study live specimens. The American Museum of Natural

History has 250,000 specimens of just one mammalian order (*Chiroptera*, the bats) and no one knows how many species that might add to the 1,300 now described. There is a trading network humming all the time between institutions, where photos, 3D images, CAT scans, specimens themselves, and facts and opinions about them go back and forth.

This is arduous work. Many specimens, especially older ones, may have been mislabeled in the field or mislabeled when they arrive, or simply left to look at later: decades or centuries may lapse. The care and inventory of collections is underfunded and some specimens are literally piled up.

A good example of the challenges involved is biologist Laura Marsh's effort to revise the saki monkeys (genus *Pithecia*). She went to 36 museums in 17 countries to study 876 skins and 690 skulls. At the Zoologische Staatssammlung in Munich, a curator pointed to a pile of monkey skins 6 feet (1.8 m) high and told her to look through it. (March ended up revising the whole genus, adding five new species and re-establishing three disputed or synonymized ones.)

Then there's the scarcity of taxonomic expertise. In particular, there are not nearly enough people who can differentiate insects. Kemp visited two scientists who had developed, through decades of work, an almost mystical ability to recognize new or different species from thousands of specimens. They can't entirely explain how they do it, although one is helping develop a computer program to at least partially automate the process.

Kemp also shows us that it's not always the specimen itself that is the discovery. A shell collected in Indonesia around 1894 was next examined in 2007 by a scientist who found an artificial pattern of scratches on it: it is 500,000 years old and the first evidence of prehumans making art.

American zoologist Kristofer Helgen, who found the first *olinguito* skull in a Field Museum collection, was part of the team that named the skywalker gibbon (*Hoolock tianxing*) in 2017 from a holotype collected by Roy Chapman Andrews in 1913. A paleontologist at the British Geological Society opened an old cabinet in 2011 and found specimens on glass slides never inspected in the 160 years since Charles Darwin collected them. Collections thus hold not only specimens but much of the history of the biological sciences.

Kemp closes with another explanation of the importance of preserving and studying these collections. Collections can identify what the historic range of a species was and how it has changed. Specimens of species most affected by climate change can indicate when conditions in their habitat were altered. Finally, they can tell us about extinctions.

A last note on content: Helgen also says he knows of 50 mammal specimens that haven't been described yet.

This is an important, unique, and accessible book: Kemp's writing and his explanations are good enough that I never once had to stop and look up a term. There are thorough endnotes. I was puzzled by the absence in his examples of the famous giant gecko (*Hoplodactylus delcourti*) discovery, and I wanted many more illustrations. Overall, though, I loved this book. Looking at old specimens with labels like "Argentina, 1900" isn't as exciting as tramping through Tasmania looking for thylacines, but sometimes it's where the action is.

Birds New to Science: 50 Years of Avian Discoveries

Brewer, David (2018: Christopher Helm Publishers, 415pp.)

This is a really amazing book, discussing hundreds of birds discovered in the sixty years prior to its publication. There are great illustrations of every species, with plenty of description and an explanation of their unique features. Brewer adds extras such as an explanation of the species concept. In addition to the wonderful ornithology, this book has certain interesting features for cryptozoologists. For example, Brewer's stories of how the different animals were located, confirmed, and described provide a great review of how biological science works with new species. Brewer includes species that no longer are considered valid and 50 species or apparent species which have yet to be described as of 2018.

The author looks at the current controversy over whether a physical specimen needs to be in hand (bird in a hand, see what I did there?) to be described, and he includes a very extensive bibliography of the kind that more writers should at least attempt. Brewer's writing is clear and interesting throughout. This is a must-have book whether your specialty is ornithology or the broader topic of how species are found and described.

Eye of the Shoal: A Fishwatcher's Guide to Life, the Ocean and Everything

Scales, Helen (2018: Bloomsbury Publishing, 320pp.)

Scales, a marine biologist, is a prolific writer on all matters marine. Based on this book, I've put all her works on my list. In *Eye of the Shoal*, she pulls off the amazing feat of introducing the fishes in one short volume. Scales begins with the favorite question, "What is a fish?" and moves on through types, ancestry, habitats, and so much more. This is no boring recitation, though: Scales writes clearly and engagingly, working in the adventures and studies of ichthyologists, traditional stories from many cultures, and some cool illustrations. There are no endnotes, but she provides a good bibliography for each chapter.

Orca: How We Came to Know and Love the Ocean's Greatest Predator

Colby, Jason (2018: Oxford University Press, 408pp.)

The killer whale is an important beast to cryptozoologists, illustrating how we can assume an animal is one species and only much later realize it's not. (This ignorance has created serious problems in captivity, where animals were thought very similar and thus compatible but weren't.) We generally condemn orca catching now, but what did the men who first captured whales think? Colby talked to men like Ted Griffin (who caught the original Namu) who started the industry. Colby's major contribution here is to record how captive orcas came to be "a thing" and how their image evolved as a result. It's a valuable book.

Spying on Whales: The Past, Present, and Future of Earth's Most Awesome Creatures

Pyenson, Nick (2018: Viking Press, 322pp.)

This is a superbly written one-volume introduction to whales through the personal experiences of the author's adventures, whether the whales in question are fossilized (the author is a paleontologist and the fossil marine mammal curator at the Smithsonian) or living individuals.

He describes numerous challenges in the fossil-hunting field, like trying to get a stunning bonanza of fossils weighing countless tons out of Chile before the area was bulldozed, and smaller but memorable moments like having his four-year-old son discover a fossil whale skull.

He relates his first adventure in trying to tag a whale (he did) and (despite his ethical qualms) studying carcasses at an Icelandic whaling station. There he and a colleague discovered that, despite centuries of killing whales, some species had a sensory organ connecting the jawbones at the tip that was not only undescribed in the literature but was a *type* of organ never described in any animal. (Think of it as a jelly doughnut with fibers [papillae] inside, all of which grow out of one side and connect to the other side.) It's amazing how recent much of our knowledge of whales is and how much we have yet to learn.

When trying to understand the behavior of whales, he explains how we don't know what "natural" behavior for the great whales looks like. No one knows how feeding, diet, migration, ranges, etc., looked like before humans started the wholesale slaughter and later brought serious acoustic disturbance to the oceans.

Pyenson effectively traces the failure of conservation efforts until recent decades and the problems whales still face. He also recounts being part of the fundamental work of figuring out the nutrients vs. metabolic costs involved in feeding. It turns out blue whales are as big as whales can be: any bigger, and the energy expended to feed can't be adequately recouped.

His work on this topic is also a reminder of how the sciences can cross-fertilize each other. When trying to understand how whales' pleated throats expanded and contracted, the whale scientists brought in Jean Piven, who designed parachutes, to help calculate how the throat expanded, what the energy expended was, etc. Pyenson also describes the information gained from his fossils at the Smithsonian, explaining technical, biological terms and functions in language non-experts can understand. While Pyenson doesn't try to cover every species, I ended up with a much better idea of what a whale really is and why whales look and act as they do. A marvelous achievement.

Ahab's Rolling Sea: A Natural History of Moby-Dick

King, Richard (2019: University of Chicago Press, 430pp.)

As an aficionado who's read *Moby-Dick* four times (yes, really), I found this a marvelous book. King takes us through Melville's tale and shows what parts of the natural science were accurate, which were misunderstood, and which were fictitious. He writes very well and includes chapters on navigation, weather, and other topics, but the greatest value of this book for this library is the way King looks at all the creatures appearing in Melville's narrative, from giant squids to barnacles, and explains what we do and don't know about them. (Ishmael described a monster squid as "furlongs in length and breadth," or at least 400 meters (1,320 feet) in each dimension!) King writes that current size estimates for the giant and colossal squid are trending upward, though not to the degree mentioned by Melville. However, he studies a famed museum specimen called Archie and finds himself "unexpectedly underwhelmed."

While King says Melville's novel is, to him, more about "the living ocean" than Captain Ahab and his monomania, this book works as both an up-to-date primer on marine science and a relatively painless introduction to Melville. King also contrasts Melville with other historical accounts and with literature like Coleridge's "Rime of the Ancient Mariner." King seems to have read everything written on Melville and also introduces us to experts who explain things like what species of sharks appear in *Moby-Dick*. King also spends considerable time tying the novel's themes into current concerns like environmentalism. This book will teach the reader a great deal about oceanic life and quite a bit about Melville, his era, and what a complex and awesome achievement his novel really is.

The Book of Eels: Our Enduring Fascination with the Most Mysterious Creature in the Natural World

Svensson, Patrik (2019: ECCO, 241pp.)

This is a unique book by an author who mingles eel science with his own story of growing up in Sweden hunting them with his father. This book relates humanity's attempts to understand these mysterious fishes. Svensson begins on the science side with Aristotle, who described eels accurately but could not figure out their reproductive process: he finally, perhaps in desperation, wrote they were born from the mud. As we follow the very slow unraveling of the eel secrets by human scientists, we learn that, among other things, Sigmund Freud spent a year dissecting eels. The hero of the story is Danish marine biologist Johanne Schmidt, who went all over the Atlantic Ocean catching thousands of eels as he strove to understand where they were born and where they died. We think today that the answers are most likely lie in the region known as the Sargasso Sea. However, eels keep a shroud of mystery wrapped around them: while our tracking of their movements as larvae and as adults shows they swim to and from the Sargasso Sea, no one has caught an eel of any age there. He writes, "a scientifically minded optimist would say it's just a matter of time." He also notes, however, that time may run out. Eels are overfished, and *decades* of effort by Japanese experts to farm them have proven a costly and frustrating failure. Svensson's philosophical observations can go a bit far afield, such as when he quotes scripture about faith in Jesus having something to do with the belief in the mystery and importance of eels. He does not attempt to explore all the species of eels, focusing mainly on those in the Atlantic and does not address some topics like the maximum size to which eels can grow. This is as much a personal journey as it is a study of the eel's journey.

Becoming Wild (2020: Henry Holt & Company, 368pp.)

Beyond Words (2015: Henry Holt & Company, 480pp.)

Safina, Carl

Anyone searching for new or "extinct" vertebrates should try to understand something of their behavior, communication, and intelligence. What is revealed in these two recent works by Dr. Carl Safina is astonishing. The animals we spend time with include elephants, chimps, scarlet macaws, killer whales, sperm whales, and wolves. Safina hits hard on the idea that not only do animals have communications that we can't decipher, but there is also communication we don't even know is taking place. Intelligence, sentience, and the need to engage in play are just some of the things Safina believes are much more widely distributed in the animal kingdom than we thought. For example, forget everything you know about wolf hierarchy and pack structure: there's no real "alpha." Sperm whales have such distinct "voices" that one scientist Safina visits can pick out individuals with unaided ears. Chimp bands are as different as human societies: one that makes certain tools and lives in a strict dominance hierarchy may live next to one which makes different tools for the same tasks and employs a more relaxed, informal structure. "Culture" is a word Safina uses a lot: if a group of animals does the same thing for generations or makes a change that is then picked up by everyone in the group, that is culture, shared and passed on as in humans. (One of the pioneering books in this field was John Bonner's *The Evolution of Culture in Animals* [Princeton, 1980], which postulated that evolutionary pressures encourage and perpetuate successful cultural developments.) Amateurs like myself can't turn themselves into trained zoologists or biologists, but books like this enable us to understand the complexity of the world we're analyzing and how much we don't know about the species we seek to study.

Some people talk to animals. Not many listen though. That's the problem. – A. A. Milne, author

Handbook of Whales, Dolphins, and Porpoises of the World

Carwardine, Mark (2020: Princeton University Press, 528pp.)

This is a monumental piece of work, with a thousand-plus illustrations by Martin Camm and others, a short "quick ID" guide, profiles of the species (about 450 pages of that), a good glossary, a long list of scientists who contributed, a species index, etc., although the bibliography is oddly short. The newest beaked whale, the *karasu* or dwarf Baird's beaked whale) is included. Carwardine also mentions the uncertainties about classifying some species and subspecies. He includes known variants that can make identification uncertain (short-finned pilot whales and Risso's dolphins that are brown instead of gray, Atlantic spotted dolphins without the spots, and many more). Killer whales get 25 pages of coverage, including all ecotypes (some of which may be species) with their ranges and distinctive marks. Carwardine has reset the standard for a portable one-volume reference with extensive information on spotting and identifying cetaceans at sea by appearance, behavior, spouts, flukes, etc. If you're interested in cetacean identity, species, reported types, questions, etc., you need this book.

Owls of the Eastern Ice: A Quest to Find and Save the World's Largest Owl

Slaght, Jonathan (2020: Farrar, Straus, and Giroux, 348pp.)

Blackiston's fish owl is the world's biggest and rarest owl. It has a wingspan approaching two meters (6.6 feet)and a fluffy, shaggy appearance that Slaght likens to a juvenile bear with feathers glued on. It's scattered in pockets of Russia, China, and Japan, keeping to sections of old-growth forest with large nesting trees and streams or rivers that don't freeze over. The total population is perhaps 2,000. Most of the world doesn't even know it's there: I've read nature books all my life and barely recognized the name.

In Russia, where the species was confirmed to nest only in 1971, it clusters along the Pacific coast. That's where Slaght, the son of diplomats and a good speaker of Russian, joined Russian scientists to find the owls, document locations, and attach GPS tags to as many as possible.

This is a book about spending months at a time, stretched over five years of hard work, in unforgiving terrain where humans keep an eye out for the Amur tiger, the huge brown bear, and the armed and dangerous poacher. Slaght, working with a rotating cast including Sergey Surmach of the Federal Scientific Center of the East Asian Terrestrial Biodiversity and Sergey Avedeuk of the Amur-Ussuri Center for Avian Diversity, set out using snowmobiles and a massive ex-military four-wheel truck to probe areas where roads are terrible (if they exist at all) and where a Western scientist is a sight rarer than the owl. Here in Russia's Primorsky Krai (Maritime Territory), they also face dangers from the land itself: fires in summer and freezing in the infamous Russian winters. They have many failures before devising a trap that works for the wily birds.

He writes, too, of the emotional peaks and valleys inherent in chasing something that may be vanishing. Slaght is an excellent writer, and people, owls, and the terrain come alive here.

Much of the owl habitat is being logged, and regulations and enforcement are spotty in this remote area. Deciding that a large wildlife preserve is politically difficult, affecting too many people's livelihoods, Slaght focuses instead on pinpointing the owls' locations and habitat needs to pursue more focused protection. He negotiates with companies and officials about leaving certain trees and areas alone and scores some successes. At the end of the book, he is cautiously optimistic. Slaght, a man who puts his life where his heart is, continues his work today with the Wildlife Conservation Society's Russia program.

Fieldwork is often regular repetition of challenging or unpleasant activities, an application of persistent pressure to a question until the answer finally emerges. – John Slaght, biologist, *Owls of the Eastern Ice*

Oxford Dictionary of Zoology

Allaby, Michael (2020: Oxford University Press, 736pp.)

This book is always handy and often indispensable. I've owned three editions. This one drops the cross-indexing of scientific and common names in the text but puts them in an appendix where you can look up the common name to find the scientific one. There are some 6,000 entries from "abductor muscles" to "hypurals" (enlarged ribs supporting the caudal fin of some bony fishes, but you knew that), to "Sciuromorpha" (a suborder of "more primitive" rodents) to the "zygomatic arch" or "zygoma," the bone that runs from beneath the orbit toward the back of the skull. The paperback is low-priced and a must for zoological research.

Monarchs of the Sea: The Extraordinary 500-Million-Year History of Cephalopods

Staaf, Danna (2020: The Experiment, 237pp.)

This book traces the origins of today's cephalopods, with excursions into the side branches like the ammonites that once flourished and are now forgotten. We learn, for example, that the origins of squid remain fuzzy because the ammonia they had developed for buoyancy essentially dissolved their tissue and thus any chance to leave imprint fossils. This is not the book if you want to know all the species, ranges, and so forth: invertebrate biologist Staaf is concerned here with where these creatures came from and how they developed their various features. From the first cephalopods that left the seafloor to drift over it like UFOs, reaching down for trilobites, to the giants of today, their evolution is far more complex and fascinating than I had realized. The language is sometimes fairly technical: while Staaf sprinkles discovery stories and wit into the mix, this is a book you really need to sit down and read, not just dip into. She speculates the development of modern squid and whales led to an arms race: the whales developing echolocation to hunt squid, the squid developing smaller "pens" (the internal shell that stiffens their bodies) to reduce their sonar echo.

Staaf also offers her opinions on the stories of monster cephalopods. She grants the giant squid a relatively modest length of 42 feet (12.8 m) overall, the colossal squid 32 (9.8 m), and the Pacific giant octopus a tentacle spread of 10 feet (3 m) and a weight of 156 pounds (7.8 kg). This generally follows the famous "Sizing Ocean Giants" paper by Craig McClain *et al.* from 2015, although the paper notes observations of much larger octopuses.

Staaf does not believe any squid has ever attacked a boat or hurt a human. She deplores the way one facetious remark by one scientist is still fomenting global headlines about how cephalopods are aliens from another world. This well-referenced book offers a solid grounding for any further study of the cephalopods.

Strange Sea Creatures

Hoyt, Erich (2020: Firefly Books, 112pp.)

Hoyt is an experienced writer on marine life. In this short but beautiful book of undersea photography with accompanying text, he showcases the work of several photographers in capturing animals both famous and obscure, including some recent discoveries. The book is divided by depth, with sections on Surface Waters of the Ocean at Night, Middle to Deep Dark Waters, and The Continental Shelf to the Abyssal Plain.

Still Alive: A Wild Life of Rediscovery

Galante, Forrest (2021: Hatchette Book Group, 238pp.)

This is a rousing tale of adventure and discovery. Galante hosts the TV program *Extinct or Alive?* and, as described here, has found some surprising answers to the title question while dealing with storms, disease, corruption, and all the other impediments to learning whether a particular species or subspecies is still with us.

The book starts with his rewarding childhood of outdoor exploration in Zimbabwe, which becomes a deadly hell in a political upheaval. Relocated to California, Galante earns a degree in wildlife biology only to find it's not a ticket to adventure. Instead, he's employed in necessary but mind-sapping jobs pulling weeds and counting ants. His break came when his ability to find edibles in the wild helped him in a TV competition program, *Naked and Afraid*, leading to his career in television.

The meat of the book is, of course, the hunt for animals whose current existence is doubtful or dismissed. This has exciting but also humorous moments, as when Galante dives in dangerous conditions searching for a missing African shark while his zoologist wife strolls along the beach with a photograph of the species and finds one for sale. He marvels at his own successes: the odds of finding something missing for decades in a two-week expedition are, despite extensive preparation, vanishingly small. His proudest moments are filming the Zanzibar leopard (*Panthera pardus adersi*) and locating a Fernandina Giant Tortoise (*Chelonoidis phantasticus*), a Galapagos Islands animal last seen in 1906.

Galante writes that biologists from the Galapagos Conservancy who was with him looking for the tortoise have unfairly downgraded his role to merely filming the discovery. This brings up an important topic. This is Galante's book and his account. Other writers and scientists have disputed some details, such as his claim of credit for the rediscovery of the Rio Apaporis caiman (*Caiman crocodilus apaporiensis*). (An important footnote on this animal is that Galante believes samples he collected show it's not as originally thought a subspecies, but a species in its own right.)

While cryptozoologists celebrate his demonstrations of how "presumed extinct" can turn out to be different from "extinct extinct," his only mention of the field is dismissive, and he has no interest in looking for Bigfoot. (He has appeared on a Bigfoot podcast, where he offered friendly advice for searching out evidence but didn't offer to join the search.) It can be argued that what Galante does *is* cryptozoology, no matter the terminology, but it can also be argued this is the kind of "mainstream zoology" work that shows cryptozoology isn't necessary.

Galante says a couple of times he's redefined "extinction" or changed the way it's declared, which is an overreach given that most of his finds had not officially been declared extinct. He also discusses other activities like catching a human-eating crocodile (the end of that tale will startle you) and documenting "wet markets" and the brutal Faroe Islands pilot whale drive. As a gadget lover, I enjoyed reading how he and his team (Galante does a good job of crediting his crew) jury-rigged gear or made on-the-spot changes of plan to pursue success. The book has a good photo section, but I would have liked some maps and an index.

SECTION 3
CRYPTO-FICTION

  The human mind enjoys impressive visions of unearthly creatures.

— JULES VERNE, *TWENTY THOUSAND LEAGUES UNDER THE SEA*

Cryptozoological fiction has a long history. There's no doubt tales of monsters predate the written word. Early humans hardly needed to make up tales as they tangled with cave bears, cave lions, saber-toothed cats, and the other predators of their day, but dragons and great serpents and sea monsters became staples of the storyteller's art. History and myth became interwoven as the Chinese told of dragons while Native Americans spoke of the thunderbird and Kraken haunted the sagas of Norsemen.

The genre has never been healthier, in quantity or quality. That is, assuming we can define crypto-fiction. I suggest that if the novel makes an attempt to depict a believable creature with a believable origin, it qualifies, even if those attempts might fall short. If the creature is central to the novel and is alleged to exist, or could exist, in the real world, it probably qualifies.

Good crypto-fiction, first and foremost, must be good fiction. The best crypto-novels are done by people who not only understand science but who tell a good people story. The theme of "ordinary people meeting extraordinary creatures" underlies much of crypto-fiction.

Is there room for more crypto-fiction? Absolutely. There is a glut around Loch Ness and Sasquatch, though the best novels will always find audiences. There are many creatures of fact and legend to work with. Some authors offer unique ideas, as Lee Murphy did with the Honey Island swamp monster mystery in *Heretofore: Unknown* (Defining Moments, 2007). There have only been a few novels probing the rich history of sea serpent sightings/mythology: interesting creatures like the buru, the Kamchatka giant bear, the various amphibious or saber-toothed cats, and many other denizens of cryptozoology remain unvisited except by the crypto-horror novelists who just want to get the beast on stage so it can start the slaughter.

Jules Verne published *The Sea Serpent: The Yarns of Jean Marie Cabidoulin* in 1901, but modern crypto-fiction novels began with Arthur Conan Doyle's **The Lost World**, written in 1912 and still in print.

I don't have a favorite for the single best crypto-novel. I have a Top Three made up of Eric Penz's *Cryptid*, Petru Popescu's *Almost Adam*, and Mira Grant's *Into the Drowning Deep*. My idea of a novel that transcends and transforms its genre is Elizabeth Kostkova's *The Historian* for vampire fiction (I'm not an Anne Rice fan), and these three come close.

Dean Koontz once wrote that novelists can ask a reader to accept one major improbability as long as all the other features of the novel, down to the smallest details, are grounded in reality. That does not rule out some reasonable liberties in geography or history, though.

Then there are the cryptids themselves. A horror writer can invoke the supernatural and get away with almost anything, but a good crypto-fiction author can't. The author has to make the creature(s) seem probable or at least plausible. Improbabilities can sink a tale for me. In James Robert Smith's enjoyable thriller *The*

Flock (Five Star, 2006), I could get past his terror birds' undetected survival but was stopped short by a scene where a critter got a mental image by reading the minds of human hunters.

Sometimes authors gloss over too much. Robert Masello in *Bestiary* (Berkley Publishing, 2006) described his prehistoric survivors well but never explained where they were for millions of years before they ended up in the care of an Iraqi dynasty. Sometimes authors go the other way, throwing a blizzard of scientific jargon at the reader in hopes said reader will thus buy into the creature's reality. An example is Dave Freedman's **Natural Selection** (Hatchette, 2006) which mixes a few real data points and many imaginary ones trying to establish his flying manta rays.

Human characterization is the hardest thing for any novelist to get right. Imagine being alone in the forest when confronted by a Sasquatch. Some of us would stand and stare in fascination: some would reach for a camera or a gun; some would high-tail it out in search of reinforcements. The author needs to think about why this person is in the woods, what shaped their character, and how they would respond.

In some novels, the author offers us a collection of two-dimensional folks who summon no sympathy even dismembered. At the other extreme, Robert Laws is so sure his characters in *Ferocity* will hold the reader's attention that his feline cryptid gets two brief mentions in the first six chapters. Likewise, one of the reasons I admire **Almost Adam** is that Popescu's characters keep us turning the pages even when his australopithecines are off-screen.

Not all characters, of course, are equal. No one wants another round of the skeptic who dismisses everything until the cryptid turns him into *Homo tartare* or the wise old Native who tells the stupid white visitors to stay out of the woods.

The crypto-fiction reader wants to be transported into a setting that is right for the animals involved and feels real to the reader. Eric Penz in **Cryptid** did this superbly, making us see, hear, and smell our surroundings with great skill.

Cryptids show up in all kinds of works, such as Edgar Rice

Burroughs's *Tarzan* series, where his great apes are just one of a horde of unknown species or survivors. There are many other novels that include cryptozoological elements as secondary or even incidental components (Michael Crichton's *Sphere* and Arthur C. Clarke's *The Deep Range*, for example), but I've included only a few such examples here.

There is an enormous amount of unplumbed material in the crypto-world. I once asked cryptid enthusiast and bestselling novelist Jonathan Maberry what creatures or monsters he thought were underused, and he replied that almost nothing outside of North American or European folklore had been written about. "There's hundreds you could use."

The great cryptid tales set up the most interesting kind of people stories—the kind where true character comes out under great stress —and offer the chance to enlighten readers on the scientific plausibility of the entire field of cryptozoology.

My Top Three

Into the Drowning Deep

Grant, Mira (pen name for Seanan McGuire) (2017: Orbit Books, 438pp.)

This is an epic top-quality marine creature novel. It beats most competitors in science, characterization, plot, and/or writing skills, and that makes it one satisfying read.

Many authors have tried to find a believable creature within the mermaid legends, but no one's done it this well. The research ship *Melusine* has been custom-built by the Imagine Network to follow up on mysterious events that overtook a much smaller ship over the Mariana Trench.

The *Melusine* has everything needed for finding, studying, capturing, and/or killing new creatures, although most of the scientists are just piggybacking on that seemingly nonsensical mission to do other research. Cryptozoologist Luis Martines and marine biologist Jillian Toth, though, believe they will find something,

Once in the search area, things get weird. A fatal submersible descent, a crewman, yanked over the side, and bizarre sonar and hydrophone readings are followed by fatal close encounters. One result, rather humorous to read, is a series of clashes between scientists with different motivations, disciplines, and methods. Then the fun is over, as the "sirens" decide this weird floating reef full of edible creatures merits an attack. Their ancestry, anatomy, and capabilities are explored here, and it all feels plausible. Everything goes to hell and the tension goes up and up and up.

I'm not calling this book *the* definitive marine creature thriller, but the science is excellent, the characters are interesting, and the creatures are cool. Grant works in intriguing ideas on everything from deafness to evolution, never preaching but letting the characters speak in ways that make sense.

MATT BILLE

. . .

Matt's Musings: If you're considering a purchase from Seanan McGuire / Mira Grant, know that the author is very sympathetic to cryptozoology. She also, when we've met at conferences, loved my Dunkleosteus collection, so I'm not unbiased. Trust me, though. This is a crypto-epic done right.

Almost Adam

Popescu, Petru (2015: William Morrow and Company, 544pp.)

For Ken Lauder, a paleoanthropologist doing research in Africa, finding some oddly recent-looking Australopithecine fossils is a gateway to adventure and an epic discovery. After much other drama —this book takes time to explore its characters' lives, and they are compelling—Lauder and geologist Ngili Ngiamena find an overlooked spot in the African Rift Valley where human ancestors have hung on. There's a great deal of scientific background presented as Lauder befriends an Australopithecus whose world faces a deadly conflict between the gracile hominins and an aggressive tribe of *Australopithecus robustus*. (This plot idea also appears in John Darnton's *Neanderthal*.) The resulting conflict parallels the Kenyan civil war disrupting humans' lives. This is a terrific book in every sense, not a slam-bang action yarn but one that presents memorable people and sound science. This book entertains even as it draws you deep into the question, "Who is human?"

Cryptid

Penz, Eric (2005: iUniverse, 312pp.)

There's a *lot* to like in this thriller, beginning with the fact that Penz has clearly done his historical and scientific homework.

I am no scholar of the Lewis and Clark period, but Penz's descriptions of this era and the re-created correspondence of the explorers and President Jefferson are convincing as he sets the stage. In the present day, the search for *Gigantopithecus* remains and the search for Sasquatch are neatly brought together in a well-plotted tale that involves a few coincidences, but nothing too unlikely.

While the size of Penz's Sasquatch, nine feet eight inches (3 m) for a subadult male, is impractical, the rest of the ape description works very well. Penz has tried hard to create a scientifically plausible tale of Giganto's evolution and migration. What is really outstanding in Penz's writing is his gift for description. Very few authors can immerse the reader in an environment, and Penz ranks with writers like Barbara Kingsolver on this point. The characters are good, from the dedicated scientist Dr. Ostman (there's a nice nod to Sasquatch history in that name) to the lovers separated by professional ambitions. The Native American hunter feels stereotypical, although he's well-drawn.

The only real mistake here, to me, is entwining the cryptozoology with a large-scale conspiracy stretching back 200 years, completely unknown yet so powerful its agents kill citizens at will.

Penz's writing style is sure-footed: he puts in the scientific and historical background without slowing the story. I greatly enjoyed this book, and I hope Penz has many more novels in him.

Other Crypto-Novels

Meg series

Alten, Steve

Alten famously re-introduced the largest-ever shark, *C. megalodon*, into popular culture. While *Meg* (1997) introduced this universe in a splashy debut and *The Trench* (1999) followed it up, I wasn't taken with the novels: they were fun, and the technology was cool, but I gave them harsh reviews on the science. However, it's the author's setting, and what the reader wants is to see is what stories he can tell in it. *Meg: Primal Waters* (2004) pulls hero Jonas Taylor into a wonderfully over-the-top reality TV show that has, of course, picked the wrong patch of ocean to film in. The Alten universe expanded with the discovery of an ancient sub-seafloor habitat in *Hell's Aquarium* (2009). It's not an easy place to believe in, but the author gets credit for describing the hypothetical geology and paleontology of his scenario.

As prose, this novel's breathless style with lots of dashes and exclamation points is a step below Alten's very good novel *The Loch*). Most of the characters in *Hell's Aquarium* are three-dimensional: Alten started off so-so in this department with *Meg* but has improved. Alten's strength, as always, is action, and there are some real page-turner moments. He also has a knack for incorporating popular culture, like the internet contest naming two captive Megalodons, Mary-Kate and Ashley. (I ask today's readers to trust me when I say this was hilarious in 2009.)

Alten likes to pile on the creatures and maximize their sizes. Well, if Peter Benchley can use a 100-foot squid, Alten can use a 122-foot *Liopleurodon*. I like his 25-foot vampire squid *Vampyroteuthis infernalis* —that would be scary as hell. It's not clear how creatures 360 million years apart ended up in this habitat, although I'll buy anything that brings *Dunkleosteus* on stage. Alten emphasizes there's a complete food web in the "aquarium," although almost everything we meet is a mega predator. All the big Mesozoic reptiles are here (evolved gills and all), along with sharks and even a giant turtle: I thought at one point about the old kaiju film *Destroy All Monsters.*

The level of cooperation and intelligence shown by some of Alten's sharks goes beyond what we know of real sharks, although they've had time to evolve, so go with it. *Hell's Aquarium* is what it's supposed to be, which is fun. It's like going to a *Transformers* film. You came to see the robots in action. You pick up an Alten novel to see the creatures in action. *Hell's Aquarium* definitely gives you what you pay for.

The last novel I've read in this series so far is **Meg: Nightstalkers.** This one is also full of creature action, indeed overstuffed, and chemosynthetic ecosystems aren't nearly as productive as shown. Alten has, though, conjured up invertebrate predators that are among the creepiest, scariest things in all of monster fiction. There is also a science fiction thread that makes sense only if you've read his thriller **Vostok.**

All that said, this is a crowd-pleaser: exotic locations, giant predators, and a mix of heroic and stupid characters getting in and out of hair's-breadth scrapes. Also, Alten turns his fondness for pop culture and reality TV up to 11.

As of 2021, the Meg universe is a seven-book saga, with **Meg: Generations** out and the capper, **Meg: Purgatory**, due out in 2022. The first book returned as **Meg: Revised and Expanded Edition** (2015), which fixed a couple of the scientific problems of the original and improved the characterization.

The Loch

Alten, Steve (2005: Tsunami Books, 496pp.)

This is Alten's best cryptozoology novel. Scottish-born marine biologist Zach Wallace is a lot like Jonas Taylor from the *Meg* series but more screwed up. He's reliant on antidepressants thanks to two near-drownings, the second involving an unclassified marine creature and the famous "Bloop" sound. Then Zack's father is jailed for a murder he insists was committed by the Loch Ness monster. The media, scientists, and others converge on Loch Ness, along with an order of sword-bearing "knights" connected to Robert the Bruce. Wallace has to face his fear of water, self-doubt, and some enormous eels to solve the mystery. The giant-eel solution to Loch Ness was always the most plausible of the "unknown species" theories, and Alten does a good job with it, including an explanation for why the creature hasn't been found before. The "triumphant" moment when Zack throws his antidepressants away with no ill effects made me wince, but I liked this one.

Vostok

Alten, Steve (2015: Next Century Publishing, 416pp.)

Steve Alten's first real science fiction novel is a lot of fun for creature aficionados. This genre-melding entry in Alten's creature sagas uses creatures from ancient whales to giant eels to the biggest crocodile you never want to meet to set the events in motion and bring his characters from the *Meg* series and *The Loch* together. From there, it's a science fiction adventure combining everything from UFOs to conspiracy theories to quantum physics. The science-fiction aspects aren't as much fun to me, but *Vostok* offers plenty of remarkable beasts, beast hunters, and beast-to-beast combat.

Devour

Anderson, Kurt (2016: Pinnacle Books, 400pp.)

Devour is unusual for a crypto-creature novel in that Anderson spends a great deal of time on his humans. His pliosaur is off-screen for whole chapters, mentioned only as a looming shadow over the human drama that occurs on a crippled gambling-excursion ship. In this novel, pliosaurs have always been with us. They have long lives (okay) and hibernate in the ice (less okay). This is one tension-filled cruise. Humans play out their dramas on a ship that is slowly sinking as a monster nudges it, picks off people foolish enough to get near the rail, and makes the chances for survival and rescue look increasingly bleak. *Devour* is a worthy addition to the sea-monster thriller genre.

Cetus Insolitus: Sea Serpents, Giant Cephalopods, and Other Marine Monsters in Classic Science Fiction and Fantasy

Arment, Chad (editor) (2008: Coachwhip Publications, 396pp.)

This is one of a series of marvelous anthologies by Arment collecting stories on subjects like monstrous primates, dinosaurs, and killer insects from a long list of publications dated (in this book) 1848 to 1928. H.G. Welles' "The Sea Raiders" might be the most famous, but there are 25 others, with story titles like "Last Stand of the Decapods" (by Frank Bullen, a name well known to marine cryptozoologists) and "Finless Death" (Robert Ernest Vernede). How could you not love a collection like this?

Bestiarium Cryptozoologicum: Mystery Animals and Unknown Species in Classic Science Fiction and Fantasy

Arment, Chad (editor) (2010: Coachwhip Publications, 302pp.)

Another cool compilation. Here Arment collects 23 crypto-fiction tales, from the classics like A. Conan Doyle's "The Horror of the Heights" (my favorite) from 1913 to the obscure, like Charles E. Howard's 1915 tale "An Alaskan Monster."

The Elusive Trilogy

Bailey, J.M. (CreateSpace Independent Publishing)
Bailey, a wilderness expert and Sasquatch hunter, shows

considerable skill as a writer in this trilogy about a human named Anna. In the opening novel, *Eve* (2012), Anna makes unintended contact with the ancient human offshoot called the "Sas-kay." Anna and a Sas-kay she names Eve cautiously, and believably, befriend each other. In *Iron Mountain Ridge* (2014), Anna is obsessed with her contact with Eve and family and must decide whether to run away from her world and her husband to find out more about them. The Sas-kay let We-lah (their word for her) see more of their family lives and rituals at an annual gathering. In *A Forever Journey* (2015), Anna and the Sas-kay collide with the human world. Anna must choose a permanent direction for her life. It's a difficult choice because Anna has evolved from the profane, often self-centered woman of the first book to someone who cares about the welfare of people and Sas-kay alike. Bailey works in all kinds of detail about the natural world of the Pacific Northwest and where these creatures would fit into it. The Sasquatches seem a little too "modern-human" in their thoughts, and they have talents no real primate does, but Bailey creates a believable culture devoted to avoiding our own.

Primordia

Beck, Greig (2017: Severed Press, 246pp.)

In a new take on the "lost world" formula, two teams of mismatched adventurers follow a letter from Sir Arthur Conan Doyle to scientist Ben Cartwright's grandfather. It won't surprise you they find Doyle's presumably fictitious lost world in South America, but Beck throws in some twists and surprises in a fast-paced adventure that sometimes gives the dinosaurs only brief screen time as humans desperately try to survive an ecosystem where seemingly everything wants to eat them. There are holes in the science, but I didn't mind as much as I usually do because the entertainment quotient is so high. This is the first in a three-book series.

Fathomless

Beck, Greig (2016: Momentum, 420 pages)

Megalodon pretty much deserves its own shelf in the fiction aisle at Barnes and Noble. From its mention in *Jaws* to a raft of novels to its appearance in *Meg* and a couple of terrible faked "documentaries," the big lug has been popular for a while now. That makes it harder to write original Meg novels, although authors like Briar Lee Mitchell (***Big Ass Shark***) have pulled it off to stand out from the horde of self-published novels by people who have never seen either a shark or an editor. Now Grieg Beck offers one hanging out in a subterranean Alaskan sea. While most authors zoom past the "how did it survive" question with impossible or rushed-through scenarios, Beck expands that part while he gives our heroes not one great adventure, but two. I can nitpick the science: Meg was not closely related to the modern great white, and "sharks don't get cancer" is a false advertising slogan, not a fact. The undersea ecosystem has too many big animals and no source of outside energy (like sunlight) to make it keep going. But is it all entertaining? Hell, yes.

Jaws

Benchley, Peter (1974: Doubleday, 278pp.)

Jaws is not technically a cryptozoological novel, featuring as it does a known species. However, it certainly set the tone and arguably created the market for all the marine zoological and cryptozoological thrillers written since.

Benchley did his homework on sharks (using 1974 science, of course) and shark fishing, which is always good. The ichthyologist character, Matt Hooper, describes Megalodon as the direct ancestor, maybe even the same species, as the great white and assigns it a length of 80-100 feet. Both notions have largely been discarded but were current when Benchley wrote the novel.

Benchley nails the setting and provides good characters who take over when the shark is offscreen: there are only four shark attacks. The shark itself is outsized, especially for a male, but it works. Its behavior and cleverness are not really explained, although Matt Hooper repeatedly says that sharks are unpredictable, and we don't know why they do a lot of things they do.

Chief Martin Brody is thoroughly believable, a decent guy trying to fight his way through an ever-increasing host of problems. The mysterious Quint is sort of a human shark, a calculating predator. His comment about his lack of a wife – "never saw the need for one" – is classic. Hooper never comes alive the way he did in Richard Dreyfuss' film version, and the chief's wife Ellen is clumsily written. Despite a few miscues, *Jaws* remains a compelling read. In the subgenre it started, the marine creature thriller, it's still the top fish on the block.

Devolution: A Firsthand Account of the Rainier Sasquatch Massacre

Brooks, Max (2020: Del Rey, 304pp.)

Brooks, the author of the bestseller *World War Z*, offers a story mixing cryptozoology with classic horror and survival tales and some potshots at modern life. It's very interesting but a bit patchy, and neither human nor Sasquatch comes out of it well.

The setup is fun. People move to the tiny ultramodern eco-community of Greenloop, where everything you want comes daily by drone and everything you do has minimal impact on the environment. A half-dozen singles or families are there. One family includes Kate Holland, whose diary is the core of the story,

The novel features a collection of colorful folks who want out of the modern human world despite having no idea how the natural world works. While there are some poky stretches before we get to the action, we can sympathize with people whose world is destroyed when Mount Rainer blows its top (its side, technically) and buries a huge area in volcanic mud. Sasquatches who've been content to live on veggies and venison realize one of the few protein sources left in their devastated habitat is huddled in Greenloop.

A lot of themes unfold in the subsequent weeks. The humans display a mixture of helplessness and imagination. (If not for a woman artist who seems to know a lot about war, they wouldn't last a day.) Some of the people evolve under pressure: some crack.

Meanwhile, the Sasquatches "devolve" into sadistic-predator mode. Despite this, Brooks gives the Sasquatches personal and family dynamics. He's read Bigfoot literature and knows how to tie this story in with the long-running mythology. Mammal eyes don't glow in the dark, but Bigfoot fans will go along.

The series of battles marking the town's last days are gripping. Tactics change as humans learn Sasquatches hate fire and Sasquatches learn not to underestimate their puny opponents if they have pointy weapons. (There are detailed instructions on making a spear out of a kitchen knife.) The ending is interesting, hinting that Sasquatches are not the only primates that can "devolve."

Brooks works in a lot of commentary, some of it delivered with a shovel, on human philosophy, nature, overdependence on gadgets, etc. There's a familiar *Jurassic Park* theme with the isolated humans, and I wish he'd made it harder to guess who's going to die first. Brooks' framing device and storytelling structure, using the journal mixed with post-disaster interviews, works well. Film rights have been sold.

Jurassic Park

Crichton, Michael (1990: Alfred A. Knopf: 448pp.)

My focus is on fiction with new or surviving cryptids, but *Jurassic Park* was so monumentally influential in launching a new generation of creature features it demands mention. Most of us remember the movies these days, but the book's human characters are quite different, with John Hammond being a profit-hungry tycoon and Ian Malcom a dour annoyance. The dinosaur-cloning is explained pretty well. (Stephen J. Gould wrote that this can't really be done, but the book offered "the most clever and realistic solution" in fiction.) Chaos theory is important from the beginning: Malcom warns piling one sophisticated security system and protocol on another, combined with the uncertainties introduced by the dinosaurs, would lead to catastrophic failure. He's right, although nobody likes a sourpuss prophet, and I thought "good riddance" when he was apparently eaten by a *T. rex*. Crichton's writing and characterization are not spectacular, but his style works well, building tension and offering some great scares, and the jargon is kept at a reasonable level. The dinosaurs are a varied and entertaining lot, true to the science of the time, and this is where the world learned the word *Velociraptor*. The sequel, **The Lost World** (1995: Alfred A. Knopf, 393pp.), written after the first movie, keeps most of the characters and brings Ian back from the seemingly dead. He's closer to Jeff Goldblum in this one, which moves (way too slowly) to Site B. There we learn more about how the dinosaur reviving was done and witness a lot more death. The *T. rex* is still the boss species, but we get interesting new ones, including a predator with previously unknown chameleon-like abilities. The *Jurassic Park* franchise catapulted dinosaurs back into popular culture, apparently to stay. Crichton wrote other crypto-fiction, like **Congo** (1980: Alfred A. Knopf, 348pp.). *Congo* is a good novel using an unknown gorilla species. I enjoyed it throughout until the catastrophic/convenient ending. **Eaters of the Dead** (1976, Alfred A. Knopf, 288pp.) was clever in its melding of wildmen (or Neanderthals?) with Vikings to retell the story of Beowulf. As a novel, though, it was a bit clunky and just didn't stick in my mind the way his later works did.

Neanderthal

Darnton, John (1996: Random House, 368pp.)

In this novel, rival scientists hunting for a missing anthropologist discover there are living Neanderthals—thousands of them—in a hidden valley in northern Asia. Humans make contact and learn there two tribes, one peaceful and one decidedly not. While the

Neanderthals have modern-human intelligence, they've stagnated technologically. They are curious and take quickly to new ideas, though, including (a nice bit) the sport of wrestling. Neanderthals also have some telepathic abilities, which of course, American and Russian intelligence agencies turn out to know something about. The book moves very quickly, with lots of thrills, throwing in sermons about how scientists are closed-minded and so on, and ending with— well, I didn't like the ending. To each their own.

The Lost World

Doyle, A. Conan (1912: many editions and versions)

This is the foundational novel of modern English-language crypto-fiction, still read today and inspiring such homages as ***The Lost World: Jurassic Park*** and Greig Beck's ***Primordia***. The book opens with love-struck reporter Edward Malone trying to impress a woman by joining the deranged Professor Challenger on a dangerous expedition. It takes almost half the book to get to the dinosaurs surviving on a South American tepui, but once we do, they are vivid. To Doyle's scientific credit, the discoverers at least wonder how so many predators can exist there and what controls the balance. Language like a cry being "vibrant with the uttermost strain of agony and horror" makes us smile now, while attitudes and language reflecting white men as the pinnacle of evolution make us cringe. The explorers return to an academic and media free-for-all until (of course) something gets loose. This book was a precursor to a flood of adventures by writers like Edgar Rice Burroughs and H. Rider Haggard, whose ***Hue-Hue, or The Monster*** (1924: Hutchinson & Co.) is an example. In *Hue-Hue*, the "White Lord" Allan Quartermain searches for a monster in Africa and meets the Hairy Folk, who are repulsive but definitely human. This group of novels as a whole is shot through with racism (Quartermain maintains the white man's superiority despite being outwitted by the Zulu wizard Zikali), but its influence is undeniable.

Below the Waves: Tales from the Deep

Dillon, Steve (editor), with Clive Barker *et al.* (2018: Tales from the Well, 425pp.)

There are many anthologies of sea-monster stories. This one offers mermaids and science fiction, as well as some straight-up marine creature stories. These range from the tale of an oil rig that plopped down in a very bad spot to the only entry that specifically references cryptozoologists. This is Aristo Couvaras' "The Natloer," a very good story about a South African cryptid which I'll bet someday makes the rounds of the Internet as a real thing.

Fragment

Fahy, Warren (2009: Delacorte Press, 530pp.)

Fahy's novel of a natural Jurassic Park spins out some interesting notions on evolution, ecosystems, and humanity's place on the planet. The characters aren't memorable, and the final third of the book crosses the line of believability, but a twisting plot, original ideas, and well-written action kept me reading to the end. Fahy's key notion is that evolution could have taken a totally different path from the early arthropods forward, with the tetrapod vertebrates never emerging. It's great fun to follow the resulting speculation as contestants on a reality series bump into an island that's been noted but never explored. What they find is an "all eat all" ecosystem where everything moves so fast that the rest of nature will never survive if the island creatures are set loose.

I usually think illustrations in a novel are indulgent, but field-guide-style animal sketches add to the fun here.

I had science nitpicks. The island is too small to sustain the ecosystem for millions of years, and there are reasons arthropods have never evolved into big, fast animals. But you'll enjoy *Fragment*.

Pandemonium

Fahy, Warren (2014: Tor Books, 448pp.)

I thought the science in *Fragment* was well researched and presented, although a bit too far out, but Fahy's worked hard here to make it more plausible even as he brings in yet another unknown ecosystem. Not all his creatures and their lifestyles convince me, but many are fascinating, and some even make you wonder why evolution didn't go in that direction. He puts his ecosystems, his characters, and his storylines together in an epic thriller of a confrontation deep in a hidden city built by the old Soviet Union. Throwing so many elements together shouldn't work, but, in Fahy's skilled hands, it does. It's a terrific book.

Primeval

Golemon, David (2011: St. Martin's Paperbacks, 448pp.)

I enjoy David Golemon's Event Group thrillers. *Primeval* gives an unusual take on Sasquatch. In Goleman's fiction, his descendants of *Gigantopithecus* (misspelled throughout, which is weird because Goleman's research is usually good) are huge and keep to themselves, but they also keep an eye on the human world. They are intelligent, able to camouflage themselves well and band together to wreak havoc on any intruders in their remote Alaskan fastness. The "sky burials" of their dead are an interesting detail, although one wonders why no one studying satellite photographs ever noticed countless huge corpses rotting in treetops. An adventure tale for the cryptozoologist and the action-lover alike.

At the Water's Edge

Gruen, Sara (2015: Penguin Random House, 416pp.)

Nessie is more plot device than plesiosaur in Sarah Gruen's superb novel, but Gruen weaves in a great deal of history and culture about the loch, its people, and its monster. The writer of *Water for Elephants* (Algonquin Books, 2007) tells a spellbinding story about love and betrayal set during World War II. To the Loch comes Ellis Hyde, a man obsessed with finding the monster, Ellis' neglected wife Madeline, and his friend Hank. Madeline will learn more about herself than the monster, but the ensuing tale leaves the door open for the mystery of the lake.

The Shadowkiller

Hansen, Matthew (2007: Simon & Schuster, 448pp.)

Better than average for cryptozoological fiction, this is a fast read with lots of action and an interesting take on Sasquatch. Hansen has read the Sasquatch literature and often pays homage to it: one character's Sasquatch encounter is clearly a rewrite of a classic account by William Roe.

This is a thriller, though, and it's larded with violence as a Sasquatch who has lost his family to human-caused wildfire opts to wreak vengeance on every human in sight. Hansen tries to give us interesting characters and generally succeeds, although amoral reporter Kris Walker is a bit over the top and the wise old Native American trope has been done to death.

Hansen's Sasquatch is gigantic (11 feet and 1,300 pounds, or 3.4 m and 590 kilograms), has a touch of psychic ability, and has switched to an all-human diet out of sheer hate. In a nonfiction afterword, Hansen pronounces himself convinced of the species' existence and acknowledges that portraying a rogue homicidal Sasquatch may irk cryptozoologists. The bottom line is that this novel succeeds as a thriller, providing an entertaining and interesting read.

Kronos Rising series

Hawthorne, Max (2013: Far From the Tree Press, 542pp.)

Creature novels often have two faults: the hand-waving of the science and the inability of the author to provide characters who keep our attention when the creature is off stage. Hawthorne's novel succeeds on the second count and is mixed on the first.

Hawthorne writes characters with color and dimension. Everyone has an interesting backstory, which helps us cheer for the heroes and humanizes the villains. The author knows the sea, and the ocean scenes are authentic and suspenseful. We feel the rocking of the waves and smell the salt air. Finally, Hawthorne is good at plotting and pacing. The book races along, and only the climax feels drawn-out.

The science, however, is iffy. Hawthorne's villain is an evolved species of kronosaur, close to 100 feet (34.5 m) long. It's common for authors using extinct creatures to postulate that evolution over millions of years has left them bigger, smarter, and so on, which is okay with me if the creature is at least possible.

The monster's almost-instant healing and echolocation abilities gave me pause and it bothered me to see a baleen whale echolocate. This and some other liberties could have been revised or written around. The kronosaurs' survival to the present is incomplete: Hawthorne presents a story that puts two kronosaurs in a volcanic cone after the K-Pg asteroid impact, but the next 65 million years is a bit fuzzy. However, he adds detail in his subsequent works.

None of the nitpicks will bother anyone looking for a fun read because *Kronos Rising* delivers on plot twists, roller-coaster suspense, colorful characters, and action. Hop aboard.

Kronos Rising: Kraken (Vol. 1)

Max Hawthorne (2018: Nook Press, 554pp.)

Max Hawthorne followed up his initial marine reptile adventure, *Kronos Rising*, with his shot at truly epic crypto-fiction with *Kraken*. This sprawling novel is the third in a five-book story (a novella called *Kronos Rising: Plague* comes in between, and *Kronos Rising: Kraken Volume 2* and *Volume 3* (subtitled *Winner Tastes All*) came out in 2020.

Kraken is essentially a kaiju novel. The loosing of the monster pliosaurs and other beasts has rewritten the rules for human use of the oceans and made hash out of the existing ecosystem. This book is basically about the clash of three giant predator species and the humans who try to study, kill, or weaponize them. In other words, it's a story of massively armed and powerful beasts bashing the hell out of each other. Hawthorne, like Steve Alten, likes to play with the pop-culture and media aspects of his creature, and the *Xiphactinus* fishing tournament is a hoot.

By the Silver Water of Lake Champlain

Hill, Joe (2014: William Morrow and Company, a short story released as a standalone ebook)

This is an atmospheric horror tale. It's a terrific story, not because it explains the science or anything, but because it doesn't need to. It won't surprise you that the monster of Lake Champlain is real, but you've never seen it written like this. Hill focuses on the children involved and their viewpoints. I've not been a ten-year-old in several decades, but every word of the dialogue rings true, and the ending will stay with you.

Esau

Kerr, Philip (1996; Henry Holt & Company, 372pp.)

This is the first thriller I've read about Yetis from a well-established writer (Kerr is especially known for historical fiction.) California anthropologist Jack Furness finds a Yeti skull while climbing in the Himalayas, and an expedition is formed to track down the creature. Funding this party is the CIA, with an ostensibly mundane objective that masks the hunt for a downed satellite. Of course, the expedition members have conflicting agendas, scientific and political, and things get nasty. Kerr's skills as a thriller writer and a researcher are on display, as there are no dull stretches in the novel. I docked him points for an unrealistic satellite crash and a mystical twist that took me out of the story, but cryptozoologists will still enjoy the book.

Prophet of Bones

Kosmatka, Ted (2014: St. Martin's Griffin, 368pp.)

Kosmatka deftly mixes thrills, terror, science, and politics in a world with one great difference from our own: science has proven the Judeo-Christian Genesis beliefs are true and the Earth is 6,000 years old (or has it)? Kosmatka takes as his real-life point of departure the Flores "hobbit" bones, and the plot rockets forward from there. I learned a great deal from the way the author takes the complex science of genetics and illustrates it in different ways, including the explanation from an autistic scientist who visualizes genetic codes as music. Meanwhile, the heroes are probing the mysteries of human origins and meeting some primates who are a long way from the harmless hobbits. The story is wholly original, the characters, human and nonhuman, are good, and it's also a very clever take on science vs. religion turned backward and sideways.

Ferocity

Laws, Stephen (2007: Leisure Books, 337pp.)

Several authors have essayed novels about the "alien big cats" reported in Britain. This is the one that sticks with me. Cath Lane and Drew Hall have both lost spouses and end up living near each other on the moors, so you can see the romance coming, but what makes it work is how well these people are drawn. We're several compelling chapters into the book before the big cat riddle Drew is trying to solve gets more than passing mention. Our heroes' efforts lead to the capture of a cat of unknown species with an odd chameleonic ability to camouflage itself. (Mr. Laws wrote me to say he deliberately left a bit of mystery about the cats' abilities.) Then comes a very tense third act involving the cats, a storm, and three very nasty human criminals who don't know there's a predator around much more dangerous than themselves. Highly satisfying.

Below

Lockwood, Ryan (2013: Pinnacle Books, 416pp.)

Lockwood is another novelist who avoids the crypto-fiction trap of focusing on the creature above all else. His technical details of the sea and diving are very interesting, the science is stretched but not absurdly so, and he takes his time introducing a believable story about believable people.

Lockwood's creatures, the Humboldt squid, are a real species, pack-hunting animals 2-3 meters (6.5-9.8 feet) long that communicate with flashes of color. Lockwood makes them a little too smart and too emotional, adding a fictitious parasite that makes them more aggressive, but they are believably scary. This species could do a lot of damage a group of them ever decided to grab some humans.

A leading cephalopod expert, Dr. Danna Staaf, wrote that she didn't think the scenario could happen, but there was some good science in it and the novel was "...an intellectually stimulating and emotionally provocative work of imagination."

The book drags in spots, with a little too much lecturing thrown in. And there are nitpicks: destroyers don't carry guns you could "fit a soccer ball" into. But overall, kudos to Lockwood. He's given us a first-rate thriller and an ecological lesson into the bargain.

What Lurks Beneath

Lockwood, Ryan (2015: Kensington Books, 416pp.)

Carrying on the theme from *Below*, Lockwood surpasses his earlier work and gives us the best fictional treatment so far of the *lusca*, the giant octopus of the Bahamas. In Lockwood's hands, good characters, great settings, believable science, realistic gadgets (ok, I wasn't sure where some of them get adequate power), and island folklore come together to create a memorable tale cryptozoologists and horror aficionados will savor. Lockwood's oceanographer Valerie Martell cites lingering doubt about the 1896 St. Augustine carcass as she explores the famous "blue holes" with troubled diver Will Sturman. They're trying to solve recent disappearances and track down what she suspects is a new species of cephalopod. She will, of course, learn that there's such a thing as being *too* right.

Lockwood's characters are good: while they have their secrets and tragedies, most have a heroic side that comes out when lives are at stake. (Points off for referring to the enemy in Iraq as the Taliban.) The major plot turns are generally not surprising, but Lockwood tells a story better than most writers, and we're taking the ride with people we care about. Much more than a "monster" tale, *Lurks* offers a multifaceted story that makes for one of the best recent crypto-fiction novels. Dive in... wait, did that coral just move?

The Dragon Factory

Maberry, Jonathan (2015: St. Martin's Paperbacks, 672pp.)

This is a very good thriller in Maberry's Joe Ledger series. It includes villains who, in pursuing DNA manipulation focused on creating super-soldiers, have developed a sideline: they bring back some extinct creatures and create some existing only in myth. (Dodo, one man observes, does not taste like chicken.) Maberry, whose wife photographed the "Yardley Yeti" in Pennsylvania a few years ago, is a well-known cryptozoology fan who coauthored *Cryptopedia* (Section 4) and enjoys putting creatures in his novels.

In the late 1990s, a team of geneticists in London were inserting snippets of DNA into the genomes of mice...one of the mice had extra digits and very broad paws. The team was able to generate an entire family line of these mutants. They called them Sasquatch, after the big-footed creature of the paranormal world. – Neil Shubin, evolutionary biologist

Big Ass Shark

Mitchell, Briar Lee (2014: Permuted Press, 146pp.)

I tossed this off as a *Meg* ripoff before I read it, but I've apologized to the author because it's much better than that. Mitchell has done some research, the characters are colorful (they don't have a lot of depth, but they are fun to follow) and there are some very funny lines. Most of the components here (giant shark near a beach, competing scientists, scoop-hungry media, etc.) are stock, but Mitchell remixes them and comes out with a fast-paced adventure. Mitchell offers some interesting speculations about why the shark wasn't discovered before and why it's seemingly easy to find now. There are flaws, the most serious being that the shark's inconsistent behavior. Watch for the in-joke based on a scene in Steve Alten's first book.

The Road to Loch Ness

Murphy, Lee (2014: Defining Moments, Kindle)
This is the best of Murphy's George Kodiak novels: the plot, setting, and characters are all terrific. The author sends his tough-guy cryptozoologist to Loch Ness for two futile years of research in a semi-submerged lab which (for reasons that could be made clearer) many local citizens oppose. The boredom, though, explodes in one short week as one of George's friends gets killed, new and old adversaries try to sabotage him, and the creature of the loch arises once and for all. This is the first novel where Kodiak has a really good supporting cast. His friend Rocky, Rocky's daughter Erika, and local and international helpers and meddlers are along. Murphy loves the latest in technology (I helped him a bit on some research) and there are plenty of cool gadgets on display. The grammar is marred by occasional changes of tense, and the sentence structure is clunky in the standalone chapter "Extinction Event." The plotting and pacing here are good, and the reader will find plenty of surprises. This is also the funniest of Lee's books.

Hopsquatch

Newton, Michael (2018: Wolfpack Publishing, 306pp.)
Newton, a thriller writer and cryptozoology researcher, has some fun with a different take on Sasquatch. He opens with a car crash that may or may not be a simple accident. Events after that spiral into a small-town melee involving more deaths, a put-upon sheriff, three oversized loggers, a dedicated cryptozoologist, an annoying FBI agent, a colorful anarchist, and the Nahanni tribe, which mainly wants to be left alone. Unlike books that explore Sasquatch itself, Newton focuses on the havoc wreaked by sightings and an apparent Sasquatch-on-human murder. There are many cryptozoological references, although there is, alas, no cryptozoology site called "ThunderbirdsareGo!" Newton is a good descriptive writer. His

characters, settings, and action are all easy to visualize. We never learn much about Sasquatch, and the book is a little less than the sum of its interesting parts, but cryptozoologists and thriller fans will enjoy it.

The Essex Serpent

Perry, Sarah (2016: Custom House, 422pp.)

This atmospheric novel follows Cora Seaborne, a widowed naturalist who moves to a small village on the Essex coast in 1893. She has arrived, it seems, just in time to begin hearing tales of the return of a legendary sea serpent. Is it a supernatural menace? An unknown species, maybe even a prehistoric monster? Or a story born of myths and expectations? Like Sara Gruen's Loch Ness novel, this is a story focusing not so much on the serpent, whatever it may be, as on the effects it has on beliefs, relationships, and life in this isolated spot. The writing is lovely but takes a little getting used to. Perry writes in a rich, poetic style that can't be skimmed through but is well worth the effort.

The Relic

Preston, Douglas, and Lincoln Childs (1996: Tor Books, 480pp.)

A terrific novel in every sense, this crypto-horror tale has a perfect setting (New York's largest museum), great characters, and an unknown South American creature that seems to have come north with a shipment of crated specimens. First come the rumors of the half-glimpsed Museum Beast hiding in the warren of sub-basements. Then two kids are found dead, then a guard, and then things accelerate as scientists and law enforcement try to accept what's happening and work out the genes that went into a bizarre hybrid. We know of big, powerful predators adapted for their roles, but what would a perfect predator look like? The science here is well-explained and up to date for the time of publication (2021 readers will snort at the "powerful" 200-gigabyte database). The museum is thoroughly authentic, as Preston wrote a book on the real equivalent, the American Museum of Natural History. Genuinely creepy stuff with one of the scariest beasts in fiction and a classic horror twist at the end.

Full Wolf Moon and others

Preston, Douglas, and Lincoln Childs (as solo writers and as collaborators)

Both authors like to add creatures to their work. In Childs' **Moon** (2017: Anchor Books, 246pp.), "enigmaologist" Jeremy Logan is trying to solve savage murders blamed on a werewolf near an Appalachian retreat. The interesting bit for cryptozoology is Logan's discovery, buttressed by very speculative but intriguing science, that the full moon does, for a handful of people, have some scary effects. In **The Forgotten Room** (2017: Corsair Books, 304pp.), an opening chapter involving Loch Ness will bring smiles to Nessie fans. In **Terminal Freeze** (2012: Anchor Books, 352pp.), scientists beset by sudden casualties in the Arctic suspect a surviving *Smilodon* but find something much nastier. There is some interesting science here. I didn't know there are hypothesized forms of ice that behave differently from the observed types, although I'm not sure about a large animal being flash-frozen so quickly that no ice crystals form in the cells. It's a fun read that's a homage to Arctic thrillers like Howard Hawks' 1951 film *The Thing*. In the Preston-Childs novel **The Lost Island** (2014: Grand Central Publishing, 368pp.), cryptozoology is front and center, as evolution has produced a strange human species vital to a clever adventure plot. In **Cabinet of Curiosities** (2014: Grand Central Publishing, 704pp.), an old mansion contains a stuffed Tusked Megalopedus, a mysterious tapir-like mammal described by Pliny the Elder (this is true) labeled as the only known specimen of its species.

The Great Zoo of China

Reilly, Matthew (2015: Pocket Books, 464pp.)

Reilly's thriller is about the ultimate cryptozoological creatures - dragons. Here they are giant, smart relations of pterosaurs, which have hibernated for millions of years (not possible, but go with it). Reilly has a lot of fun showing the reader different species of varying appearance and behavior. The dragons, of course, escape from the confinement systems of the zoo and wreak havoc. Reilly's human characters are good, and he's put a lot of thought into how the Dragon Zoo would be designed to maximize revenue and (oops) safety. He writes action very well. Reilly says at one point that dragon legends around the world tell of beasts with four legs plus wings, a very odd thing to say in China, where the dominant form of folklore dragon has no wings. A bigger distraction for me was the physics: the size, speed, and carrying capability of the dragons don't work, at least not on Earth. If you're looking for a fun read with a great premise, though, this one delivers.

The Bone Labyrinth

Rollins, James (2017: William Morrow and Company, 512pp.)

Rollins likes to include cryptozoology in his bestselling thrillers, so here are two examples. In **Labyrinth,** Rollins offers his usual globe-trotting adventure, thrilling escapes, and high-tech gadgets. While the characters include a genetically modified gorilla named Baako, Rollins mentions the Yeti and one surviving human ancestor. This is a bit muddled: the ape (not human) *Meganthropus* was not eight feet (2.4 m) tall, or seven, or six. In *Ice Hunt* (2003: William Morrow and Company, 416pp.), Rollins explores a secret Arctic base where grendels, his bigger, nastier versions of the cetacean ancestor *Ambulocetus,* have survived 50,000 years in hibernation in the ice.

That doesn't really work (one character voices a bit of sci-babble about it), but it leads to scary fun.

The challenge for the science-minded reader is that Rollins presents both good science and fringe/crackpot science and says (as in the Afterword in *Labyrinth*) that he believes some of the latter to be true. But readers come to Rollins for thrills, and he keeps them coming.

Sea Raptor

Rust, John (2015: Severed Press, 246pp.)

There's a lot here to like. Rust writes well, and he gives us good characters, lots of action, and fun gadgets. Rust takes the time to give us a twisting plot where personal and monetary interests can lead people to kill, steal, and spy. The novel's well-funded cryptozoology investigation society, with its own boats and other hardware, would be most welcome in real life. The sea monster, though, could have been better. It seems chimerical, without a logical fossil ancestor, and it's hard to believe it could be undiscovered given its living and eating habits. If you want a cryptid-chasing adventure, though, this is an exciting book: I couldn't put it down for long stretches.

The Abominable

Simmons, Dan (2013: Little, Brown and Company, 672pp.)

This is epic novel writing. As with most Simmons books, the detail is astonishing: you'll feel like an expert in pre-World War II mountain climbing, among other things, and Simmons knows how to pace things, so the details never stop the story.

Climbing Mount Everest back then, we learn, was grueling beyond the imagination of us armchair adventurers. Simmons pits four climbers against a larger, better-armed party determined to stop them from finding a lost climber's body and the secret the dead man was carrying. The history of mountaineering is told in the buildup to a deadly cat and mouse game. Those wanting to learn about the Yeti will not find a lot of detail, but the subject is pivotal at two points. To keep from spoiling it, I won't say whether Simmons' novel presents the *metohkangmi* as real animals. If you are interested in tackling a long and unique novel with some cryptozoological bits, you won't be disappointed.

The Wolfen

Strieber, Whitley (1978: Bantam Books, 275pp.)

In the group just below my top three is this excellent thriller about intelligent, pack-living predators evolved from wolves (which they consider beautiful but stupid). The Wolfen thrive in America's wilderness but have learned how to pick off homeless and forgotten humans in a city without fuss. When two impetuous youngsters kill policemen, that begins to change. The pacing is perfect, the characters (human and otherwise) well-written, the creatures believable, and the tension and dread maintained throughout. The movie was a mess, but I don't know who wouldn't enjoy this novel.

Matt's Musings: The Wolfen *made such an impression on me that 30 years later, when I started my novel* The Dolmen, *about beasts of legend loose in Los Angeles, I was about halfway through before I realized I was channeling Strieber much more than I'd thought. I rewrote several chapters.*

Warrener's Beastie: A Novel of the Deep

Trotter, William (2006: Carroll & Graf Publishers, 496pp.)

This is a sprawling epic about a boring professor interested in cryptozoology and how he steps out of his comfortable corner to find the adventure of a lifetime. Allen Warriner will deal with Norse myths, personal dramas, betrayals, love, a porn film director, the awesomeness and power of the oceans, long-necked sea serpents, and something called the "Vardinoy Monster." Set in and around the Faeroe Islands, this novel plumbs the human heart and imagination. There's sometimes too much detail, although the pacing gets better as it goes along. Well worth the time investment.

Invasive Species

Wallace, Joseph (2013: Berkley Publishing, 496pp.)

Wallace has done everything right in the scariest "creature" novel ever written. This thriller offers good characters, a killer premise, and scary details, and it proves cryptids don't need to be big to be terrifying. Wallace writes the scientific part very well. His "thieves" are several evolutionary steps beyond any real wasps, but he makes them terrifyingly plausible. The hive-mind intelligence gets a little far out when it's connecting individuals separated by entire continents, but even here, he grounds the thieves' capabilities in what we know about hive minds and mentions the genuine scientific questions we still have about how they might work. His concepts of how parasitic hosts exploit and control their prey have real analogs in nature, including those hellishly alien fungi that control the minds of ants. The pacing is perfect, the descriptions are thorough without being overly detailed, and he creates characters we care about and yet is never afraid to kill them. It's clear no one is safe in this chilling novel.

Daedalus and the Deep

Willis, Matthew (2012: Cotero Publishing, 248pp.)

This is a unique entry in the field of sea-creature novels. Willis takes as his starting point a true event, the report of a sea serpent by the HMS *Daedalus* in 1848. He fictionalizes Captain Peter McQuahe as Robert MacQuarrie, and the other names used are all fictitious. Our protagonist here is Ensign Colyer, a teenage girl passing herself as her dead brother Tom. Such things did happen in the Royal Navy, and Colyer is an engaging hero.

Willis asks what might have happened if the captain had not merely reported the serpent but chased it hell-bent, determined to secure it for the honor of England, its Navy, and the *Daedalus*. Along the way, we get all kinds of detail on how such a ship was equipped and sailed in those days. Indeed, there's a little too much detail at times.

While trying not to spoil the plot too much, it's important to say there is a science fantasy element in this book. It's not by accident that the *Daedalus* and the creature came together, and their running fight over many days and thousands of miles is driven by the creature as much, or more than, by Captain MacQuarrie.

The result is a very enjoyable read. Willis writes well: there are only a couple of clunky sentences here and there. You will put this book down, having enjoyed a rousing adventure story, an original slant on the sea serpent, and an engaging introduction to the days of sail.

SECTION 4
A MARVELOUS MISCELLANY

Here are some books that don't quite fit into the main categories but are too important, interesting, or enjoyable to skip. Some are nonfiction, while others include fiction containing magic or other elements outside physical cryptozoology.

Wilderness Skills and Tracking Books

This entry breaks my "personally reviewed rule. Having no field experience, I asked Loren Coleman of the International Cryptozoology Museum and the three Bigfoot-hunters he named as Cryptozoologists of the Year in 2019 to suggest one top book each. Loren recommended *Tom Brown's Field Guide to Nature Observation and Tracking* by Tom Brown, Jr. (1986: Berkley Publishing, 288pp.). Craig Woolheater offered up Jane Goodall's *My Life with the Chimpanzees* (1996: Aladdin, 140pp.). I thought that was interesting since it's for junior readers. As I've said, though, when new to a science or a skill, start with books that lay out the basics in a way you understand, whoever they are written for. Ken Gerhard suggested the ***National Audubon Society Field Guide to Mammals of North America*** by

John L. Whitaker (1996: Alfred A. Knopf, 942pp.). Lyle Blackburn was the only one to suggest a cryptozoology-specific book, *Bigfoot Observer's Field Manual: A practical and easy-to-follow step-by-step guide to your very own face-to-face encounter with a legend,* by Robert W. Morgan (2008: Pine Woods Press, 136pp.).

Mysteries

Blashford-Snell, John (1983: The Bodley Head, 251pp.)

Blashford-Snell is an explorer who recounts ventures into the most remote parts of the world. He has an interest in cryptozoology and tells of his innovative but unsuccessful searches at Loch Ness and Loch Morar. He also discusses dinosaur legends in New Guinea, his encounters with outsized monitor lizards, and his meeting with "Oliver," the curious chimp. Captivating adventure reading.

Alien Animals

Bord, Janet and Colin (1982: Stackpole Books, 258pp.)

The Bords, who are primarily known as paranormal investigators, have written a book that's mainly about apparitions of animals. I do think it's useful, though, for the numerous accounts of flesh-and-blood cryptids. There are endnotes for all the cases, and many of the sources are worth checking in themselves.

Unfortunately, researchers are only peripherally interested in the thousands of species discovered so far and given unpronounceable Latin names. Countless more species are waiting in vain to be discovered. – Peter Wohlleben, forester, *The Hidden Life of Trees*

Working for Bigfoot

Butcher, Jim (2015: Subterranean Press, 136pp.)

This collection of three stories takes place in Butcher's Harry Dresden universe. Harry, a private investigator/wizard, ends up with Bigfoot for a client. (The erudite hominid explains that Native Americans help him with things like making phone calls.) Butcher doesn't work much of cryptozoology's history into this, but his Sasquatch, Strength of a River in his Shoulders, is a great character. River Shoulders has a fondness for junk food and a relationship with a human woman who bore a son who looks human but isn't. At one point, he and Harry have some fun pranking Sasquatch hunters (Butcher, by the way, is genuinely curious about Sasquatch). River Shoulders displays a magical talent, the ability to make himself "less and less relevant to the situation" until he's no longer there. So it's not cryptozoology, but it's a lot of fun, and it's one more indication of how much the Big Guy has permeated popular culture. Relax and laugh along. There's also a graphic novel about the dogman in this universe, moving that cryptid to the American South. The three Bigfoot stories have been rewritten into a single story for a graphic novel, *Dresden Files: Bigfoot*, due out in 2022.

A Natural History of the Unnatural World

Cryptozoological Society of London (1990: St. Martin's Press, 224pp.)

An elaborate spoof mixing zoology, cryptozoology, myth, and outright fiction, all presented in a mock scientific tone. For entertainment value only, as the Society does not (unfortunately) exist.

MATT BILLE

Cryptozoology Anthology: Strange and Mysterious Creatures in Men's Adventure Magazines

Deis, Robert, David Coleman, and Wyatt Doyle (editors) (2015: Men's Adventure Library, 316pp.)

Men's adventure magazines like ARGOSY, TRUE, and a dozen others were the "real man's" literature in the 1940s-1970s, sharing stories of horrible creatures, willing women, and brawny (white) adventurers. The editors here collect 13 items, from a short story by Arthur C. Clarke to serious articles by Ivan Sanderson and John Keel to outright nonsense, sometimes with a disclaimer that the magazine could not vouch for the facts but presented the story (of course) for the readers to decide for themselves. I was interested to learn that some of the classic Sasquatch stories first popped up in these magazines. There are wild men, giant lizards, a dinosaur, and various other critters. The thunderbird article is a favorite of mine. It has a lot of details science is "afraid to discuss" (reasonable, since author Jack Pearl made them up) but features a mythical ornithologist's soberly-written "scientific" discussion. The lurid and sexist covers are also reproduced here. Monsters always know exactly how much of a lady's clothing they can rip off without destroying her modesty, which is considerate of them. The editors treat the magazines with some respect, not stooping to ridicule even when there's plenty to ridicule. The whole business belongs in another era, but it tells us something about that era, and the creatures are fun.

Red Earth, White Lies: Native Americans and the Myth of Scientific Fact

Deloria Jr., Vine (1997: Fulcrum publishing)

Deloria, a Standing Rock Sioux professor and historian, starts from the premise that Native American accounts and inherited knowledge of nature have been passed over by scientists. That's hard to argue with: the eminent George Gaylord Simpson in 1943 harshly rejected the idea the people who'd been on the continent longest knew anything about its extinct animals. Deloria, though, goes on to take issue with the entire scientific enterprise, arguing the approach to nature by Native Americans is equally valid, often more so. He argues indigenous people were created on this continent and that modern analysis of dates and layers is fatally flawed because it overlooks Native traditions of great floods and other catastrophes. While such views are almost universally rejected by scientists, this is important reading for people wanting to understand how the science that doesn't at least listen to traditional beliefs is incomplete and why indigenous peoples may reject its findings.

After Man: A Zoology of the Future

Dixon, Dougal (1998: St. Martin's Griffin, 124pp.)

While this speculative look at what might evolve 50 million years after the Age of Man has no direct connection to cryptozoology, it's a unique introduction to animal evolution and how creatures might adapt to fill niches in their environments.

On the Trail of Bigfoot

Dupler, Mike (2020: New Page Books, 224pp.)

This book is heavy on the paranormal content (Dupler thinks Sasquatch is flesh and blood, but some sightings concern paranormal beings) but worth reading. Dupler explores the Sasquatch-hunting culture and the major groups, Sasquatch in pop culture, and what he considers the most important incidents and evidence. Among other things, he thinks "stick structures" are very important. He includes personal Sasquatch photos, although they don't impress me. This is an easily digested view of the Sasquatch phenomenon, not just the cryptid.

Serpents of the Sky, Dragons of the Earth

Holiday, F. W. (1993: Horus House, 247pp.)

F. W. "Ted" Holiday's books are generally too weird to be cited as references, which you'd expect from a man who believed in interdimensional creatures and once had a priest exorcise Loch Ness. However, this one has two valuable nuggets. One is a good collection of legends related to Nessie and other monsters. The other is a unique recounting of efforts to capture creatures reported in tiny Irish lakes. This is one of the few cases where cryptozoologists were able to search an entire habitat using nets and dynamite and definitively rule out a creature's existence there. Holiday thinks Nessie descends from a bizarre 30-cm-long creature called *Tullimonstrum gregarium* that died out 300 million years ago, a topic he also covered in *The Dragon and the Disc* (1973) and *The Great Orm of Loch Ness* (1970).

Matt's Musings: Here's an obscure fact: Tullimonstrum is the Official State Fossil of Illinois. Meanwhile, Ohio honors Isotelus, a genus of very large Late Ordovician trilobites, and has recently added the more spectacular Dunkleosteus terrelli from the Cleveland Shale formation. My home state of Colorado uses Stegosaurus armatus, while North Carolina, which has a famous fossil-hunting area called Topsail Beach, honors our favorite monster shark Megalodon.

Panthers of the Coastal Plain

Humphreys, Charles (1994: The Fig Leaf Press, 200pp.)

Humphreys' aim here is to present reports of supposedly-extinct Eastern cougars in North Carolina. The author may be too quick to accept all the witnesses' statements, but he has assembled a valuable database of 160-plus accounts. Humphreys, who sent me a copy gratis after reading my 1995 *Rumors of Existence*, self-published this book when that was a relatively complicated and costly thing to do.

> But the cat came back the very next day,
> Thought he was a goner, but the cat came back
> He just wouldn't stay away.
>
> — AMERICAN FOLK SONG

Cryptopedia

Kramer, David, and Jonathan Maberry (2007: Citadel Press, 320pp.)

An enjoyable gorgeously illustrated romp through definitions and short articles on cryptids, aliens, demons, and miscellaneous creatures from folklore, religion, myth, and so forth all over the world. I wish the authors had added references, but it is what it is, and that's fun.

The Big, Bad Book of Beasts: The World's Most Curious Creatures

Largo, Michael (2013: William Morrow and Company, 464pp.)

Mr. Largo clearly had a grand time writing this book, a romp through strange creatures of zoology, cryptozoology, legend, and hoax. He offers a selection of 120 or so creatures, a bevy of good illustrations, some interesting tidbits of science like the workings of the electric eel, and considerable humor (I wish I'd thought of calling the platypus "nature's combo platter"). It's marred by the author's carelessness with facts. Saying that a prehistoric shark's jaws were in constant motion, for example, makes no sense. Suggesting dragons could be a folk memory of late-surviving dinosaurs isn't logical absent any reason to believe there were late-surviving dinosaurs. Still, this book is a lot of fun if you read it with a bit of caution.

Deadlands: Ghostwalkers

Maberry, Jonathan (2015: Tor Books, 477pp.)

The first in the Deadlands series based on a gaming universe offers a horde of creatures along with dastardly villains, brave heroes (the Native American named Looks Away is a crackup), and an airship (of course, there's an airship). These elements appear in a you-are-there desert setting reminiscent of Stephen King's *The Dark Tower*. There are also wild inventions based on the mysterious "ghost rock" exposed by the great earthquake of 1868. When we get to the beasts and monsters, we get a lot of them. The ghost rock seems to have reanimated a lot of things, and gunfighter Grey Torrance has to use his weapons and wits to elude or destroy raptors, tyrannosaurs, pterodactyls, and enough other critters to start the West Coast Jurassic Park. There's a new danger or terror around every rock and in every cave. There are some anachronistic phrases and no hint of a workable food chain, but never mind: saddle up and ride into the weirdest Western tale I've ever read.

Investigating the Impossible: Sea-Serpents in the Air, Volcanoes that Aren't, and Other Out-of-Place Mysteries

Magin, Ulrich (2011: Anomalist Books, 241pp.)

Magin is interested in everything odd and has his own view of what can and can't be filed under the generic label "folklore." In the cryptozoology sections of this book, Magin turns up some interesting facts. He writes there is no clear "sea serpent" reports from residents of the Iberian Peninsula, but there are stories from passing English ships, which leads him to muse on the cultural origins of such creatures. In a long-ago sea monster case Bernard Heuvelmans wrote off as a hoax, Magin argues instead for a most interesting phenomenon, a Mediterranean undersea volcano. Magin includes no illustrations, which is unfortunate given he does talk about some images in the text. There are a few mistakes here that seem to have slipped through editing, and the print on some pages was oddly faint. These detracted from my enjoyment of the book, but it's still an interesting disquisition on the impossible, improbable, or simply unique.

The Cryptid Creatures of Florida

Marlowe, Scott (2011: CFZ Press, 116pp.)

Cryptozoologists love Florida. It has a very colorful natural "personality," with all kinds of odd, invasive, and reported wildlife. Longtime Florida cryptozoologist Marlowe (who once put me in a calendar called "Men of Cryptozoology") here offers a tour of the state's reported cryptids. Marlowe doesn't attempt in-depth zoological analysis, but the plethora of anecdotes provides a nourishing sampler of Florida's cryptozoological attractions.

Planet Ocean: A Story of Life, the Sea, and Dancing to the Fossil Record

Matsen, Brad, and Ray Troll (1994: Ten Speed Press, 133pp.)

This delightful book will goggle the eyes even as the text provides entertaining scientific information on the evolution of the ocean and its creatures. Ray Troll's illustrations of creatures great and small are done in a unique style he calls "scientific surrealism." It's a blend of Victorian, scientific illustration, and cartoon influences, and it makes creatures pop out from every page. The text mixes anecdotes, facts, and observations in the service of a necessarily brief but engaging and informative tour of the subject.

Deadlands: BoneYard

McGuire, Seanan (2017: Tor Books, 336pp.)

BoneYard is another novel in the Deadlands universe, where the natural and supernatural mix. As a ramshackle circus creaks into Oregon, oddities-keeper Annie Pearl and her ailing daughter are looked at as prey by human and nonhuman creatures. The wolflings (smart wolves with handlike paws) are a fun creation, and the things kept in Annie's show wagon are memorable. They include the nibblers, essentially North American piranhas, the foot-long pit wasps, and the "terrorantulas," which are just what you think they are. There's a lot of imagination in these critters, and you'll be glad you haven't met them.

McGuire also writes the *InCryptid* series, in which the Price/Healy family is charged with keeping magical cryptids a secret. While she's not focusing on plausible animals, she tells good stories and tosses off lines like, "The problem with people who say monsters don't really exist is that they're almost never saying it to the monsters." It's a wild, funny, and original series.

Chasing American Monsters

Offutt, Jason (2019: Llewellyn Publications, 384pp.)

America has a rich folklore, still developing in the present day, of monsters, lake serpents, and just plain odd creatures. To take an enjoyable tour of this richness, we have *Chasing American Monsters*.

All fifty state entries have some interesting nuggets, even if you've read collections like this before. In my favorite spot, Alaska, he mentions some recent sightings of the Lake Iliamna monster, although he's another writer who refers to early Russian reports without details or sources. Offutt repeats some falsehoods (e.g., that a monster photo appeared in a certain issue of the Tombstone *Epitaph*). There are few primary sources, making this an example of what Sharon Hill calls "cut-and-paste cryptozoology." Some of the creatures are absurd, and it's not always certain what Offutt wants us to swallow and what he offers just for fun. It is an enjoyable read, though.

Do Abominable Snowmen of America Really Exist?

Patterson, Roger (1966: Franklin Press, 169pp.)

Before Patterson was famous for his film, he wrote a book on the title question. While assuming that all the reports and footprints he discusses are genuine, he tells a good story. He describes the people he's met and the prints he's seen, tells some of the touchstone stories in Bigfoot lore (Ape Canyon, Albert Ostman, etc.), and illustrates the book with his own well-done pencil drawings. Some reprints of newspaper and magazine articles are included. *The Bigfoot Film Controversy* (2005: Hancock House Publishers, 264pp.) reprints Patterson's book plus two chapters of updates and analysis by Christopher Murphy.

The Bigfoot Book: The Encyclopedia of Sasquatch, Yeti, and Cryptid Primates

Redfern, Nick (2016: Visible Ink Press, 381pp.)

I read this one because it had some impact on the field, but it had less impact on me. Redfern states upfront he's a believer in the paranormal, and that permeates the book. There are many primate sightings and stories from around the world, and some of them are intriguing. The research that went into those, however, is swamped by the talk of apparitions and portals and so on. I'm always irked by books that mention things like quantum physics and wormholes with no details to show the science is workable (it isn't.) Saying the Ketchum DNA case debate was ongoing, years after geneticists ended it, doesn't help. This could have been a useful reference on cryptid primates, but to me, it rarely is.

Monster Files: A Look Inside Government Secrets and Classified Documents on Bizarre Creatures and Extraordinary Animals

Redfern, Nick (2013: New Page Books, 288pp.)

There's little in here that really qualifies as classified, although it includes stories of people saying they've seen classified documents on this or that. Still, this romp through reports with some government or military affiliation is my favorite of Redfern's cryptozoology books. Some non-cryptid stories, like the CIA's bionic spy cat, are here, too. (That one really was classified because no one wanted to admit they'd had any part in it.) Royal Navy encounters with sea serpents are here, along with claims of a secret Sasquatch autopsy, soldiers hunting British big cats, some cool stories of monsters faked by soldiers to scare superstitious enemies, and much more. There's a decent bibliography, and those who like their cryptozoology with a hint of Men in Black will really enjoy this book.

Mysterious Sea Monsters of California's Central Coast

Reinstedt, Randall (1993: Ghost Town Publications, 72pp.)

This is my favorite example of the mini-books sometimes written about cryptozoological tales surrounding particular seaports or coasts. Reinstedt has a lot of fun with this and offers some genuinely intriguing tales from local fishermen. These are mostly told anonymously, so there's not much verifiable information here, but Reinstedt is convinced by some of these tales. He suggests some stories arise from seeing oarfish or sea elephants, but others...? Come meet the Old Man of Monterey Bay, the white-haired sea beast, and more, brought to life in Ed Greco's wonderful pencil drawings. Be ye hardened skeptic or wide-eyed monster lover, you're in for a great time.

Rare Animals of the World

Salvadori, Francesco (1990: Mallard Press, 192pp.)
This tour of the world's rarest creatures, illustrated with Piero Cozzaglio's paintings, includes a number of animals declared extinct but found again. These include, among other species, the Seychelles owl, the Persian fallow deer, and the bridled nail-tailed wallaby.

ShukerNature 2: Living Gorgons, Bottled Homunculi, and Other Monstrous Blog Beasts

Shuker, Karl (2019: Coachwhip Publications, 462pp.)
Everything from the Chupacabras to a miniature llama (really) to Dr. Doolittle's pushme-pullyou and those old giant-grasshopper postcards pops up in this entertaining sequel to *ShukerNature 1*.

Mysteries of Planet Earth

Shuker, Karl (1999: Carlton Books, 192pp.)
Shuker here mixes cryptozoology with unrelated phenomena. Whatever one thinks of apparitions and ancient engineering, there's enough well-written cryptozoology in here to make the book worth having. Shuker's topics range from animals with odd coloration to suspected hybrids to lake monsters. Shuker is good at turning up overlooked or little-known cryptid reports. We all know about Nessie, but this is the first book I read that covered the "whale-fish" of Lake Myllesjon in Sweden. Paintings by Bill Rebsamen add to the book's appeal.

From Flying Toads to Snakes with Wings

Shuker, Karl (1997: Llewellyn Publications, 222pp.)

This book is based on cryptozoology articles Shuker published from 1988 to 1997. The most fascinating item is an account of a titanic jellyfish (with estimated 200-foot tentacles) impaled on the bow of a steamship in 1973. Unfortunately, no one has printed the analysis which supposedly confirmed this identity or the names of the experts who performed it. Shuker throws in some non-zoological items, such as "ghost dogs," but this collection is so interesting the zoologically-minded reader will readily forgive a few such wanderings.

Dragons: A Natural History

Shuker, Karl (1995: Barnes and Noble, 120pp.)

A tour through dragons of myth, fable, and legend, mixed with cryptozoological reports of creatures that may have inspired dragon stories or been inspired by them. Shuker differentiates the types of dragons and includes pictures of dragon-like creatures from many cultures.

Supernatural Mysteries and Other Tales

Snow, Edward Rowe (1974: Dodd, Mead & Company: 268pp.)

Snow was a prolific chronicler of folklore, history, and sea stories, especially those concerning New England. Here he includes a major section on "His majesty, the sea serpent." Snow devotes chapters to two famous incidents, the *Pauline*'s report of a sea monster strangling a whale and a sea serpent captured in 1852 by the whaler *Monongahela*. Snow writes, based on reading an account posted home by Captain Jason Seabury, that the *Monongahela* events are factual, although the ship sank before it landed the cargo. Snow also inspected the Scituate, Massachusetts, "monster" carcass washed ashore in 1970. Snow declares it a real monster based on seeing "fur" and "talons," rejecting the idea it was a basking shark (which it was). We also learn its flesh was served up by a restaurant in "Sea Serpent Soup!" It's a charming book by a great storyteller.

Mysteries and Monsters of the Sea

Spaeth, Frank (editor) (1998: Gramercy Books, 242pp.)

    I included this collection of articles from *FATE* magazine because *FATE* has published cryptozoology articles since 1948, longer than any other source still in existence. Its standards range from flexible to ephemeral, and the issue that carried my article on possible outsized versions of known species had a cover so horrible I refuse to even describe it. But along with Atlantis and ghost ships, there are sections on lake monsters, sea monsters, and non-serpentine ocean giants with a few items worth perusing. One is Karl Shuker's article on lesser-known lake monsters, from Canada to Tibet. Others touch on Champ, Ogopogo, and of course Nessie. Sea serpent articles cover classic stories, possible monstrous invertebrates, Cornwall's Morgawr, and most controversially, Brian McCleary's 1965 claim in "My Escape from a Sea Monster." Shuker's articles on giant sharks and jellyfish are fun, and Michael Goss has an article disputing the famous squid encounter by the ship *Pearl*. There is some obsolete and some undocumented material, but read it and enjoy.

Monster Hunt: The Guide to Cryptozoology

Storm, Rory (2008, Metro Books, 207pp.)

    This is a charming item, a faux field notebook stuffed with illustrations, maps, and well-written summaries of dozens of cryptids organized by continent. There's a section on famous monster-hunters (starting with Herodotus (!) and running to Loren Coleman), a Q&A section about cryptozoology, maps, and other goodies. Fun to browse through and a great gift for the budding cryptozoologist on your Christmas list.

Mysterious Creatures

TIME-LIFE (1998: TIME-LIFE, 164pp.)

Definitely worth having for the visuals. It opens with gorgeous illustrations of mythical and then recently-discovered beasts. The next section covers sea serpents, with pretty standard text, which, as in the following sections, also calls out the hoaxes. The *Zuiyo Maru* account leans toward a plesiosaur, but skeptics like Maurice Burton and Ronald Binns are cited in the Nessie text. All the major Loch Ness photos, a spectacular series of illustrations of giant squid, a splashy set of photos on Roy Mackal's chase of *mokele-mbembe*, an actual-size spread of a photographed *almas* footprint, lots of Bigfoot tracks, and more are on display, with some closing shots from monster movies. One annoying mistake is a picture claimed to be of a coelacanth showing a fish that doesn't resemble it at all. Decent bibliography.

The Extinction Club

Twigger, Robert (2002: William Morrow and Company, 222pp.).

This book is nominally about the recovery of Père David's deer, also known as the *milu*. This unique water-loving cervid, the only member of its genus, was first seen by a Westerner in 1866 when missionary Armand David slipped into a walled preserve in Beijing. Twigger tells the story of how specimens were sent to Europe and maintained while the original group was hunted out of existence. I say the book is "nominally" about this because the history of the deer is buried in a strange mosaic of writing about travels, books, extinction, the fate of humanity, a fictitious villain, writing a book, publishing a book, and some things I'm sure I'm forgetting. I finished it a bit exhausted, but I did learn more about the deer.

Zoology Coloring Books

I've said several times that learning can come from any sort of book written for anyone. These coloring books provide a very useful introduction to animals and (in the case of the marine bio book) the world they live in. In my experience, the effort needed to color in an object makes it stick in the mind a bit better. There are several other books in this series.

The Zoology Coloring Book by Lawrence M. Elson (1982: Collins Reference, 240pp.)

The Marine Biology Coloring Book by Thomas M. Niesen (2000: Collins Reference, 248pp.)

People with a psychological need to believe in marvels are no more prejudiced and gullible than people with a psychological need not to believe in marvels. – Charles Fort, author

These people call what they do 'cryptozoology' – '-zoology' meaning 'the study of animals,' and 'crypto-' meaning 'shit we made up.' – Penn Jillette, magician and skeptic

AFTERWORDS

The inclination to believe in the fantastic may strike some as a failure in logic, or gullibility, but it's really a gift. A world that might have Bigfoot and the Loch Ness Monster is clearly superior to one that definitely does not. – Chris Van Allsburg, author and illustrator

Cryptids and Me

In these reviews, I've avoided offering my opinion in the various cryptids as much as I can, so I should mention the major ones here and let readers decide how much my opinions have affected my descriptions of the books.

There are a few large cryptids that may be found alive. Those include the orang-pendek, the giant fish of Alaska's Lake Iliamna (likely sturgeons, but big ones), Marcus van Roosmalen's black and white jaguar (surely a variant and not a species, but still) and Australia's introduced big cat, most likely the puma. There are also animals that are probably extinct and but just might, against high odds, still be found. The thylacine and the yarri fall in that group. An animal I wouldn't bet on but don't rule out is some kind of eel or eel-like fish (or a larger version of a known species), measuring eight meters (26 feet) or longer, that might cause some sea serpent reports. My longshot sentimental favorite, unlikely though it may be, is a robust wolflike North American predator, called *waheela* and other names: this may be another case of recent extinction. I think the other big-name cryptids, despite many sincere witnesses and other evidence, are more likely to be mistake and myth rather than monster. I've talked to reliable people who are certain they got a good look at Sasquatch, but I can't get past the lack of fossils or recent remains, so all I can say is that I don't know what they saw. I've often been wrong in this life, and I hope more mystery creatures, no matter how unlikely they seem, will still turn up someday. I can put it no better than author Thomm Quackenbush in his humorous *Holidays with Bigfoot*:

These animals are not disputed but 'hidden.' It is an optimistic mission statement. It would be quixotic to seek gremlins that exist no further than storybooks. Bigfoot exists, along with Nessie and the Jersey Devil. Their formal discovery will happen tomorrow, or next week at the latest, and won't you feel silly when they are?

There was the ending still unfinished, the finale buried in the future—and in this we find the fascination of Nature and Science. – William Beebe, naturalist and marine explorer

A Few Contributions of My Own

I have, so far, published two books and a novel with cryptozoological facets. I'm proud of all of them. I have another novel and a book on marine monsters and myths in the queue. Each book below includes my favorite review quote and the blurbs used when the books first came out.

Rumors of Existence: Newly Discovered, Supposedly Extinct, and Unconfirmed Inhabitants of the Animal Kingdom

1995: Hancock House Publishers, 192pp.
"*A lovely little book, jam-packed with fascinating material.*" – Richard Ellis

Despite the intensive exploration of our planet, there remain surprising gaps in our knowledge of the animal world. New birds, mammals, reptiles, fishes, and amphibians are still described every year. Matthew Bille seeks to introduce readers to the discoveries, rediscoveries, and sightings of unclassified creatures made since the 1960s. The animals being presented include large mammals from Vietnam, a Tasmanian pouched wolf, pygmy elephants, and a dolphin with two dorsal fins. Exhaustively researched and scientifically accurate, *Rumors of Existence* is a testimonial to the variety of life existing on this planet and a plea to explore and preserve what remains of the wild.

Shadows of Existence: Discoveries and Speculations in Zoology

2006: Hancock House Publishers, 318pp.
"*Bille is knowledgeable. This effort took substantial research, and it shows. He is also realistic, takes evidence into account and, yet is hopeful that new, amazing discoveries are out there.*" – Sharon Hill, science writer and educator, *Modern Cryptozoology*

The age of zoological discovery has not passed. Every year, spectacular and exciting new species are being located and classified, adding to our knowledge of the animal kingdom. New whales, deer, snakes, sharks, and birds are just some of the creatures we have learned about in the past decade. Moreover, the seas and forests continue to conceal unsolved mysteries of zoology. Are there undiscovered big cats and unclassified apes hidden in the world's forests? Do large animals of unknown type lurk in deep lakes or in the oceans? The discoveries, rediscoveries, controversies, and mysteries of modern zoology are collected here in *Shadows of Existence*, a thoroughly researched guide to the wonders of zoology.

The Dolmen

2014: Wolfsinger Publications, 210pp.

"*The most gripping monster novels ... make them as plausible as possible, to the point that a reader can start to believe they actually might exist. This is no easy task, but Matt Bille accomplishes it with style.*" – John K. Patterson, author

When attorney Julie Sperling's fiancée is murdered while researching a controversial museum exhibit, she calls on her ex-lover, science writer Greg Preston, for support. The exhibit is a dolmen—an entire megalithic tomb moved illegally from England to Los Angeles. A murder mystery turns into a nightmarish pursuit as very real predators from ancient folktales try to hunt down anyone with knowledge of their existence. For Greg and Julie, the City of Angels has become the gateway to hell...

Exotic Zoology

I published a newsletter from 1994-99, first under the title *Cryptozoology Newsletter* and then, as a homage to Willy Ley, *Exotic Zoology*. It covered new-species news, cryptids famous and obscure, and possible survivals. I included book reviews and short descriptions of articles in major magazines and two issues concerning research on the newfangled internet. I even published a subscriber directory. The last issue carried the first picture and discussion of a new species of coati, courtesy of my friend Peter Hocking (alas, the animal did not turn out to be a species.) There's a lot of value in it still, and Isaac Koi has, with my permission, uploaded the entire archive.

https://isaackoiup.blogspot.com/2021/07/exotic-zoology-and-cryptozoology.html

Finally, my own pages of interest:

Website: www.mattbille.com

Twitter: MattWriter

Matt's Sci/Tech Blog, with news and reviews on zoology, space exploration, and other topics:

https://mattbille.blogspot.com/

My community for science, reviews, and comment about the awesome marine predator *Dunkleosteus terrelli*, aka God's own staple remover:

https://www.facebook.com/DunkleosteusTerrelli/

Go to Hangar1Publishing.com to learn more about the Author and stay up to date with their newest releases.

ACKNOWLEDGMENTS

As some of these reviews date back 30 years, the number of people who've recommended books, provided information on their own books, answered questions or helped me sort through cryptozoological and other scientific literature and information is enormous, and I've unfortunately forgotten some. Those that have not been forgotten, including those no longer with us, are listed below.

Dr. Anne Larsen deserves special mention because of her help in editing this book and applying her knowledge of scientific history to correct some errors. Others:

Max Anton; Chad Arment; J. M. Bailey; Dr. Robin Baird; Marissa Balfour; Lyle Blackburn; William Bratton; Markus Bühler; Suzanne Braun; Henry Bauer; Brooke Bessensen; Dr. Troy Best; Michael Bright; Nate Brislin; Celia Cackowski; Bruce Champagne; Mark Chrovinsky; Dr. Russell Ciochon; Loren Coleman; William Corliss; Paul Cropper; Dr. Merel Dalebout; Dr. David Daniell; Jonathan Downes; Richard Ellis; Dr. Louise Emmons; Mark Fetherman; Angel Morant Fores; Dr. Karin Forney; Richard Freeman; Arlene Gaal; Dr. Gary Galbreath; Ken Gerhard; William Gibbons; Professor J. Richard Greenwell; Dr. Colin Groves; Dr. James Halfpenny; Doug Hajicek; Mark A. Hall; Craig Heinselman; Markus Hemmler; Sharon Hill; Peter Hocking; Charles Humphreys; Dr. Bernard Heuvelmans; Patrick Huyghe; Dr. Cheri Jones; John Kirk III; Dr. Grover Krantz; Dr. Paul LeBlond; Daniel Loxton; John and Linda Lutz; Dr. Roy Mackal; Scott Marlowe; Scott Mardis; Carl Marshall; Debbie Martyr; Dr. Mireya Mayor; Marc Miller; Dr. Cherie McCollough; Cameron A.

McCormick; Dr. Jeff Meldrum; Richard Muirhead; Lee Murphy; Dr. Darren Naish; Gayle Horner Neufeld; Michael Newton; Scott Norman; June O'Neill; Chris Orrick; John Patterson; Dr. Charles Paxton; Dr. Ronald Pine; Robert Pitman; Dr. Frank Poirier; James Platz; Dr. Alan Rabinowitz; Ben Radford; Aurora Rayn; Michel Raynal; Dick Raynor; Bill Rebsamen; Nick Redfern; Dr. Marc van Roosmalen; Lorenzo Rossi; Lori Sakshaug; Bobbie Short; Liane Gentry Skye; Kirsty Smith; Michelle Souliere; Dr. Karl Shuker; Ben Speers-Roesch; Bret Swancer; Dr. Robert Timm; Craig Woolheater; Dr. Janet Voight; and Peter Zahler.

David Hancock provided additional books from his publishing firm, Hancock House Publishers. Finally, my supporters in cryptozoological writing include my family (Deb Bille, Jane Bille, Don Bille, Chris Bille, Corinne Bille, Lauryn Bille, and George and Eileen Kantner); supportive friends like Deb Fiedler, Liz Ruth, Ed and Joy Aldridge, Robyn Kane, Paul Kolodziejski, Liane Gentry Skye, Kris Winkler Davis, Kathy Brandt, Tonya Atkinson, Laurie Baker, Cicily Janus, my comrades at the Pikes Peak Writers Club and the National Association of Science Writers, and so many others.

My apologies to anyone I've overlooked. There are doubtless many of you, especially in the FaceBook world, and I appreciate you all.

How I Selected the Books

Most of these books are ones I'd already reviewed. Some were from the 1994-99 newsletter *Exotic Zoology*, some from *Matt's Sci/Tech Blog*, and a few from Amazon reviews I'd written. I did read some 60 additional books in the year this project was in work. To select those, I scoured lists of top books in the sciences, Loren Coleman's annual *10 Best Cryptozoology Books* lists, reviews by people like Darren Naish, Karl Shuker, and Sharon Hill, the catalogs of cryptozoology publishers, and new and used bookstores. I asked for recommendations via FaceBook groups and other forums. I didn't have the time and money to get to nearly everything I wanted to read:

I have a huge list of cryptozoology-related books I couldn't fit in, and the same is true of other sciences.

Note on Publishers

Some cryptozoology books are published by the "Big 5" major publishers, but there aren't many. Several small publishers have stepped into the gap. The newest is Doug Haijeck's Hangar 1, which did such a great job with this book. Chad Arment's Coachwhip Publications provides an important service by republishing out-of-print cryptozoology books along with new ones. The Centre for Fortean Zoology (CFZ Press) is the major cryptozoological publisher in the United Kingdom. Cosimo offers the "Loren Coleman Presents" series of reprinted cryptozoology books, with 18 out so far. Prometheus publishes some of the skeptical books, while Anomalist Books and Hancock House (publisher of my first two books) are very cryptozoologist-friendly.

INDEX

Index Section 1 Cryptozoology, 1-123

Titles

1. *Abominable Snowmen: Legend Come to Life - The Story of Sub-Humans on Five Continents from The Early Ice Age Until Today.* Sanderson, Ivan, 15-17
2. *American Monsters: A History of Monster Lore, Legends, and Sightings in America.* Godfrey, Linda, 107
3. *Animal Fakes & Frauds.* Dance, Peter, 93-94
4. *Animal Legends.* Burton, Maurice, 90
5. *Animal Treasure: A Naturalist in Search of Strange Creatures.* Sanderson, Ivan, 51
6. *Anthropology and Cryptozoology: Exploring Encounters with Mysterious Creatures.* Hurn, Samantha, 55-56
7. *Arthur C. Clarke's Mysterious World.* Welfare, Simon, and John Fairley, with Arthur C. Clarke, 94
8. *Beast of Boggy Creek: The True Story of the Fouke Monster, The.* Blackburn, Lyle, 42-43
9. *Beast of Exmoor, The.* Francis, Di, 59

10. *Beasts of Britain*. McGrath, Andy, 67
11. *Beyond the Secret Elephants: On mystery, elephants and discovery*. Patterson, Gareth, 66-67
12. *Bigfoot*. Napier, John, 20-21
13. *Bigfoot Casebook: Updated Sightings and Encounters from 1818 to 2004, The*. Bord, Janet and Colin, with Loren Coleman, 41
14. *Bigfoot Exposed*. Daegling, David, 39-40
15. *Bigfoot in Maine*. Souliere, Michelle (Introduction by Loren Coleman)
16. *Bigfoot Sasquatch Evidence*. Krantz, Grover, 36-37
17. *Bigfoot! The True Story of Apes in America*. Coleman, Loren, 38-39
18. *Big Footprints: A Comprehensive Bibliography Concerning Bigfoot, the Abominable Snowman, and Related Beings*. Perez, Danny, 32-33
19. *Big Footprints: A Scientific Inquiry into the Reality of Sasquatch*. Krantz, Grover, 35
20. *Biological Anomalies: Mammals I*. Corliss, William, 97-98
21. *Boilerplate Rhino, The*. Quammen, David, 96
22. *Book of Sea Monsters, The*. Eggleton, Bob and Nigel Suckling, 84
23. *Bunyips & Bigfoots: In Search of Australia's Mystery Animals*. Smith, Malcolm, 99
24. *Canadian Bestiary: A Collection of People, Places, and Beasties from Canadian Folklore, Cryptozoology, Native Religion, and Mythology, A*. Fisher, Todd, 108
25. *Case for the Sea Serpent, The*. Gould, Rupert, 10-11
26. *Copper State Monsters: Cryptids and Legends of Arizona*. Weatherly, David, 56-57
27. *Cryptid Creatures: A Field Guide*. Halls, Kelly Milner, 111-112
28. *Cryptozoology A to Z*. Coleman, Loren and Jerome Clark, 100
29. *Cryptozoology and the Investigation of Lesser-Known Mystery Animals*. Arment, Chad, 104

30. *Cryptology: Science and Speculation.* Arment, Chad, 102-103
31. *Dictionary of Cryptozoology, A.* Coghlan, Ronan, 103
32. *Discovering Cadborosaurus.* LeBlond, Paul, John Kirk, and Jason Walton, 73-74
33. *Drums Along the Congo.* Nugent, Rory, 97
34. *Eastern Panther: Mystery Cat of the Appalachians, The.* Parker, Gerry, 63
35. *Encyclopedia of New and Rediscovered Animals.* Shuker, Karl, 5-6
36. *Enigma of Loch Ness, The.* Bauer, Henry, 13-14
37. *Essential Guide to Bigfoot, The.* Gerhard, Ken, 45-46
38. *Exotic Zoology.* Ley, Willy, 5
39. *Extreme Expeditions: Travel Adventures Stalking the World's Mystery Animals.* Davies, Adam, 105
40. *Far-Out, Shaggy, Funky Monsters: A What-It-Is History of Bigfoot in the 1970s.* Green, Daniel, 26-28
41. *Field Guide to Bigfoot, Yeti, and Other Mystery Primates Worldwide, The.* Coleman, Loren, and Patrick Huyghe, 22
42. *Field Guide to Lake Monsters, Sea Serpents, and Other Mystery Denizens of the Deep, The.* Coleman, Loren, and Patrick Huyghe, 69-70
43. *Field Guide of Whales and Dolphins.* Morzer Bruyuns, Willem, 93
44. *Fish Caught in Time, A.* Weinberg, Samantha, 84-85
45. *Flight of the Iguana, The.* Quammen, David, 95
46. *Florida's Unexpected Wildlife.* Newton, Michael, 112-113
47. *Fossils for Kids.* Hall, Ashley
48. *Ghost Grizzlies.* Peterson, David, 61
49. *Ghost with Trembling Wings: Science, Wishful Thinking, and the Search for Lost Species, The.* Weidensaul, Scott, 101-102
50. *Giants, Cannibals and Monsters: Bigfoot in Native Culture.* Strain, Kathy Moskowitz, 28-29
51. *Gold Rush in the Jungle: The Race to Discover and Defend the Rarest Animals of Vietnam's "Lost World".* Drollette, Dan, 52-54

Index

52. *Great New England Sea Serpent, The.* O'Neill, June, 68
53. *Hunting Monsters: Cryptozoology and the Reality Behind the Myths.* Naish, Darren, 117-118
54. *In Pursuit of the Abominable Snowman.* Tchernine, Odette, 19
55. *In Search of Prehistoric Survivors.* Shuker, Karl, 98-99
56. *In Search of the Ivory-Billed Woodpecker.* Jackson, Jerome, 104
57. *In the Domain of the Lake Monsters: The Search for Denizens of the Deep.* Kirk, John, 68
58. *In the Tracks of the Yeti.* Hutchison, Robert, 34-35
59. *In the Valleys of the Noble Beyond: In Search of the Sasquatch.* Zada, John, 47
60. *In the Wake of Bernard Heuvelmans.* Woodley, Michael, 70-71
61. *In the Wake of the Sea-Serpents.* Heuvelmans, Bernard, 11-12
62. *Karl Shuker's Alien Zoo.* Shuker, Karl, 114-115
63. *Lake Monster Traditions: A Cross-Cultural Analysis.* Meurger, Michel, and Claude Gagnon, 82
64. *Last Tasmanian Tiger, The.* Paddle, Robert, 64
65. *Last Unicorn: A Search for One of Earth's Rarest Creatures, The.* de Buys, William, 54-55
66. *Living Dinosaur?, A.* Mackal, Roy, 58
67. *Living Fossil: The Story of the Coelacanth.* Thomson, Keith, 82-83
68. *Living Fossils: The Survival of Homo gardarensis, Neandertal Man, and Homo erectus.* Hall, Mark, 37-38
69. *Living Wonders: Mysteries and Curiosities of the Animal World.* Michell, John, and Robert J.M. Rickard, 94-95
70. *Lizard Man: The True Story of the Bishopville Monster.* Blackburn, Lyle, 65
71. *Loch Ness Monster: The Evidence, The.* Campbell, Steuart, 83-84
72. *Loch Ness Mystery Solved, The.* Binns, Ronald, 80-81
73. *Loch Ness Story, The.* Witchell, Nicholas, 79
74. *Lore and Legend of the Yeti.* Rall, Kesar, 33

Index

75. *Lost Grizzlies, The.* Bass, Rick, 61
76. *Making of Bigfoot, The.* Long, Greg, and Karl Korff, 40
77. *Mammoth Hunt.* Blashford-Snell, John, and Rula Lenska, 62
78. *Manlike Monsters on Trial: Early Records and Modern Evidence.* Halpin, Marjorie (editor), 31
79. *Medusa's Gaze and the Vampire's Bite: The Science of Monsters.* Kaplan, Matt, 106
80. *Meet the Sasquatch.* Murphy, Christopher, with John Green and Thomas Steenburg, 41
81. *Menagerie of Mysterious Beasts, A.* Gerhard, Ken, 108-109
82. *Mermaids and Mastodons.* Carrington, Richard, 90-91
83. *Mirabilis: A Carnival of Cryptozoology and Natural History.* Shuker, Karl, 117
84. *Monster Hunt.* Dinsdale, Tim, 78-79
85. *Monster of Loch Ness, The.* Mackal, Roy, 79-80
86. *Monsters & Marine Mysteries.* Hawthorne, Max, 88-89
87. *Monsters of Patagonia.* Whittall, Austin, 66
88. *Monsters of Texas.* Gerhard, Ken, and Nick Redfern, 105
89. *Monsters of the Deep.* Helm, Thomas, 78
90. *Monsters of the Deep.* Redfern, Nick, 87
91. *Monsters of the Gévaudan: The Making of a Beast.* Smith, Jay, 52
92. *Monsters of the Last Frontier: Cryptids and Legends of Alaska.* Weatherly, David, 122-123
93. *Monsters of the Sea.* Ellis, Richard, 12-13
94. *Monster Wrecks of Loch Ness and Lake Champlain.* Zarzynski, Joseph, 81
95. *Monstrous Commotion, A.* Williams, Gareth, 14-15
96. *Mothman and Other Curious Encounters.* Coleman, Loren, 64
97. *My Quest for the Yeti.* Messner, Reinhold, 38
98. *Mysterious America.* Coleman, Loren, 95
99. *Mysterious Creatures: A Guide to Cryptozoology.* Eberhart, George, 101
100. *Mystery Creatures of China.* Xu, David, 118-119

Index

101. *Mystery Monsters, The.* Soule, Gardner, 91
102. *Mythical Monsters.* Gould, Charles, 97
103. *Natural Acts.* Quammen, David, 96-97
104. *Natural History of Hidden Animals, The.* Heuvelmans, Bernard and Peter Gwynvay Hopkins, editor, 109-110
105. *Natural History of Unicorns, The.* Laver, Chris, 121-122
106. *Nature of The Beast: The First Genetic Evidence on The Survival of Apemen, Yeti, Bigfoot and Other Mysterious Creatures into Modern Times, The.* Sykes, Bryan, 24-25
107. *Natural Mysteries: Monster Lizards, English Dragons, and Other Puzzling Animals.* Hall, Mark, 58-59
108. *Neanderthal: The Strange Saga of the Minnesota Iceman.* Heuvelmans, Bernard, translated by Paul LeBlond, Afterword by Loren Coleman, 44
109. *Nessie: The Surgeon's Photograph Exposed.* Martin, David, and Alastair Boyd, 84
110. *No Mercy: A Journey to the Heart of the Congo.* O'Hanlon, Redmond, 63
111. *North America's Great Ape: The Sasquatch.* Bindernagel, John, 21
112. *On the Track of the Sasquatch.* Green, John, 30
113. *On the Track of Unknown Animals.* Heuvelmans, Bernard, 3-4
114. *Onza!* Carmony, Neil, 62
115. *Orang Pendek: Sumatra's Forgotten Ape.* Freeman, Richard, 106
116. *Out of the Shadows: Mystery Animals of Australia.* Healy, Tony, and Paul Cropper, 59-61
117. *Proceedings of the Eastern Cougar Conference, 1994.* Tischendorf, Jay, and Steven J. Ropski, 62-63
118. *River Monsters: True Stories of the Ones that Didn't Get Away.* Wade, Jeremy, 85-86
119. *Sasquatch Central: High Strangeness at a Minnesota Homestead.* Quast, Mike, 50
120. *Sasquatch: Legend Meets Science.* Meldrum, Jeffrey, 17-19

121. *Sasquatch Seeker's Field Manual, The*. Gordon, David, 43
122. *Sasquatch: The Apes Among Us*. Green, John, 25-26
123. *Scientific Americans: The Culture of Amateur Paranormal Researchers*. Hill, Sharon, 110-111
124. *Sea Monsters on Medieval and Renaissance Maps*. Van Duzer, Chet, 86-87
125. *Sea Serpents and Lake Monsters of the British Isles*. Harrison, Paul, 85
126. *Seal Serpent (Revised): The Search for a Long Necked Pinniped, The*. Cornes, Rob, and Gary Cunningham, 75-76
127. *Search for Bigfoot, The*. Byrne, Peter, 30
128. *Search for the Last Undiscovered Animals, The*. Shuker, Karl, 102
129. *Searching for Sasquatch: Crackpots, Eggheads, and Cryptozoology*. Regal, Brian, 41-42
130. *Sherpa and the Snowman, The*. Stonor, Charles, 29-30
131. *Shuker Nature Book 1: Antlered Elephants, Locust Dragons, and Other Cryptic Blog Beasts*. Shuker, Karl, 120-121
132. *Something Hidden Behind the Ranges*. Taylor-Ide, Daniel, 35-36
133. *Song of the Dodo, The*. Quammen, David, 95
134. *Soviet Sasquatch, The*. Porshnev, Boris, 47-48
135. *Species Seekers: Heroes, Fools, and the Mad Pursuit of Life on Earth, The*. Conniff, Richard, 115-116
136. *Still in Search of Prehistoric Survivors: The Creatures That Time Forgot?* Shuker, Karl, 7-8
137. *Still Living? Yeti, Sasquatch, and the Neanderthal Enigma*. Shackley, Myra, 32
138. *Sun, Sand, and Sea Serpents*. Goudsward, David, 76-77
139. *Tales of Giant Snakes: A Historical Natural History of Anacondas and Pythons*. Murphy, John, and Robert Henderson, 99-100
140. *Tetrapod Zoology*. Naish, Darren, 116-117
141. *There Are Giants in the Sea: Monsters and Mysteries of the Depths Explored*. Bright, Michael, 82

142. *Things and More Things: Myths, Mysteries, and Marvels!* Sanderson, Ivan, 113-114
143. *Thylacine: The Tragedy of the Tasmanian Tiger.* Guiler, Eric, 57-58
144. *Tom Slick and the Search for the Yeti.* Coleman, Loren, 34
145. *Tracking the Man-Beasts.* Nickell, Joe, 23-24
146. *True Giants: Is Gigantopithecus Still Alive?* Hall, Mark, and Loren Coleman, 22-23
147. *Untold Story of Champ, The.* Bartholomew, Robert, 72-73
148. *Varmints: Mystery Carnivores of North America.* Arment, Chad, 65
149. *Weird Waters: The Lake and Sea Monsters of Scandinavia and the Baltic States.* Thomas, Lars, with Jacob Rask, 71-72
150. *Where Bigfoot Walks.* Pyle, Robert, 36
151. *Wild Man: China's Yeti.* Zhenxin, Yuan, and Huang Wanpo, 31-32
152. *Yeti: An Abominable History.* Hoyland, Graham, 44-45

Authors

Arment, Chad, 65, 102-103, 104
Bartholomew, Robert, 72-73
Bass, Rick, 61
Bauer, Henry, 13-14
Bindernagel, John, 21
Binns, Ronald, 80-81
Blackburn, Lyle, 42-43, 65
Blashford-Snell, John, 62
Bord, Janet and Colin, 41
Boyd, Alastair, 84
Bright, Michael, 82
Burton, Maurice, 90
Byrne, Peter, 30
Campbell, Steuart, 83-84
Carmony, Neil, 62

Index

Carrington, Richard, 90-91
Clark, Jerome, 100
Clarke, Arthur C., 94
Coghlan, Ronan, 103
Coleman, Loren, 22-23, 34, 38-39, 41, 49-50, 64, 69-70, 95, 100
Conniff, Richard, 115-116
Corliss, William, 97-98
Cornes, Rob, 75-76
Cropper, Paul, 59-61
Cunningham, Gary, 75-76
Daegling, David, 39-40
Dance, Peter, 93-94
Davies, Adam, 105
deBuys, William, 54-55
Dinsdale, Tim, 78-79
Drollette, Dan, 52-54
Eberhart, George, 101
Eggleton, Bob, 84
Ellis, Richard, 12-13
Fairley, John, 94
Fisher, Todd, 108
Francis, Di, 59-61
Freeman, Richard, 106
Gagnon, Claude, 82
Gerhard, Ken, 45-46, 105, 108-109
Godfrey, Linda, 107
Gordon, David, 43
Goudsward, David, 76-77
Gould, Charles, 97
Gould, Rupert, 10-11
Green, Daniel, 26-28
Green, John, 25-26, 30, 41
Guiler, Eric, 57-58
Hall, Ashley, 133-134
Hall, Mark, 22-23, 37-38, 58-59

Index

Halls, Kelly Milner, 111-112
Halpin, Marjorie, 31
Harrison, Paul, 85
Hawthorne, Max, 88-89
Healy, Tony
Helm, Thomas, 78
Henderson, Robert, 99-100
Heuvelmans, Bernard, 3-4, 11-12, 44, 109-110
Hill, Sharon, 110-111
Hopkins, Peter Gwynvay, 109-110
Hoyland, Graham, 44-45
Hurn, Samantha, 55-56
Hutchison, Robert, 34-35
Huyghe, Patrick, 22, 69-70
Jackson, Jerome, 104
Kaplan, Matt, 106
Kirk, John, 68, 73-74
Korff, Karl, 40
Krantz, Grover, 35, 36-37
Laver, Chris, 121-122
LeBlond, Paul, 44, 73-74
Ley, Willy, 5
Lenska, Rula, 62
Long, Greg, 40
Mackal, Roy, 58, 79-80
Martin, David, 84
McGrath, Andy, 67
Meldrum, Jeffrey, 17-18
Messner, Reinhold, 38
Meurger, Michel, 82
Michell, John, 94-95
Morzer Bruyuns, Willem, 93
Murphy, Christopher, 41
Murphy, John, 99-100
Naish, Darren, 116-118

Index

Napier, John, 20-21
Newton, Michael, 112-113
Nickell, Joe, 23-24
Nugent, Rory, 97
O'Hanlon, Redmond, 63
O'Neill, June, 68-69
Paddle, Robert, 64
Parker, Gerry, 63
Patterson, Gareth, 66-67
Perez, Danny, 32-33
Peterson, David, 61
Porshnev, Boris, 47-48
Pyle, Robert, 36
Quast, Mike, 50
Quammen, David, 95-97
Rask, Jacob, 71-72
Rall, Kesar, 33
Redfern, Nick, 87, 105
Regal, Brian, 41
Rickard, Robert J.M, 94-95
Ropski, Steven J., 62-63
Sanderson, Ivan, 15-17, 51, 113-114
Shackley, Myra, 32
Shuker, Karl, 5-8, 98-99, 102, 114-115, 117, 120-121
Smith, Jay, 52
Smith, Malcolm, 99
Soule, Gardner, 91
Souliere, Michelle, 49-50
Steenburg, Thomas, 41
Stonor, Charles, 29-30
Strain, Kathy Moskowitz, 28-29
Suckling, Nigel, 84
Sykes, Bryan, 24-25
Taylor-Ide, Daniel, 35-36
Tchernine, Odette, 19

Index

Thomson, Keith, 82-83
Tischendorf, Jay, 62-63
Thomas, Lars, 47-48, 71-72
Van Duzer, Chet, 86-87
Wade, Jeremy, 85-86
Walton, Jason, 73-74
Weatherly, David, 56-57, 122-123
Weidensaul, Scott, 101-102
Weinberg, Samantha, 84-85
Welfare, Simon, 94
Whittall, Austin, 66
Williams, Gareth, 14-15
Witchell, Nicholas, 79
Woodley, Michael, 70-71
Xu, David, 118-119
Zada, John, 47
Zarzynski, Joseph, 81
Zhenxin, Yuan, and Huang Wanpo, 31-32

Index of Books Section 2 Sciences, 124-220

Titles

1. *Ahab's Rolling Sea: A Natural History of Moby-Dick*. King, Richard, 212-213
2. *Alligators, Caimans, Crocodiles, and Gharials of the World, The*. Stevenson, Colin
3. *All Yesterdays – Unique and Speculative Views of Dinosaurs and Other Prehistoric Animals*. Daish, Darren, with C.M. Koseman and John Conway, 136-137
4. *Animals of East Africa*. Leakey, Louis, 167
5. *Antelopes, Deer, and Relatives: Fossil Record, Behavioral Ecology, Systematics, and Conservation*. Vrba, Elisabeth and George Schaller, editors, 179
6. *Astonishing Elephant, The*. Alexander, Shana, 179-180

Index

7. *Barefoot Through the Amazon – On the Path of Evolution.* Van Roosmalen, Marc, 201-202
8. *Beak of the Finch, The.* Weiner, Jonathan, 128
9. *Bears of the World.* Domico, Terry and Mark Newman, 169
10. *Becoming Wild.* Safina, Carl, 214
11. *Beyond the Last Village: A Journey of Discovery in Asia's Forbidden Wilderness.* Rabinowitz, Alan, 181-182
12. *Beyond Words.* Safina, Carl, 214-215
13. *Big Cats and Their Fossil Relatives.* Turner, Alan, 129-130
14. *Birds at Risk.* Whitlock, Ralph, 168-169
15. *Birds New to Science: 50 Years of Avian Discoveries.* Brewer, David, 209-210
16. *Book of Eels: Our Enduring Fascination with the Most Mysterious Creature in the Natural World, The.* Svensson, Patrik, 213-214
17. *Brilliant Abyss: Exploring the Majestic Hidden Life of the Deep Ocean, and the Looming Threat that Imperils It, The.* Scales, Helen, 163-164
18. *Call of the Siren, The.* Dietz, Tim, 171
19. *Carolina Parakeet: Glimpses of a Vanished Bird, The.* Snyder, Noel, 185
20. *Catch Me a Colobus.* Durrell, Gerald, 166-167
21. *Certain Curve of Horn: The Hundred-Year Quest for the Giant Sable Antelope of Angola, The.* Walker, John, 183
22. *Collins Guide to the Rare Mammals of the World, The.* Burton, John, and Bruce Pearson, 169
23. *Coral Seas.* Steene, Roger, 153
24. *Crocodiles and Alligators of the World.* Alderton, David, and Bruce Tanner, 185
25. *Deep Atlantic: Life, Death, and Exploration in the Abyss.* Ellis, Richard, 152
26. *Deep Blue Home: An Intimate Ecology of Our Wild Ocean.* Whitty, Julia, 195-196
27. *Demon Fish: Travels Through the Hidden World of Sharks.* Eilperin, Juliet, 198-199

28. *Dinosaur Artist, The.* Williams, Paige
29. *Dinosaur in a Haystack: Reflections in Natural History.* Gould, Stephen J, 129
30. *Dinosaurs: How They Lived and Evolved.* Naish, Darren, and Paul Barrett, 139-140
31. *Diversity of Life, The.* Wilson, Edmund, 171-172
32. *Dolphins and Porpoises: A Worldwide Guide.* Sylvestre, Jean-Pierre, 173
33. *Eels: An Exploration, from New Zealand to the Sargasso, of the World's Most Mysterious Fish.* Prosek, James, 196
34. *Eighth Continent: Life, Death, and Rediscovery in the Lost World of Madagascar, The.* Tyson, Peter, 154-155
35. *Empty Ocean, The.* Ellis, Richard, 155
36. *End of the Megafauna: The Fate of the World's Hugest, Fiercest, and Strangest Animals.* MacPhee, Ross, 142-143
37. *Endless Novelties of Extraordinary Interest: The Voyage of HMS Challenger and the Birth of Modern Oceanography.* MacDougall, Doug, 161-162
38. *Every Living Thing: Man's Obsessive Quest to Catalog Life, From Nanobacteria to New Monkeys.* Dunn, Rob, 190
39. *Evolution in Minutes.* Naish, Darren, 140-141
40. *Evolution: The Triumph of an Idea.* Zimmer, Carl, 131-132
41. *Explorations.* Ballard, Robert, 151
42. *Extreme Life of the Sea, The.* Palumbi, Stephen and Anthony Palumbi, 203
43. *Eye of the Shoal: A Fishwatcher's Guide to Life, The Ocean, and Everything.* Scales, Helen, 210
44. *Fathoming the Ocean: The Discovery and Exploration of the Deep Sea.* Rozwadowski, Helen, 155-156
45. *Finders, Keepers: Treasures and Oddities of Natural History.* Purcell, Rosamond, and Stephen Jay Gould, 172-173
46. *Fire Under the Sea.* Cone, Joseph
47. *Fishes: A Guide to Their Diversity.* Hastings, Philip, with Harold Walker, Jr., and Grantly Galland, 197

Index

48. *Fishes of the Open Ocean: A Natural History and Illustrated Guide.* Pepperell, Julian, 196-197
49. *Fossil Legends of the First Americans.* Mayor, Adrienne, 132-133
50. *Gap in Nature: Discovering the World's Extinct Animals, A.* Flannery, Tim, and Peter Schouten, 182
51. *Gone: A Search for What Remains of the World's Extinct Creatures.* Blencowe, Michael, 164-165
52. *Great Auk, The.* Fuller, Errol, 177
53. *Great Sperm Whale: A Natural History of the Ocean's Most Magnificent and Mysterious Creature, The.* Ellis, Richard, 199-200
54. *Great White Shark.* Ellis, Richard, and John E. McCosker, 171
55. *Green Laurels: The Lives and Achievements of the Great Naturalists.* Peattie, Donald, 147-148
56. *Handbook of Whales, Dolphins, and Porpoises of the World.* Carwardine, Mark, 215-216
57. *High Frontier, The.* Moffett, Mark, 150
58. *Hope is the Thing With Feathers: A Personal Chronicle of Vanished Birds.* Cokinos, Christopher, 180
59. *Horseshoe Crabs and Velvet Worms: The Story of the Animals and Plants That Time Has Left Behind.* Fortney, Richard, 135-136
60. *Human Evolution: A Very Short Introduction.* Wood, Bernard, 145-146
61. *Immense Journey, The.* Eisley, Loren, 166
62. *In Oceans Deep: Courage, Innovation, and Adventure Beneath the Waves.* Streever, Bill, 162-163
63. *In Search of Deep Time: Beyond the Fossil Record to a New History of Life.* Gee, Henry, 130
64. *In the Shadow of Man.* Goodall, Jane, 135
65. *Kingdom of Might: The World's Big Cats.* Brakefield, Tom, 174
66. *Kingdom Under Glass: A Tale of Obsession, Adventure, and One*

Man's Quest to Preserve the World's Great Animals. Kirk, Jay, 197-198
67. *Kraken: The Curious, Exciting, and Slightly Disturbing Science of Squid*. Williams, Wendy, 200-201
68. *Last Chance to See*. Adams, Douglas, and Mark Carwardine, 170
69. *Life in the Treetops: Adventures of a Woman in Field Biology*. Lowman, Margaret, 154
70. *Lives of Hawai'i's Dolphins and Whales: Natural History and Conservation*, The. Baird, Robin, 205
71. *Lizard Man Speaks, The*. Pianka, Eric, 174
72. *Lost Species: Great Expeditions in the Collections of Natural History Museums, The*. Kemp, Christopher, 207-209
73. *Lost Wild America*. McClung, Robert, 150-151
74. *Mammals of Australia*. Strahan, Ronald, editor, 176
75. *Mammals of Madagascar*. Garbutt, Nick, 178
76. *Mammals of New Guinea*. Flannery, Tim, 175
77. *Monarchs of the Sea: The Extraordinary 500-Million-Year History of Cephalopods*. Staaf, Danna, 218-
78. *Naming Nature: The Clash Between Instinct and Science*. Yoon, Carol Kaesuk, 191-193
79. *National Audubon Society Guide to Marine Mammals of the World*. Reeves, Randall, editor, 183
80. *Natural History Museum Book of Animal Records, The*. Carwardine, Mark, 202-203
81. *Nature's Ghosts: Confronting Extinction from the Age of Jefferson to the Age of Ecology*. Barrow, Mark, 157-158
82. *New Human: The Startling Discovery and Strange Story of the "Hobbits" of Flores, Indonesia, A*. Morwood, Mike, and Penny van Oosterzee, 188-190
83. *New York Times Book of Science Literacy, Volume II: The Environment From Your Backyard to the Ocean Floor, The*. Wade, Nicholas, and Cornelia Dean and William A. Dicke, editors, 151
84. *New Zoo, The*. Shuker, Karl, 183

85. *No Turning Back: The Life and Death of Animal Species.* Ellis, Richard, 184-185
86. *Ocean of Life: The Fate of Man and the Sea, The.* Roberts, Callum, 159
87. *Octopus's Garden: Hydrothermal Vents and Other Mysteries of the Deep Seas, The.* Van Dover, Cindy Lee, 152
88. *Octopus: The Oceans Intelligent Invertebrate.* Mather, Jennifer, with Roland Anderson, and James Wood, 198
89. *Old Fourlegs: The Story of the Coelacanth.* Smith, J.L.B., 125-127
90. *100 Heartbeats: The Race to Save Earth's Most Endangered Species.* Corwin, Jeff, 193-194
91. *Orca: How We Came to Know and Love the Ocean's Greatest Predator.* Colby, Jason, 210-211
92. *Other Origins: The Search for the Giant Ape in Human Prehistory.* Ciochon, Russell, with John Olsen and Jamie James, 127-128
93. *Owls of the Eastern Ice: A Quest to Find and Save the World's Largest Owl.* Slaght, Jonathan, 216-217
94. *Oxford Dictionary of Zoology.* Allaby, Michael, 217
95. *Parrot Without a Name, A.* Stap, Don, 170
96. *Pictorial Guide to the Living Primates, The.* Rowe, Noel, 176
97. *Pink Boots and a Machete.* Mayor, Mireya, 158-159
98. *Prehistoric Animals.* Augusta, Joseph, 127
99. *Prehistoric Life: The Definitive Visual History of Life on Earth.* DK Publishing, various, 137
100. *Private Life of Sharks, The.* Bright, Michael, 178
101. *Quest for the African Dinosaurs.* Jacobs, Lewis, 128
102. *Rare Birds of the World.* Mountfort, Guy, 169
103. *Rarest Bird in the World: The Search for the Nechisar Nightjar, The.* Head, Vernon, 203-204
104. *Rarest of the Rare: Vanishing Animals, Timeless Worlds.* Ackerman, Diane, 175
105. *Rise and Fall of the Dinosaurs: A New History of a Lost World, The.* Brusatte, Steve, 143-144

106. *Science Times Book of Fish, The.* Wade, Nicholas, editor, 177
107. *Science Times Book of Mammals, The.* Wade, Nicholas, editor, 178
108. *Sea Dragons.* Ellis, Richard, 131
109. *Seals and Sea Lions of the World.* Bonner, Nigel, 186
110. *Search for the Giant Squid, The.* Ellis, Richard, 177
111. *Search for the Golden Moon Bear: Science and Adventure in Pursuit of a New Species.* Montgomery, Sy, 183-184
112. *Sex in the Sea: Our Intimate Connection with Sex-Changing Fish, Romantic Lobsters, Kinky Squid, and Other Salty Erotica of the Deep.* Hardt, Marah, 206
113. *Shadow and a Song: The Struggle to Save an Endangered Species, A.* Walters, Mark Jerome, 173
114. *Shadows in the Sea: the Sharks, Skates, and Rays.* McCormick, Harold, 168
115. *Sibley Guide to Bird Life and Behavior, The.* Sibley, David, editor, 182
116. *Sibley Guide to Birds, The.* Sibley, David, 180-181
117. *Singing Whales and Flying Squid: The Discovery of Marine Life.* Ellis, Richard, 186-187
118. *Sixth Extinction: An Unnatural History, The.* Kolbert, Elizabeth, 159-160
119. *Soul of an Octopus: A Surprising Exploration into the Wonder of Consciousness, The.* Montgomery, Sy, 206-207
120. *Spying on Whales: The Past, Present, and Future of Earth's Most Awesome Creatures.* Pyenson, Nick, 211-212
121. *Still Alive: A Wild Life of Rediscovery.* Galante, Forrest, 219-220
122. *Story of Life in 25 Fossils: Tales of Intrepid Fossil-Hunters and the Wonders of Evolution, The.* Prothero, Donald, 138-139
123. *Strange Sea Creatures.* Hoyt, Erich, 219
124. *Swift as a Shadow: Extinct and Endangered Animals.* Purcell, Rosamond Wolff, 154
125. *Tasmanian Tiger: The Tragic Tale of How the World Lost Its Most Mysterious Predator.* Owen, David, 186

Index

126. *Three Stones Make A Wall: The Story of Archaeology.* Cline, Eric, 144-145
127. *Throwim Way Leg.* Flannery, Tim, 153
128. *Tribe of Tiger, The.* Thomas, Elizabeth Marshall, 174
129. *Undersea Frontiers: Exploring by Deep-Diving Submarines.* Soule, Gardner
130. *Under the Sea: A Treasury of Great Writing About the Ocean Depths.* Soule, Gardner, 148-150
131. *Universe Below, The.* Broad, William, 153
132. *Vanished Species.* Day, David, 170
133. *Vaquita: Science, Politics, and Crime in the Sea of Cortez.* Bessensen, Brooke, 160-161
134. *Walker's Primates of the World.* Nowak, Ronald, 179
135. *Walking Whales, The.* Thewissen, Hans, 137-138
136. *Whales, Dolphins, and Other Marine Mammals of the World.* Shirihai, Hadoram, and Brett Jarrett, 187-188
137. *Whales, Dolphins, and Porpoises: A Natural History and Species Guide.* Berta, Annalisa, editor, 204-205
138. *Whales, Dolphins, and Porpoises: The Visual Guide to All the World's Cetaceans.* Carwardine, Mark, 175-176
139. *When Fish Got Feet, Sharks Got Teeth, and Bugs Began to Swarm: A Cartoon Prehistory of Life Long Before Dinosaurs.* Bonner, Hannah, 133-134
140. *Where the Wild Things Were: Life, Death, and Ecological Wreckage in a Land of Vanishing Predators.* Stolzenburg, William, 156-157
141. *Wild Blue: A Natural History of the World's Largest Animal.* Bortolotti, Dan, 191
142. *Wild Cats of the World.* Alderton, David, 184
143. *Wild Echoes.* Bergman, Charles, 170-171
144. *World is Blue: How Our Fate and the Ocean's Are One, The.* Earle, Sylvia, 158
145. *World Ocean Census.* Crist, Darlene Trew, with Gail Scowcroft, James Harding, Jr., and Sylvia Earle, 194-195

146. *Your Inner Fish: A Journey into the 3.5-Billion-Year History of the Human Body.* Shubin, Neil, 134

Authors

Ackerman, Diane, 175
Adams, Douglas, 170
Alderton, David, 184, 185
Alexander, Shana, 179-180
Allaby, Michael, 217
Anderson, Roland, 198
Augusta, Joseph, 127
Baird, Robin, 205
Ballard, Robert, 151
Paul Barrett, 139-140
Barrow, Mark, 157-158
Bergman, Charles, 170-171
Berta, Annalisa, 204-205
Bessensen, Brooke, 160-161
Blencowe, Michael, 164-165
Bonner, Hannah, 133-134
Bonner, Nigel, 186
Bortolotti, Dan, 191
Brakefield, Tom, 174
Jarrett, Brett, 187-188
Brewer, David, 209-210
Bright, Michael, 178
Broad, William, 153
Brusatte, Steve, 143-144
Burton, John, 169
Carwardine, Mark, 170, 175, 202-203, 215-216
Ciochon, Russell, 127-128
Cline, Eric, 144-145
Cokinos, Christopher, 180
Colby, Jason, 210-211

Index

Cone, Joseph
Conway, John, 136-137
Corwin, Jeff, 193-194
Crist, Darlene Trew, 194-195
Day, David, 170
Danna, Staaf
Dean, Cornelia, 151
Dicke, William A., 151
Dietz, Tim, 171
Domico, Terry, 169
Dunn, Rob, 190
Durrell, Gerald, 166-167
Earle, Sylvia, 155-156, 158, 194-195
Eilperin, Juliet, 198-199
Eisley, Loren, 166
Ellis, Richard, 131, 152, 155, 171, 177, 184-185, 186-187, 199-200
Flannery, Tim, 153-154, 175, 181
Fortney, Richard, 135-136
Fuller, Errol, 177
Galante, Forrest, 219-220
Galland, Grantly, 197
Garbutt, Nick, 178
Gee, Henry, 130
Goodall, Jane, 135
Gould, Stephen J., 129, 172-173
Harding, Jr., James, 194-195
Hardt, Marah, 206
Hastings, Philip, 197
Head, Vernon, 203-204
Hoyt, Erich, 219
Jacobs, Lewis, 128
James, Jamie, 127-128
Kemp, Christopher, 207-209
King, Richard, 212-213
Kirk, Jay, 197-198

Index

Kolbert, Elizabeth, 159-160
Koseman, C. M., 136-137
Leakey, Louis, 167
Lowman, Margaret, 154
MacDougall, Doug, 161-162
MacPhee, Ross, 142-143
Mather, Jennifer, 198
Mayor, Adrienne, 132-133
Mayor, Mireya, 158-159
McClung, Robert, 150-151
McCormick, Harold, 168
McCosker, John E., 171
Moffett, Mark, 150
Montgomery, Sy, 183-184, 206-207
Morwood, Mike, 188-190
Mountfort, Guy, 169
Naish, Darren, 136-137, 139-140, 140-141
Newman, Mark, 169
Nowak, Ronald, 179
Olsen, John, 127-128
Owen, David, 186
Palumbi, Anthony, 203
Palumbi, Stephen, 203
Pearson, Bruce, 169
Peattie, Donald, 147-148
Pepperell, Julian, 196-197
Pianka, Eric, 174
Prosek, James, 196
Prothero, Donald, 138-139
Purcell, Rosamond Wolff, 154, 172-173
Pyenson, Nick, 211-212
Rabinowitz, Alan, 181-182
Reeves, Randall, 183
Roberts, Callum, 159
Rowe, Noel, 176

Index

Rozwadowski, Helen, 155-156
Safina, Carl, 214-215
Scales, Helen, 163-164, 210
Schouten, Peter, 182
Scowcroft, Gail, 194-195
Shirihai, Hadoram, 187-188
Shuker, Karl, 183
Sibley, David, 180-181, 182
Schaller, George, 179
Shubin, Neil, 134
Slaght, Jonathan, 216-217
Smith, J.L.B., 125-127
Snyder, Noel, 185
Soule, Gardner, 148-150
Staaf, Dana, 218
Stap, Don, 170
Steene, Roger, 153
Stevenson, Colin
Stolzenburg, William, 156-157
Strahan, Ronald, 176
Streever, Bill, 162-163
Sylvestre, Jean-Pierre, 173
Svensson, Patrik, 213-214
Tanner, Bruce, 185
Thewissen, Hans, 137-138
Thomas, Elizabeth Marshall, 174
Turner, Alan, 129-130
Van Dover, Cindy Lee, 152
Van Oosterzee, Penny, 188-190
Van Roosmalen, Marc, 201-202
Vrba, Elisabeth, 179
Wade, Nicholas, 151, 177, 178
Walker, Jr., Harold, 197
Walker, John, 183
Walters, Mark Jerome, 173

Index

Weiner, Jonathan, 128
Whitlock, Ralph, 168-169
Whitty, Julia, 195-196
Williams, Paige, 141-142
Williams, Wendy, 200-201
Wilson, Edmund, 171-172
Wood, Bernard, 145-146
Wood, James, 198
Yoon, Carol Kaesuk, 191-193
Zimmer, Carl, 131-132

Index of Section 3 Crypto-Fiction, 221-254

Titles

1. *Abominable, The*. Simmons, Dan, 251-252
2. *Almost Adam*. Popescu, Petru, 226
3. *At the Water's Edge*. Gruen, Sara, 240
4. *Below*. Lockwood, Ryan, 244-245
5. *Below the Waves: Tales from the Deep*. Dillon, Steve, editor, 238
6. *Bestiarium Cryptozoologicum: Mystery Animals and Unknown Species in Classic Science Fiction and Fantasy*. Arment, Chad, editor, 231
7. *Big Ass Shark*. Mitchell, Briar Lee, 246
8. *Bone Labyrinth, The*. Rollins, James, 250-251
9. *By the Silver Water of Lake Champlain*. Hill, Joe, 242
10. *Cabinet of Curiosities*. Preston, Douglas, and Lincoln Childs
11. *Cetus Insolitus: Sea Serpents, Giant Cephalopods, and Other Marine Monsters in Classic Science Fiction and Fantasy*. Arment, Chad, editor, 231
12. *Congo*. Michael Crichton
13. *Cryptid*. Penz, Eric, 226-227
14. *Daedalus and the Deep*. Willis, Matthew, 253-354
15. *Dragon Factory, The*. Jonathan Maberry, 246

Index

16. *Devolution: A Firsthand Account of the Rainier Sasquatch Massacre.* Brooks, Max, 234-235
17. *Devour.* Anderson, Kurt, 230-231
18. *Eaters of the Dead.* Crichton, Michael
19. *Elusive Trilogy, The. (Eve, Iron Mountain Ridge, A Forever Journey)* Bailey, J.M., 231-232
20. *Esau.* Kerr, Philip, 243
21. *Essex Serpent, The.* Perry, Sarah, 248
22. *Fathomless.* Beck, Greig, 233
23. *Ferocity.* Laws, Stephen, 244
24. *Forgotten Room, The.* Preston, Douglas, and Lincoln Childs
25. *Full Wolf Moon.* Preston, Douglas, and Lincoln Childs, 249
26. *Fragment.* Fahy, Warren, 238
27. *Great Zoo of China, The.* Reilly, Matthew, 250
28. *Hell's Aquarium.* Alten, Steve
29. *Hopsquatch.* Newton, Michael, 247-248
30. *Hue-Hue, or The Monster.* Haggard, H. Rider
31. *Ice Hunt.* Rollins, James
32. *Into the Drowning Deep.* Grant, Mira, 225-226
33. *Invasive Species.* Wallace, Joseph, 253
34. *Jaws.* Benchley, Peter, 233-234
35. *Jurassic Park.* Crichton, Michael, 235-236
36. *Kronos Rising.* Hawthorne, Max, 241
37. *Kraken.* Hawthorne, Max, 242
38. *The Loch.* Alten, Steve, 229-230
39. *Lost Island, The.* Preston, Douglas, and Lincoln Childs
40. *Lost World, The.* Crichton, Michael
41. *Lost World, The.* Doyle, Arthur Conan, 237
42. *Meg.* Alten, Steve, 228-229
43. *Meg: Generations.* Alten, Steve, 228-229
44. *Meg: Nightstalkers.* Alten, Steve, 228-229
45. *Meg: Primal Waters.* Alten, Steve, 228-229
46. *Neanderthal.* Darnton, John, 236-237
47. *Pandemonium.* Fahy, Warren, 239
48. *Primeval.* Goleman, David, 239

49. *Primordia.* Beck, Greig, 232
50. *Prophet of Bones.* Kosmatka, Ted, 243
51. *Relic, The.* Preston, Douglas, and Lincoln Childs, 248-249
52. *Road to Loch Ness.* Murphy, Lee, 247
53. *Sea Raptor.* Rust, John, 251
54. *Shadowkiller, The.* Hansen, Matthew, 240
55. *Terminal Freeze.* Preston, Douglas, and Lincoln Childs
56. *Trench, The.* Alten, Steve
57. *Vostok.* Alten, Steve, 230
58. *Warrener's Beastie: A Novel of the Deep.* Trotter, William, 252-253
59. *What Lurks Beneath.* Lockwood, Ryan, 245
60. *Wolfen, The.* Strieber, Whitley, 252

Authors

Alten, Steve, 228-230
Anderson, Kurt, 230-231
Arment, Chad, 231
Bailey, J.M., 231-232
Beck, Greig, 232-233
Benchley, Peter, 233-234
Brooks, Max, 234-235
Childs, Lincoln, 248-249
Crichton, Michael, 235-236
Darnton, John, 236-237
Dillon, Steve, 238
Doyle, Arthur Conan, 237
Fahy, Warren, 238-239
Goleman, David, 239
Grant, Mira (McGuire, Seanan), 225-226
Gruen, Sara, 249
Haggard, H. Rider, 237
Hansen, Matthew, 240
Hawthorne, Max, 241-242

Hill, Joe, 242
Kerr, Philip, 243
Kosmatka, Ted, 243
Laws, Stephen, 244
Lockwood, Ryan, 244-245
Jonathan Maberry, 246
Mitchell, Briar Lee, 246
Murphy, Lee, 247
Newton, Michael, 247-248
Penz, Eric, 226-227
Perry, Sarah, 248
Preston, Douglas, 248-249
Popescu, Petru, 226
Reilly, Matthew, 250
Rollins, James, 250-251
Rust, John, 251
Simmons, Dan, 251-252
Strieber, Whitley, 252
Trotter, William, 252-252
Wallace, Joseph, 253
Willis, Matthew, 253-254

Index of Section 4 A Marvelous Miscellany, 255-271

Titles

1. *After Man: A Zoology of the Future.* Dixon, Dougal, 259
2. *Alien Animals.* Bord, Janet and Colin, 256
3. *Big, Bad Book of Beasts: The World's Most Curious Creatures, The.* Largo, Michael, 261-262
4. *Bigfoot Book: The Encyclopedia of Sasquatch, Yeti, and Cryptid Primates, The.* Redfern, Nick, 265
5. *Bigfoot Film Controversy, The.* Murphy, Christopher and Roger Patterson
6. *Bigfoot Observer's Field Manual: A Practical and Easy-to-*

Follow Step-by-Step Guide to Your Very Own Face-to-Face Encounter With a Legend. Morgan, Robert W.
7. *Chasing American Monsters.* Offutt, Jason, 264-265
8. *Cryptid Creatures of Florida, The.* Marlowe, Scott, 263
9. *Cryptopedia.* Kramer, David, and Jonathan Maberry, 261
10. *Cryptozoology Anthology: Strange and Mysterious Creatures in Men's Adventure Magazines.* Deis, Robert, David Coleman, and Wyatt Doyle, editors, 258
11. *Deadlands: BoneYard.* McGuire, Seanan, 264
12. *Deadlands: Ghostwalkers.* Maberry, Jonathan, 262
13. *Do Abominable Snowmen of America Really Exist?* Patterson, Roger, 265
14. *Dragons: A Natural History.* Shuker, Karl, 268
15. *Extinction Club, The.* Twigger, Robert, 270-271
16. *From Flying Toads to Snakes with Wings.* Shuker, Karl, 268
17. *InCryptid Series.* McGuire, Seanan
18. *Investigating the Impossible: Sea-Serpents in the Air, Volcanoes that Aren't, and Other Out-of-Place Mysteries.* Magin, Ulrich, 262-263
19. *Marine Biology Coloring Book, The.* Niesen, Thomas M.
20. *Monster Files: A Look Inside Government Secrets and Classified Documents on Bizarre Creatures and Extraordinary Animals.* Redfern, Nick, 266
21. *Monster Hunt: The Guide to Cryptozoology.* Storm, Rory, 269-270
22. *My Life with the Chimpanzees.* Goodall, Jane
23. *Mysteries.* Blashford-Snell, John, 256
24. *Mysteries and Monsters of the Sea.* Spaeth, Frank, editor, 269
25. *Mysteries of Planet Earth.* Shuker, Karl, 267
26. *Mysterious Creatures.* TIME-LIFE6, 270
27. *Mysterious Sea Monsters of California's Central Coast.* Reinstedt, Randall, 266
28. *National Audubon Society Field Guide to Mammals of North America, The.* Whitaker, John L.

29. *Natural History of the Unnatural World, A.* Cryptozoological Society of London, 257
30. *On the Trail of Bigfoot.* Dupler, Mike, 259
31. *Panthers of the Coastal Plain.* Humphreys, Charles, 260-261
32. *Planet Ocean: A Story of Life, the Sea, and Dancing to the Fossil Record.* Matsen, Brad and Ray Troll, 263
33. *Rare Animals of the World.* Salvadori, Francesco, 267
34. *Red Earth, White Lies: Native Americans and the Myth of Scientific Fact.* Deloria, Jr., Vine, 258-259
35. *Sasquatch/Bigfoot.* Hunter, Don with Rene Dahinden
36. *Serpents of the Sky, Dragons of the Earth.* Holiday, F.W., 260
37. *ShukerNature 2: Living Gorgons, Bottled Homunculi, and Other Monstrous Blog Beasts.* Shuker, Karl, 267
38. *Supernatural Mysteries and Other Tales.* Snow, Edward Rowe, 268-269
39. *Tom Brown's Field Guide to Nature Observation and Tracking.* Brown, Tom
40. *Working for Bigfoot.* Butcher, Jim, 257
41. *Zoology Coloring Book, The.* Elson, Lawrence M, 271

Authors

Blashford-Snell, John, 256
Bord, Janet and Colin, 256
Brown, Tom, 255
Butcher, Jim, 257
Cryptozoological Society of London, 257
Deis, Robert, 258
Deloria, Jr., Vine, 258-259
Dixon, Dougal, 259
Dupler, Mike, 259
Elson, Lawrence M., 271
Goodall, Jane, 255
Holiday, F.W., 260
Humphreys, Charles, 260-261

Index

Hunter, Don
Kramer, David, 261
Largo, Michael, 261-262
Maberry, Jonathan, 261-262
Magin, Ulrich, 262-263
Marlowe, Scott, 263
Matsen, Brad, 263
McGuire, Seanan, 264
Morgan, Robert W., 256
Murphy, Christopher, 265
Niesen, Thomas M., 271
Offutt, Jason, 264-265
Patterson, Roger, 265
Redfern, Nick, 265-266
Reinstedt, Randall, 266
Salvadori, Francesco, 267
Shuker, Karl, 267-268
Snow, Edward Rowe, 268-269
Spaeth, Frank, 269
Storm, Rory, 269-270
Troll, Ray, 263
Twigger, Robert, 270-271
Whitaker, John L., 256

Printed by Libri Plureos GmbH in Hamburg, Germany